An Unexpected Light

Princeton Theological Monograph Series

K. C. Hanson, Charles M. Collier, and D. Christopher Spinks,
Series Editors

Recent volumes in the series:

Richard Valantasis et al., editors
The Subjective Eye: Essays in Honor of Margaret Miles

Anette Ejsing
A Theology of Anticipation: A Constructive Study of C. S. Peirce

Caryn Riswold
Coram Deo: Human Life in the Vision of God

Paul O. Ingram, editor
Constructing a Relational Cosmology

Michael G. Cartwright
Practices, Politics, and Performance: Toward a Communal Hermeneutic for Christian Ethics

David Hein
Geoffrey Fisher: Archbishop of Canterbury, 1945–1961

Gabriel Andrew Msoka
Basic Human Rights and the Humanitarian Crises in Sub-Saharan Africa: Ethical Reflections

T. David Beck
The Holy Spirit and the Renewal of All Things: Pneumatology in Paul and Jurgen Moltmann

An Unexpected Light

Theology and Witness in the Poetry and Thought of Charles Williams, Micheal O'Siadhail, and Geoffrey Hill

DAVID C. MAHAN

☙PICKWICK *Publications* • Eugene, Oregon

AN UNEXPECTED LIGHT

Theology and Witness in the Poetry and Thought of Charles Williams, Micheal O'Siadhail, and Geoffrey Hill

Princeton Theological Monograph Series 103

Copyright © 2009 David C. Mahan. All rights reserved. Except for brief quotations in critical publications or reviews, no part of this book may be reproduced in any manner without prior written permission from the publisher. Write: Permissions, Wipf and Stock Publishers, 199 W. 8th Ave., Suite 3, Eugene, OR 97401.

Pickwick Publications
A Division of Wipf and Stock Publishers
199 W. 8th Ave., Suite 3
Eugene, OR 97401

www.wipfandstock.com

ISBN 13: 978-1-55635-507-3

Cataloging-in-Publication data:

Mahan, David C.

An unexpected light : theology and witness in the poetry and thought of Charles Williams, Micheal O'Siadhail, and Geoffrey Hill / David C. Mahan. With a Foreword by Ben Quash.

xvi + 230 p. ; 23 cm. — Includes bibliographical references.

Princeton Theological Monograph Series 103

ISBN 13: 978-1-55635-507-3

1. Williams, Charles, 1886–1945. 2. O'Siadhail, Micheal, 1947–. 3. Hill, Geoffrrey. 4. Theology in literature. 5. Christianity in literature. I. Quash, Ben. II. Title. III. Series.

BT1102 M25 2009

Manufactured in the U.S.A.

To my most "excellent" wife Karen

and

To Mrs. Wood, my second grade teacher
Pullen Elementary School, Mt. Pleasant, Michigan
In fulfillment of a 40 year old promise

"Indifference to art is the most serious sign of decay in any institution; nothing bespeaks its old age more eloquently than that art, under its patronage, becomes literal and self-imitating."

—Susanne K. Langer, *Feeling and Form*

"Poetry is spiritual nourishment. But it does not satiate, it only makes man more hungry, and that is its grandeur."

—Jacques Maritain, *Creative Intuition in Art and Poetry*

Contents

Acknowledgements / ix

Permissions / xi

Foreword by Ben Quash / xiii

1 Introduction: "Can Poetry Matter" [to Christian Theology]? / 1

2 "From the Exposition of Grace to the Place of Images": Incarnational Witness and "the Way of Images" in Charles Williams' Arthuriad / 25

3 Poetry as Remembrance: The Poetics of Testimony and Historical Redress in Micheal O'Siadhail's *The Gossamer Wall* / 89

4 Geoffrey Hill's "Pitch of Attention" and "Poetic Kenosis" in *The Triumph of Love* / 141

5 Conclusion / 199

Bibliography / 223

Acknowledgements

THE NAME BENEATH THE TITLE OF THIS BOOK IS MY OWN, BUT THE product is the fruit of more contributors and supporters than I can ever adequately acknowledge. I do, however, wish to thank in ink the following persons for their advice, encouragement, and persistent gentle prodding: my colleagues at the Rivendell Institute (Yale University), James and Stephani Shivers, Nicholas Wolterstorff, Peter Hawkins, Glen Cavaliero, and Bishop Peter Walker, all of whom helped to make this venture possible. I also wish to thank Micheal O'Siadhail and Geoffrey Hill whose kind attention to my study of their art provided critical insight and much needed reassurance. And I would like to thank especially my supervisor Rev. Dr. Ben Quash for his tireless support, sensitivity, always-constructive criticism, and inspiration; I regard him as both mentor and friend.

Lastly, I wish to express my deep gratitude to my parents Hal and Mary Mahan, to my wife Karen—who walked this path with me every step of the way ("*an excellent wife*" I have found!), and to my children Jessica, Tristan, and Natalie (for their love, and because they wanted to see their names in print).

Permissions

Excerpts from *Taliessin Through Logres* and *The Region of the Summer Stars* by Charles Williams. First published 1938 by Oxford University; second impression 1948; third impression 1954. Used by permission of the estate of Charles Williams, Watkins/Loomis Agency, New York, NY.

Excerpts from *The Region of the Summer Stars* by Charles Williams. First published by Editions Poetry London, 1944; reset by Oxford University Press, 1950; reprinted 1952 and 1960. Used by permission of the estate of Charles Williams and the Watkins/Loomis Agency, New York, NY.

Excerpts from *The Gossamer Wall: Poems in Witness to the Holocaust* by Micheal O'Siadhail Copyright © 2002 by Bloodaxe Books Ltd. (www.bloodaxebooks.com). Used by permission of the publisher.

Excerpts from *The Triumph of Love* by Geoffrey Hill, Copyright © 1998 by Houghton Mifflin Company. Used by permission of the publisher.

Portions of the chapter on Micheal O'Siadhail appear in *Musics of Belonging: The poetry of Micheal O'Siadhail*, Copyright © 2007 by Carysfort Press. Used by permission of the publisher.

Foreword

ONE OF THE MOST VALUABLE TASKS THAT CAN BE UNDERTAKEN BY Christian thinkers in our present time is the re-equipping of people's imaginations—helping Christians and non-Christians alike to have imaginations that are capable of responding to the divine dynamics of their reality. Today's Christianity may try to achieve this education of the imagination in various ways. It may find help by returning afresh to its sources in Scripture, liturgy and prayer. Or it may do so (and this is not incompatible with the first possibility) by renewing and deepening its relationship with other religious traditions and their practices. But just as promising as both of these must be the possibilities held out to theologians, preachers and teachers by the *arts*. Literary, visual, musical, architectural—each artistic form harbours particular resources for breaking open our set assumptions about the way the world is, and our functionalist reductionism about how we are to live well in it.

This sensitive and inspiring book chooses immersion in the literary arts, and especially the work of three modern poets, as the medium in which to develop its theological insights. The wonderful thing about the book is that it really *is* an immersion, and not a co-option of the poetry for merely illustrative or didactic purposes. In a way that is rare in theological dialogue with the arts, David Mahan respects the complex integrity of the poetry—both the generative strictures of its forms, and the seriousness of its intentions. He shows himself to be an exemplary reader of poems, with the contemplative's capacity to abide with material that is initially—so it seems—intractable to understanding. He can follow with patient attention the contours and sinews of the poetic worlds and figures that Charles Williams, Micheal O'Siadhail, and Geoffrey Hill conjure up. He appreciates the eloquence of the tiniest poetic manoeuvre deep in the text of these long poem cycles, and yet at the same time is capable of grasping the poetry's large vistas: the magnificence of Williams's vision of a sacramental imperium; O'Siadhail's determination to sustain an openness to the full horror of the Shoah by honouring the voices of so great a multitude of its victims; Hill's highly-charged attention to the layered depths of Western history which make his poems like literary cross sections through countless geological strata (which are in fact *human* strata—with all their knots and twists, profane and religious, vicious and exalted) in order to lay open the fragile possibilities we have for responsible life *now*.

Why should the theologian pay any attention to the poet, at least in our present circumstances? The answer must begin with the fact that the poet can evoke *wonder*. The poet can bring conceptual concerns (which always remain to some extent merely schematic) back into contact with living, breathing, concrete reality. But at the same time, the poet can lift our relationship to this reality from the merely workaday to a new "pitch of attention" (Hill's words). In this moment, what would otherwise be related to as mundane can be seen as shot through with matters of existential import: matters like, for example, the place of faith and hope and love in our world, and in our life in the world.

As it happens, the triumvirate of poets considered here in this book are supremely good educators in how a certain pitch of attention may be achieved through perception and language. And faith, hope and love are allowed by them to be themes of overriding authority—not just because a religion tells them it should be, but because the world they scrutinise with their poetic sensibility *requires* faith, hope and love to be such themes. (Authority, after all, is not so much something we attribute to whatever we care to, as something we encounter that will not let us go.) Williams is a poet of visionary sight, of a seeing of the unseen, which is the characteristic of *faith*. O'Siadhail sets himself perhaps the hardest challenge to *hope* that we can imagine, as though to test whether and how it can be held to without untruthfulness. And Hill obliquely, but with fierce honesty, probes the durability and power of *love*.

None of these poets is glibly pious in the way he approaches these themes, religiously-freighted though they evidently are. The poets are too in touch with a world that experiences much darkness and asks many difficult questions: the modern world that is the Christian's too. Mahan implies that Christians may too readily have adopted strategies to evade the darkness and difficulty of modern experience; a sort of emotional and intellectual insulation. So another reason he commends the reading of this poetry (which, it must be admitted, is not the accessible and undemanding fodder of much popular culture) is that it holds the religious mind back from naivety or complacency.

There is, however, more to make these poets Christianly-interesting than their themes—weighty though those themes are. There must be in any really open engagement between theology and the arts a readiness to learn from the *way the art-form works* and not just from *what it says*. The latter would inevitably risk a betrayal of the art form's particularity in the interests of a "translation," or even a "generalization," of some supposed core message. What Mahan does in this book is show us that the form cannot be dispensed with. The poets' concerns incarnate themselves in the forms of their poems, and any high view of incarnation requires that bodies be respected. The forms adopted by his poets, Mahan will argue, instruct us. They represent a discipline of sensitivity —a sensitivity that comes about in part by the simultaneously spare and adventurous use of language, by which expression can be at once exact and multivalent. They demonstrate the power of the careful disposal of words in order to summon, evoke, judge, and illuminate, with the result that any rendering into a different medium (a prose treatise, for example) would also be a loss. The demands imposed by the human tasks of perception and communication are met by this poetry in a way that Christians can learn from. And Mahan's view is that the area where this learning might pre-eminently take place is the area where Christians are most concerned to communicate well: the area of mission. So this book is a significant contribution to the sort of theology that Rowan Williams calls "communicative"—a theology that "experiments with the rhetoric of its uncommitted environment."

In the end, theology like Mahan's can "experiment" in such a way because it believes that the profoundest truths spoken about in Christian tradition are the profoundest truths of the world created by God, and thus also meditated upon by artists. There is an affirmation here of a doctrine of creation—a belief that there is a "grain" to the universe inhabited by believer and non-believer alike—such that those concerned to honour the God who made the heavens and the earth will prize good looking and good listening wherever they are found, and know they can receive insight from them. This is wisdom (the biblical genre in which poetry is most at home). But at the same time, the world of Christians and non-Christians alike is the world in need of *redemption*. The revelation of what God has done in Christ gives Christians a particular charge to remind the world of this need, and not simply to concur with its self-assessments. But even here, they may be helped (through the critical exposure of the world's pain and wickedness by the poets who look at it) not to forget the full scope of what redemption means.

This book has learnt from its poets, and its author shares many of their virtues: he is an intensely responsible, careful, and faithful perceiver of a world he loves and has hope for. He invites us here to make the language of Christian apologetics more worthy of its subject matter, and this means also, more reciprocal, more nuanced, and more beautiful. May those who have ears to hear, hear.

—Ben Quash

Introduction

"Can Poetry Matter" [to Christian Theology]?

Poetry as Christian Theology and Witness?

AN ESSAY WRITTEN IN 1991 FOR *THE ATLANTIC MONTHLY*[1] BY THE POET and literary critic Dana Gioia generated thunderous reaction, sending rumbles through the offices of academics and public intellectuals alike. Gioia's theme was as straightforward as it was provocative. He asked, simply: "Can Poetry Matter?" Inquiring after the decline in poetry's "cultural importance" Gioia laid down a gauntlet of sorts, one charged with implications not only for the status of poetry in contemporary Anglo-American society at large, but for a diverse range of more specified intellectual enterprises as well. It is not the aim of my book to explore his concern in all of its facets, nor to defend in a broad sense the importance of poetry to culture, but to take up Gioia's challenge and apply it to one area of inquiry in particular. The question I want to raise is: *Can poetry matter to Christian theology?*

For generations Christian thinkers, including Christian poets, have thoughtfully engaged the question of poetry's contribution to human thought and culture, often with both implicit and explicit religious overtures. One of Britain's most intellectual poets, Samuel Taylor Coleridge, once claimed, "No man was ever yet a great poet, without being at the same time a profound philosopher. For poetry is the blossom and the fragrancy of all human knowledge, human thoughts, human passions,

---

1. Reprinted in Gioia, *Can Poetry Matter?*

emotions, language."[2] The genius of the poet, he adds—like all human genius—displays a "*mind that feels the riddle of the world, and may help to unravel it.*"[3] This is high praise for poets and their art, suggesting an expansive scope of qualities including the role of the poet as one of the world's most sensitive interpreters. Coleridge's estimation echoes that of his predecessor William Blake, who advanced the even more forceful claim, "If it were not for the poetic or Prophetic character the Philosophic and Experimental would soon be at the ratio of all things, and stand still, unable to do other than repeat the same dull round over again."[4]

Some may regard such sweeping acclamation as anachronistic, the bygone naïveté of Romantic exuberance. But poets in more recent times have voiced similar enthusiasm for the potency of poetry, and some have done so with equally trenchant metaphysical or spiritual implications. In his 1950 essay "What Dante Means to Me," for example, T. S. Eliot asserts: "the great poet should not only perceive and distinguish more clearly than other men, the colours or sounds within the range of ordinary vision or hearing; he should perceive vibrations beyond the range of ordinary men, and be able to make men see more at each end than they could ever see without his help."[5] The great poets, and any who would seek to emulate them, adds Eliot, share

> the obligation to explore, to find words for the inarticulate, to capture those feelings which people can hardly even feel, because they have no words for them; . . . .
> . . . The task of the poet, in making people comprehend the incomprehensible, demands immense resources of language; and in developing the language, enriching the meaning of words and showing how much words can do, he is making possible a much greater range of emotion and perception for other men, because he gives them the speech in which more can be expressed.[6]

The poet as interpreter and articulator of the extraordinary as well as the ordinary; the poet as explorer, as philosopher and visionary, as an

2. Coleridge, *Biographia Literaria*, 532.
3. Ibid., 475; my italics.
4. Blake, *Complete Writings*, 97.
5. Eliot, *To Criticize the Critic*, 134.
6. Ibid.

"enricher" of speech as well as its special servant—without doubt, in the estimation of these poets poetry mattered a great deal; but in what sense for Christian theology? Their accolades clearly register a spiritual or religious temperament regarding the significance of poetry. Furthermore, in regard to the witness of Christians, who among them would not similarly aspire "to make men see more" and "comprehend the incomprehensible," or to "make possible a much greater range of emotion and perception for others"? R. S. Thomas once proposed a more explicit connection in this regard. In his essay "A Frame for Poetry" he states: "it is within the scope of poetry to express or convey religious truth, and to do so in a more intense and memorable way than any other literary form is able to. Religion has first of all to do with vision and revelation, and these are best told of in poetry."[7]

Space does not permit us to weigh the merits of all these claims. But I seize upon one set of attributes that Eliot ascribes to poets and the yield of their art as a standard for my own convictions about why, and how, poetry matters to Christian theology. In sum, poets (most especially "great" poets) are masters of speech, with a distinct capacity, as Eliot puts it, for "developing the language, enriching the meaning of words and showing how much words can do." By virtue of this proficiency, I would argue, they offer a model to the witnessing Church. Poetry matters to Christian theology, in other words, because it presents the Church with gifts of speech that intersect vitally with its most prominent public task: the holding forth of the gospel in ways that enable others to perceive its meaning (the "extraordinary" within the "range of the ordinary"). For reasons I will introduce here, then seek to demonstrate in our studies of three long poems by Charles Williams, Micheal O'Siadhail, and Geoffrey Hill, the poet's gift of speech emerges as a cardinal attribute that commends its appropriation within Christian theology.

Making a case for such assertions proves far from straightforward, however. To say that poetry manifests a form of Christian theology and provides a vital resource for Christian witness raises questions not only about poetry but about the tasks of theology as well. Theologians, for example, may find little difficulty with esteeming poetry as a resource of *some* kind, certainly as it pertains to various forms of Christian practice or manner of expression. And yet, to up the stakes a further notch,

---

7. Thomas, *Selected Prose*, 69.

the question may be asked: Are poetry and poetic studies even subjects proper to Christian theology? Theological inquiry at its best is expressly an intellectually rigorous enterprise, and often a highly technical one at that. How, then, do products of the creative imagination such as poems figure as resources within the characteristically "rational" discourses of theological investigation? Hence, the question also arises not only whether or how but *where* specifically within the disciplines of academic theology, and by extension the Church, poetry proves valuable as a resource.

In contending that poetry and its study have an integral place *within* the broader curricula of theology, readers may note that I already have injected one significant delimitation that further exacerbates the concern some academic theologians may feel at this point. Specifically, my focus rests on the contribution of *poems* to Christian reflection and practice, and not, for example, "poetics" as a theoretical category. This distinction prompts us to consider and address a range of attitudes, and to anticipate a possible objection. On the one hand, most Christian thinkers and scholars would readily acknowledge that poetry has always held a place in Christian experience and practice. The prevalence of poems and poetic forms in Scripture, liturgy and Christian worship, along with the millennia-long tradition of Christian poetry and hymnody, irrefutably establish poetry's contribution to Christianity's public expression. Why, we may therefore wonder, is it even necessary to argue for the inclusion of poetry in Christian theology, given this legacy?

In response, I would point out that, on the other hand, the assumption that poems represent a focus of study suitable to the rigors of "serious" theological inquiry faces certain longstanding biases about what constitutes genuinely intellectual theology. Certainly it is evident that the study of verse and verse forms proves to be an important factor in biblical exegesis or an element in the study of the tradition. But more generally, some may argue: Is it not the case that poetry's contribution (even in its biblical forms) lies in its ability to *enhance* theological ideas, propositions and arguments, as a sort of aesthetic punctuation point helpful for generating authentic religious emotions about the subject being presented or discussed? This being the case, the argument may continue, we should not confuse an emotive form of expression with the more serious intellectual content that such an expression merely embellishes. To address a view of this kind I offer two further clarifications and a challenge, as preliminary points for the larger aims of my book.

First, we note that despite the growing interest in literary studies as a focus for theological inquiry, a "cognitive" bias with regard to poetic verse continues to pervade the attitudes of theological scholarship.[8] We see this most evidently in the relative absence of poetic studies in current theological curricula, as one important tool for the development of well-equipped theological minds.[9] To be sure, in recent decades a plethora of projects spanning nearly all the disciplines of academic theology and religious studies have highlighted the value of at least "the poetic" as a theoretical category significant for Christian theology.[10] Only rarely, however (with the notable exception of scholarship in the area of biblical poetics) have these investigations included an extensive, formal study of poems. In making such an observation I do not intend to diminish the value of these appropriations of poetic theory for the purposes of Christian reflection; but it does recognize a gap. The question of how *poetry* matters to Christian theology asks, among other things, what poems *do* that proves significant or valuable. To pose such a question does not declare a preference for the practical over the theoretical. Rather, it trades one set of theoretical concerns for another. Accordingly, my project regards not how *poetics* represents a helpful category for Christian theology, but how an analysis of poetic *performance*—not, strictly, that of the poets but of their *poems*—comprises a further application of a theoretical as well as a practical interest in poetic studies on the part of theological thinkers.[11]

In this vein, secondly, the question of what poems do also invokes a methodological consideration central to the ambition of my study, and which is integral to the *gap* my book aims to fill. Put simply, when

---

8. Obviously, this kind of bias does not reflect an attitude towards poetry (as well as other literary genres and artistic media) exclusive to academic theologians. For similar critiques in the areas of philosophy and ethics see, e.g., Cavell, *Disowning Knowledge*; and Nussbaum, *Love's Knowledge*.

9. There are notable exceptions to this situation. My own alma mater Yale Divinity School, e.g., offers a Master's concentration track in religion and the arts, which includes literature.

10. I have included a number of these works in the bibliography.

11. For an insightful discussion of poetry's, and language's, performative properties as a theological response to the epistemological challenges advanced by contemporary literary critics, see Dawson, *Literary Theory*.

we pursue the possibility that poems make a substantial contribution to theological reflection and articulation, then only by a protracted study of their form and style can we discover what specifically that contribution includes. In short, such an undertaking calls for the *close reading* of poems. In the area of biblical studies, Robert Alter has made these points the premise of his analysis of the Bible's poetry. As he summarizes his objective in the concluding chapter of his book *The Art of Biblical Poetry*, worth quoting at length:

> The aim of my own inquiry has been not only to attempt to get a firmer grasp of biblical poetics but also to suggest an order of essential connection between poetic form and meaning that for the most part has been neglected by scholarship. . . . [P]oetry is quintessentially the mode of expression in which the surface is the depth, so that through careful scrutiny of the configurations of the surface—the articulation of the line, the movement from line to poem, the imagery, the arabesques of syntax and grammar, the design of the poem as a whole—we come to apprehend more fully the depth of the poem's meaning.
>
> The choice of the poetic medium for the Job poet, or for Isaiah, or for the psalmist, was not merely a matter of giving weight and verbal dignity to a preconceived message but of uncovering or discovering meanings through the resources of poetry. In manifold ways . . . poetry is a special way of imagining the world or, to put this in more cognitive terms, a special mode of thinking with its own momentum and its own peculiar advantages.[12]

He then adds, with an eye to the extra-biblical poetic tradition in the West, that like that poetry the Bible too "uses poetry to *realize meanings*," yielding the recognition that "the spiritual, intellectual, and emotional values of the Bible that continue to concern us so urgently are *inseparable from the form they are given in the poems*."[13]

The direction Alter takes in his study—beginning with the form of a poem and then proceeding to "uncover" or "discover" in it the meanings that *emerge* from these poetic surfaces—represents the method by which I will proceed in the study of our three twentieth-century "Christian" poems. In this respect, one may regard my project as a demonstration in pursuit of a method. In other words, I seek first to demonstrate what

---

12. Alter, *Art of Biblical Poetry*, 205.
13. Ibid.; my italics.

poets do in their poetry (as well to elucidate what these poets think about poetry) in order to show how poetic creativity manifests a significant way of *doing* theology. In the process—and this is both the challenge I have engaged and a challenge my project returns to others—I will show further how Christian theology properly conducts an investigation into the contribution of poetry with regard to theology's native interests; that is, by reading poems. Accordingly, this procedure will also indicate the set of skills needed: skills which include sensitivity to features of the poetic medium (such as Alter outlines above), the ability to perceive and formulate connections between poetic form and theological meaning, and then to apply the results of such studies to particular contemporary theological priorities. By virtue of this approach we understand that poetry's contribution to serious theological inquiry comprises an *emergent property*. Whether or not poetry and poetic studies represent a properly intellectual focus of investigation for serious theology is a matter that cannot be adequately engaged or decided without first doing the work of seeing, through close inspection, how such an intellectual yield in fact emerges in poems themselves. This is one burden of my book, and its outcome will be one of the fruits of my focus on poetic form.

At the same time, to return to the issue of where to locate poetry and its study within Christian theology, questions about the task of theology lead us to ask: Which theological interests and tasks in particular does the study of poetic verse especially enable? More is at stake than claiming for poetry or for its study an intellectual stature. Our answer to the question, "Can poetry matter for Christian theology?" must also demonstrate that poetry contributes to what *matters* to the Christian Church in this age.

However Christian theologians may debate the definition or scope of their task, few (if any) would resist the contention that theology is by nature a *responsive* as well as a descriptive and declarative discipline. This recognition also bears with it the understanding that theology is by necessity an *integrative* discipline. Both features prove critical to theology's tasks whether in response to its own texts and traditions, or to the culture(s) in which theologians live. The constant flux of issues that confront the Church in any age or culture demands flexibility on the part of its interpreters when formulating adequate responses to the emergent needs of believers as well as their unbelieving neighbors. Together with the effort to make provision for these ever-shifting conditions, theologians have also to incorporate a variety of creative forms and diverse resources into their respective projects.[14] Nowhere has this need appeared with such urgency than in that area highlighted above: the Church's public witness.

In addition to the abiding concern to articulate the substance of the faith in its biblical and historical aspects, Christian thought has always sought to give an account for its claims within and with respect to its cultural setting. Paul's injunction "But we persuade men" summarizes the ambition of the witnessing Church for all ages and in all cultural situations, as does the exhortation from I Peter 3:15 to "always be prepared to give an account/defense for the hope that is within you." With either declaration, the "equipping of the saints" as well as the disposition and needs of the uncommitted are brought to the fore. Suffice it to say, theological inquiry involves responsive, and responsible, service to both audiences. Furthermore, because Christianity has shown itself to be an eminently translatable faith, able to adjust to all variety of cultural situations without loss to its essential message, the question for a responsive theology becomes: What are the particular needs of the witnessing Church and its audience in this age and culture, and how might Christians effectively engage people in light of these conditions?[15]

That this is a question proper to theology seems indubitable. As Rowan Williams has asserted about theology's "communicative" task,

> Theology seeks also to persuade or commend, to witness to the gospel's capacity for being at home in more than one cultural environment....
>
> The Christian movement ... is a *missionary* movement: that is, it works on the assumption that it has something to say that is communicable beyond its present boundaries and is humanly attractive or compelling across these boundaries. It assumes that it has the capacity and the obligation to seek to persuade

---

14. It is on the basis of this sense of the theologian's vocation that David Tracy issues his plea for "the necessity for interdisciplinary methods in theology"; *Analogical Imagination*, 448.

15. I here restrict the scope of my own concern to the conditions obtaining for the contemporary "Western" Church in "North Atlantic" societies (as Rowan Williams labels them), although any culture manifesting those same conditions falls within this purview.

persons from all imaginable human backgrounds that it is decisively relevant to their humanity....[16]

To extend Williams' account to my own focus specifically, we may then ask: How can poetry enable the Church to address and attract people "across the boundaries" in order to persuade people about the decisive relevance of the Christian gospel? My initial answer, already given, regards poetry's "gift of speech"—its development of language that enriches the meaning of words, as T. S. Eliot contended. Some refinement of that assertion is in order. Naturally, the answer we formulate to this question depends upon which boundaries exist and which conditions we identify as particular challenges to Christian witness today. Accordingly, within those societies we designate as "modern" or "late-modern," we may ask further: How do the attitudes, sensibilities and needs of people whom we characterize in these terms present a challenge to Christian persuasion, which the formal study of poetry distinctly enables Christian witnesses to address? The combination of these three elements—that of Christian witness and the equipping role of theology in its communicative task, the conditions of late-modernity which give direction and particular urgency to this task, and the potential of poetry to effect a boundary crossing by virtue of its formal performance—represents the nexus of my methodological approach to poetic studies. It is in this sense that I advocate the study of poetry as a mode of theological inquiry, and commend poetry (at least the poetry I examine here) as a manifestation of a robust public theological witness.

Having framed my discussion within theology in these terms, what remains to be examined by way of introductory remarks involves further clarification of those cultural conditions which require the kind of theological *redress* that poetry affords. In the final section, I will then indicate the contribution of the poets and poetry I have selected, and describe how I intend to proceed through my study of this primary material in reading poetry as a mode of theological discourse specially suited to the needs of the witnessing Church.

---

16. Williams, *On Christian Theology*, xiv, 230.

Poetry and Christian Witness in Late-modernity: Resonance and Recognition

No small amount of material has been put forward for Christian thinkers to sift when attempting to assess the outlook(s) of contemporary "late-modern" people and societies. Christian "modernity critiques," as Oliver O'Donovan has labeled them, abound, and to such an extent and with such diversity of focus and interpretation that any effort to surmise what "truly" characterizes the mindset and attitudes of modern or late-modern people seems fraught with hazards. As Nicholas Lash points out, "In the confused condition of European [and we may add, North American] culture, generalisation is a risky business."[17] Agreeing with Lash, Oliver O'Donovan warns about "modernity criticism": "It is an enterprise with glaring intellectual risks. The illumination that is shed upon our times may be paid for by a very high level of historical generalisation and selectivity. The interpretative decisions that are reached are unsusceptible of confirmation or rebuttal, and can only be, as it were, ventured."[18] Despite such risks, O'Donovan insists that "there are compelling reasons to proceed to a task at once impossible and inescapable," among which, he elaborates, is the understanding that, "To be alert to the signs of the times is a Gospel requirement, laid upon us as upon Jesus' first hearers."[19]

Keeping in mind the risk as well as the requirement, we can identify certain features common to a late-modern outlook and perception of Christianity, as well as some less commonly perceived implications to be drawn from my observations of these conditions. Both indicate how a responsive theology and the Church it serves need to shape a witness to the gospel within these societies. In addition, the challenges to Christian persuasion that ensue in light of these features help to specify further the value of poetry as a resource for Christian witness. Because of the more narrow focus of my project, I will highlight only two.

First, few would debate the conclusion that Christianity faces a credibility crisis in its public reception among late-modern populations. The centuries-long erosion of confidence in Christian truth claims has led to the perception among uncommitted (as well as some

---

17. Lash, "Religion," 53.
18. O'Donovan, *Desire of the Nations*, 272.
19. Ibid., 272–73.

committed) people that Christianity, or for that matter any organized religion, no longer qualifies as an authoritative interpretive framework for all of human existence. This is not a new situation, but its cumulative effect has resulted in what Nicholas Lash calls "the exclusion of the business of religion from the realm of public truth"; not commonly, he clarifies, "as the 'censoring' or 'suppression' of religion, but rather as its displacement."[20] The recovery of Christian persuasion in the public square thus faces the twofold demand of having to re-articulate its claims about universal reality,[21] while simultaneously having to negotiate the unacceptability of any such claims, especially when cast in religious terms. In this regard, we might either accept the much-disputed view advanced by "post-modern" critics that people express "incredulity towards metanarratives," or say more modestly that late-modern people tend to suspect the authority of any overarching framework (especially one expressive of an institutionalized outlook or norm). Both positions have some descriptive merit. However we construe the situation, the widespread *loss* of credibility—not, of course, wholly undeserved—confronts the Church with a unique challenge.

Never before in its history has Christianity become passé in societies where so many people are only vaguely familiar with its message, and yet dismissive, or more typically suspicious, of its claims to disclose the truth about God and human existence. The process whereby the public authority of Christianity and the persuasive power of its vision have dissipated is of course centuries old, and it is a story well documented and perennially analyzed by Church historians and Christian modernity critics alike. One conclusion among many, however, seems not to have been analyzed enough. The situation as it now stands confronts the witnessing Church with the challenge not only of having to persuade people towards belief (which, many would justifiably argue, does not constitute the *ultimate* responsibility of the Christian witness), but of *attracting the attention of unbelieving people at all*. As a symptom of Christianity's credibility crisis, the matter of how to overcome people's

---

20. Lash, *"Religion,"* 110. Others have emphasized this condition in their own "modernity critiques," and I have included a number of such works in my expanded bibliography.

21. As David Tracy insists, "the central subject matter of all theology, the reality of God, demands by the very universality of its claims to meaning and truth a public explication of such claims" (*Analogical Imagination*, 62).

resistance to listen attentively to the gospel has become one of the single greatest demands for Christian witness in late-modern societies.

To be sure, the requirement to address a demand of this kind is not wholly unique to modernity, when viewed from the perspective of the Church's historical understanding of its evangelistic mission. It has, however, acquired new urgency and complexity in our "post-*Christendom*" era. When Paul declares, "I have become all things to all men, that I may indeed win some" (1 Cor 9:22), he underscores the conviction that the *winsomeness* of gospel witness involves the ability to demonstrate the relevance of Jesus Christ to people's lives in terms that resonate with their own sensibilities. This age-old and biblically attested principle of effective witness has never lacked its proponents and exemplars. But with the demise of a publicly accepted Christian framework and claim to authority (or, indeed, in the absence of *any* generally shared framework or authority at all), the demand for *personal* resonance has risen to heretofore-unknown levels of expectation among the Church's late-modern contemporaries. (How efforts to meet this expectation accord with a witness to the *gospel* is a matter I will take up shortly.)

The need to inculcate *resonance*, and with it, renewed *recognition*, as integral elements in the effort to move late-modern uncommitted people to reconsider their outlook on life in light of the gospel, has not escaped the notice of Christian modernity critics. Rowan Williams has articulated this need succinctly when he prescribes for theology's "communicative style" the endeavor to become "a theology experimenting with the rhetoric of its uncommitted environment."[22] He observes that this feature of Christian witness has been present in the Church from its earliest formation, and has continued to characterize the Church's own mission, when most effective, to the present—understood in part as the pursuit of a dialogical relationship with the cultures in which it exists. Such a perspective, he adds, displays "confidence that the fundamental categories of belief are robust enough to survive the drastic experience of immersion in other ways of constructing and construing the world," and at the same time recognizes that the Church must find ways to communicate the content of its faith to "a public to whom that vocabulary is basically strange."[23]

---

22. *On Christian Theology*, xiv.
23. Ibid., xiv, xv.

In his book *Sources of the Self*, Charles Taylor advances a view similar to Williams' as it pertains to the need for resonance—in my terms, the need of witnesses to a particular vision of life to make that vision familiar, or recognizable, again to others in terms that resonate with them. It is, assuredly, a position Taylor indexes to a more exhaustive analysis of the modern outlook than Williams'. His historical account of Western notions of identity and its implication for moral vision leads him to conclude that, given the demise of "a publicly established order of references," and the evaporation of confident reference to a God and a cosmic order as the grounding for beliefs, modern people now pursue "the exploration of order through personal resonance."[24] Specifically, he clarifies, such explorations involve "the search for moral sources *outside* the subject through languages which resonate *within* him or her, the grasping of an order which is inseparably indexed to a personal vision."[25] Taylor weds this search to the effort to achieve a position of "seeing good," one which reciprocates "an affirming power, which can help to realize the good by recognizing it."[26] Resonance, then, in Taylor's construal, becomes the vehicle for recognition.[27]

Against the backdrop of his persuasive description of modern notions of the self, Taylor speculates about the kind of language or languages that are needed in order to enable people to, as he puts it, "*realize* the contact."[28] Of some relevance to my own project, he urges that renewed attention be given to what he labels "epiphanic art," specifically those forms of imaginative articulation that feature what (he notes) Shelley referred to as the "subtler language" of poetry.[29] "Realizing an epiphany," Taylor elaborates, "is a paradigm case of what I called recovering contact with a moral source."[30] For him the means as well as their result have become a crucial line of inquiry, given the conditions

---

24. Taylor, *Sources of the Self*, 491, 511. For Taylor's protracted discussion of this phenomenon, see the section "Fractured Horizons" (309ff.).

25. Ibid., 510; cf. 428.

26. Ibid., 454.

27. Rowan Williams places a similar emphasis on the importance of recognition in his book *Lost Icons*, in which he explores the loss of social structures that once enabled what he calls "exchanges of recognition" (58).

28. Taylor, *Sources of the Self*, 512.

29. Ibid., 381.

30. Ibid., 425.

that now characterize the outlook of people in modern societies. He describes the relationship thus: "As our public traditions of family, ecology, even polis are undermined or swept away, we need *new languages of personal resonance* to make crucial human goods alive for us again."[31]

However we assess the merits of a category like "epiphanic," Taylor has nonetheless put his finger on a dynamic that seems crucial for an effective Christian response to those who insist upon "the exploration of order through personal resonance." What he advances in the form of speculation I want to extend in the manner of a demonstration through my study of poetry and poetic style and form; and what he applies to the matter of recovering contact with moral sources, I want to apply to theology's witnessing task as the endeavor to help people "realize contact" with the Christian gospel. When, for example, one notes Taylor's perception that resonance serves as a vehicle for recognition, does one not find here a reiteration, in its modern context, of the gospel's intrinsically incarnational (that is "Incarnational"[32]) nature and of the value Paul placed on "becoming all things to all men" as a necessary and effective mode of witness? The experience of an "epiphany" may not be paradigmatic for the aims of a gospel witness, but resonance surely is. Only now it has become a more urgent principle to be applied in the wake of Christianity's collapse as an organizing vision for people's lives, as one antidote to the indifference or antipathy people feel towards an outlook they now react *against*.

Still, some may argue, does this endeavor to generate resonance with the gospel really constitute a faithful witness to it, or does it merely accommodate the sensibilities of the age (as a lazy or anemic form of "relevance")? Moreover, others may add, doesn't the appropriation of Taylor's emphasis on articulation and the quest for "new *languages*" severely restrict the fuller sense of witness as an *Incarnational* enterprise? (The latter challenge has obvious implications for my commendation of poetry as a resource for Christian witness.) Let me briefly take each of these challenges in turn.

First, viewed from one perspective, the gospel does not readily accommodate a demand for personal resonance, at least not in the ways

---

31. Ibid., 513; my italics.

32. Because "incarnational" has become a common idiom in a variety of disciplines, and especially in literary studies, I will capitalize "Incarnational" *passim* in order to distinguish its peculiar Christian reference and meaning.

that it is commonly expressed. The vision conveyed by Christ is neither an individualistic outlook nor is it one that champions self-assertion. In both respects, Christians rightly insist, the opposite is the case.[33] On the other hand, because the gospel *is* at heart "Incarnational"—advancing universal claims about universal human needs, but addressing individuals and individual communities, and each in human terms (John 1:14ff.; Heb 1:1–3)—neither the individual nor his or her particular needs remain absent from a gospel account of humanity's relationship to God. Among those needs, which the gospel uniquely addresses, is the human incapacity to apprehend God apart from God's initiative to disclose himself to us.[34] In this respect, the gospel in its original manifestation represents *God's* accommodation to us. That its witnesses seek to extend that process by *translating* the gospel (in both a literal and figurative sense) into an idiom or manner of expression that speaks again to the personal situation(s) and sensibilities of their diverse audiences, reflects, and respects, the provenance of their message. In sum, the task of Christian witness seeks not to *conform* the gospel to the sensibilities of an age or culture, but to *confirm* its enduring significance on behalf of the Church's many diverse audiences, and to do so in ways that enable that connection.

Among the Church's trained thinkers, as well as its thoughtful adherents, this is a commonplace observation. I would argue, however, that the Church in late-modern societies, including especially its official educational institutions, has yet to promote and explore fully all of the creative resources available to effect this vital connection. Hence, the "gap," which my project aims to fill, not only consists of including new objects and substantiating new methods of theological inquiry in Christian academic practices. It also aims to include poetry in the Church's "extensive" mission[35] to revitalize its Incarnational witness,

---

33. Indeed, one can make a biblical case that there are times when God seems determined to leave people in a state of spiritual dullness and rebellion, and even pursues a strategy of confirming them in, or "giving them over" to, that condition. My ensuing argument does not presume to resolve the kind of tension these moments produce. In fact, especially with regard to tendencies towards self-assertion, all of our poems *generate* tension along these lines as an integral element in their poetic witness.

34. Put otherwise, the apprehension of God does not, in the final analysis, depend upon our ability to know God but upon God's ability, and willingness, to *make himself known*.

35. In his book *Finding the Church*, Dan Hardy delineates two mutually energizing elements in the public life of the Church, calling the one "intensity"—which regards the

as one creative resource among many needed to enable Christian witnesses and their "publics"[36] to "realize the contact" between the human condition and the work of Christ.

To address the second challenge above, I acknowledge, on the one hand, that Christian witness does consist of more than the verbal testimony of believers. As a *re*-incarnation of Christ's body, the Church testifies most fully to its message when it most fully reflects the interests, attitudes and behavior of Jesus Christ. Moreover, it is through their Christ-likeness in its human manifestation that Christians demonstrate the relevance of Christ to those around them, and in a way that indeed resonates most immediately with people who might otherwise prove dismissive of the gospel's claims.[37] That "the messenger is the message" (as the saying goes) stands without dispute within a distinctive Christian understanding. To acknowledge this, however, only situates Christian witness within its evident human context. Thus, on the other hand, to say that the messenger and the community of messengers embody the gospel calls for clarification when the issue of Christian persuasion comes to hand: What *kind* of community do we have in mind—that is, one characterized by which features and capable of what forms of expression that prove winsome as well as faithful?

Lives of moral integrity and of Christian love and wisdom, powerful in their testimony to the reality of God in Christ, at the same time do not *replace* the speech that is also intrinsic to Christian witness. If anything, the biblical testimony insists that speech represents one of the major loci for all of these Christ-*like* qualities, and no less prominently in the Church's public witness (1 Pet 3:15b; Col 4:6). Furthermore, because resistant non-believers not only do not share the religious outlook of believers, but often are also, by choice, less and less exposed to the lives and communities of Christians who embody it, speech represents one of the

---

spiritual life of believers as they engage God through worship and wisdom practices—and the other "extensity," which recognizes Christianity's inherent " "spread-out-ness," " not in vague terms but "in the historical lives of people in very different situations" (110).

36. David Tracy's nomenclature in *Analogical Imagination* to designate theology's three audiences: the Church, the Academy, and the world (or society).

37. This is the thrust of Stanley Hauerwas' response to the crisis of Christian credibility in modernity. See especially *Resident Aliens*. For a similar emphasis on this same principle applied within systematic theology specifically, see the section "The Identity and Relevance of Faith" in Moltmann, *Crucified God*.

few avenues by which witnessing Christians and communities of faith are obliged to pursue their extensive mission. In so far as this also is the case there can be no dichotomy between lived lives and language for the task of arousing the uncommitted to reconsider the gospel.[38] Hence, the question of what kind of community invokes, by necessity, the further question: What kind or quality of efficacious speech does the witnessing Church require in this age and in these societies? Viewed from the vantage points of those features of a late-modern mindset that I have highlighted *and* that of the Incarnational thrust of a witness capable of garnering renewed attention to the message of Christ (as awakened recognition through resonance), Charles Taylor's plea for "new languages" becomes a constitutive feature in the witnessing Church's urgent call. As T. S. Eliot said of poets, so too Christian witnesses are to "give people the speech" by which they may "comprehend the incomprehensible," and within that purview to solicit renewed attention to that which God has made *comprehensible* in Christ.

The calling of the poet, in this respect, parallels the calling of the Christian theologian, educator, church officer, missionary or lay witness, and with salutary implications. But these respective callings also converge. As evidence of this association, when we ask how might we further characterize the challenges for Christian witness as I have described them, I would elaborate that the challenge is threefold. We may first construe it as a rhetorical challenge, in the sense of finding efficacious speech to engage the attention of late-modern unbelieving people. Nicholas Lash makes this challenge explicit when he advocates "the need for education in attentiveness or reverence and in alertness to the languages we use," and so, exhorts the Church to engage in the "unending discipline in learning how to speak."[39] Secondly, the challenge, as Rowan Williams contends, "is to do with imagination."[40] Williams echoes John Henry Newman's perceptive observation that

---

38. Nicholas Lash gives a crisp summary of the combination of elements the Church needs when he writes, "sustained engagement with the destructive forces threatening to overwhelm the world and humankind . . . demands the construction of the kind of *culture* which can embody, sustain and *communicate* the tale" ("*Religion*," 235; my italics).

39. Ibid., 110, 127. Lash reiterates this view in his concluding reflections, stating, "The first thing we can learn to do is watch our language, be careful what we say" (ibid., 231).

40. *Lost Icons*, 85.

in the confrontation between Christian faith and nineteenth-century rationalism, "it is not reason that is against us, but imagination."[41] In its late-modern context, new variables have not weakened the cogency of Newman's insight. How people imagine their lives, what animates their sensibilities and commitments, and what registers as a belief or outlook worthy of being held (with or without careful self-reflection), represents as trenchant a set of factors in the matter of persuasion as do the rational arguments which Christian apologists put forward in defense of a "reasonable" faith.[42]

Taken together, the rhetorical and imaginative challenges signal the nature of the third. That is, the witnessing Church faces the challenge of producing creative speech and a compelling idiom in order to overcome the resistance of its late-modern audiences to listen to, and in due measure to heed, its gospel message. The reciprocal force of this challenge directs the Church's thinkers and educators to incorporate into their pedagogy—as an integral element in their heuristic task—those resources which help to cultivate such creative modes of persuasive expression. At issue is the *equipping of the imagination* of Christians as a means of re-equipping the imagination of non-Christians for the reception of a Christian vision of life.[43] What, therefore, can poetry teach theological educators as well as their students and readers about creative and, as Lash advocates, "disciplined" speech? How do poets educate the educators in "attentiveness, reverence, and alertness" to language, and the development of creative modes of expression so urgently needed for the Church's public witness in this age? And how does the poetic imagination re-enact the possibilities of that vision in a culture that has grown resistant to it? The implication I draw from such questions insists that the study of poetry neither detracts from the serious business of theology nor is it the mere indulgence of a creative inclination. Rather, in this historical moment of the Church in late-modernity,

---

41. Quoted, with approval, in Lash, "Religion," 82.

42. Lash emphasizes this element in his discussion of the Christian confrontation with "secular" narratives and "myths" of autonomous freedom. Drawing upon John Milbank's *Theology and Social Theory*, he writes, "If, then, there is another way of acting out the world, another way of being human, than as the agent or the victim of the will to power, . . . it will be shown, enacted, in the performance of a better myth, a more persuasive tale" (ibid., 227).

43. I owe some of this way of phrasing the matter to my supervisor at Cambridge, Ben Quash.

poetry represents a mode of articulation intrinsic to the public, persuasive task of Christian theology.

Thus, within a Christian theological understanding, in so far as Christian witness in late-modernity involves rhetorical and imaginative challenges, the poet at work as we discover this labor in his or her poems becomes the focus of a striking possibility: that of revitalizing the language of faith in ways that are at once faithful and compelling. Can this be demonstrated? The larger burden of my thesis is to show that it can, spurred by the observation that this possibility has neither been fully explored in current theological practices nor with methods suitable to the undertaking. As noted, the innumerable problems that such assertions provoke can be, and in many ways are being addressed through various theoretical categories and within numerous theoretical projects. The concentration of my study as an excursus into the theological significance of poetic performance—not as stylized theology but as a substantive theological *style* in its own right—does not consist of surmounting all of these problems. Rather, my project brings into focus through my method of close reading how poems disclose their own possibilities, and how at the same time they also serve, in the idiom of Christian artist/poet David Jones, to "lift up valid signs" for those who currently remain unmoved by the Church's public witness.[44] It is the ability of poetry to command or arrest attention, and to issue a summons to the reader/listener through its "patterning of particulars,"[45] which displays its power for Incarnational witness. Poetry, in other words, opens up new possibilities through and *for* language to speak to the particular situations of others in ways that they can hear resonances with their own lives. Or to approach this matter from a different angle, borrowing a phrase from Dietrich Bonhoeffer from which I take the title of this book, poetry can enable others to be "exposed to *an unexpected*

---

44. Commenting on the modern difficulty to once more show "the eternal things," Jones writes: "The whole complex of these difficulties is primarily felt by the sign-maker, the artist, because for him it is an immediate, day by day, factual problem. He has, somehow or other, *to lift up valid signs*; that is his specific task" (*Epoch and Artist*, 119; my italics).

45. Ben Quash uses this phrase to describe the formal nature of art, suggesting how it is that art generates its compelling power and reflects an "Incarnational" sense through its effects (in Begbie, *Sounding the Depths*, 98). In *Finding the Church*, Dan Hardy applies this same description to the Eucharist (246).

light," that is, the light of God as revealed in Christ and his gospel.[46] This very capacity underscores its benefit to those who would learn further how to engender such connectedness in the face of resistance or indifference; who would, in short, seek to discover how to make the gospel "*readable*" or legible again.

Poetry as Theology and Witness in the Verse of Charles Williams, Micheal O'Siadhail, and Geoffrey Hill

To say that poetry might represent a form of theological discourse and witness may seem as obvious as it is, in certain contexts and from certain perspectives, objectionable. Most poets would admit that poetry does indeed bear witness to something or someone, and seek only to clarify what in particular poetry regards.[47] When, however, we put forward the view that poetry represents a form of *Christian* witness, other issues arise for both the theologian who studies it and for the poets whose work he or she investigates. What, for example, do we mean by "Christian" poetry, or for that matter, a "Christian" poet? Moreover, in light of my own intention to focus on poetic form, how do we specify—or *need* we specify—the distinctively Christian characteristics present in the verse; and is it even possible to do so?

In regard to the first set of questions, some explanation is in order regarding my selection of these particular poets and, within their larger poetic corpus, my selection of particular poems only. I have chosen the work of these poets with three criteria in mind. First, I wanted only excellent verse, that is, poetry manifestly able to arrest attention, to inspire interest, and to challenge the intelligence as well as the outlook of readers. Second, I sought the work of poets who consciously confront the conditions of modernity in the West, and who interact with the effects of the modern situation from a Christian perspec-

---

46. Bonhoeffer, *Letters and Papers*, 362; my emphasis. In this passage Bonhoeffer considers the possibility of speaking about God in a "non-religious" way, not concealing but revealing the world's godlessness, thereby exposing it to the "unexpected light" of Christ and the gospel. We will return to Bonhoeffer's thought and its relevance to contemporary theology and witness in the concluding chapter.

47. The Polish poet Czeslaw Milosz has weighed in on the matter in his Norton Lectures *The Witness of Poetry*, in which he defends his choice of title "not because," he says, "we witness [poetry], but because it witnesses us" (4). See also Heaney, Seamus, *Redress of Poetry*, 2–3.

tive. Thus, I looked for poets who are "Christian" not only in terms of their self-identification (whether public or private), but who manifest a distinctively Christian understanding of the subjects they address in their art as well as their critical reflection. As this feature pertains to my concerns about Christian witness, I wanted, thirdly, poets who in some measure confront the "trauma" of modernity as it has affected the confidence of Christians to speak meaningfully about their faith, and so provide examples of how to address late-modern people specifically in a compelling manner. In this vein, I sought poets whose verse facilitates careful reflection on language and its intersection with the Church's public theological concerns. Regarding all of these aspects, though with varying emphases, the work of Charles Williams, Micheal O'Siadhail, and Geoffrey Hill satisfy these criteria.

In sum, I have attempted to gather an eclectic assemblage of modern "Christian" poems, or poetic sequences, not with any presumption to be representative, but in order to give a fuller treatment of the many and diverse ways in which poetic performance manifests a theologically significant enterprise. Accordingly, my effort to explore the formal features of poetry and to demonstrate with any substance how these features inculcate the advantages I have outlined required me to restrict my close reading to a limited number of examples—not only with respect to the diverse body of recent Christian poetry, but also with respect to the poetic corpus of the poets themselves. The hoped for result is that what my book lacks in breadth it will compensate for in significant depth.

What, then, can we demonstrate about the distinctively Christian character of a poem's formal elements? It must be admitted that the study of poetry as a theological enterprise involves a reciprocal relationship between these disciplines. That is, a Christian reader maintains both an interest in the ways in which poetry speaks to theology and addresses theological concerns, and an alertness to the ways in which theology speaks to poetry in terms of its own categories. The danger, of course, is that through the process of such an exchange the results prove neither faithful to the integrity of the work of art nor adequate to the interests of a specifically Christian theological outlook. From one perspective, to read a poem for what *it* does is not the same thing as reading it in regard to what it does *for* a different set of interests, unless it be shown that the latter is a constitutive element of the former. (To avoid possible confusion on this point, I prefer to speak of a poem as a particular "*mode* of" or "*vehicle* for" Christian expression, rather than of poetry's "*usefulness*.") From another perspective, Christian observers of a project that seeks to show how the study of poetry interacts with their theological concerns are justified when they insist that any claims made in defense of such an undertaking prove manifestly Christian. The effort to "legitimize" art and artistic practices in terms of Christian systematic categories offers one kind of response to this expectation, but not without problems.[48] My own project to align the study of poetry with the goals and practices of Christian theology does not aim at legitimacy in such essentialist terms. Rather, as an effort to demonstrate what a poem does—and not what it is—which reveals its *Christian* attributes, I seek to show how these poets are *doing* theological work by virtue of what they enact through their art.

At this point, I have only suggested certain advantages that I believe poetry possesses as a vehicle for inculcating new resonances for the gospel through language (again, when it is observed that such an aim and effect prove intrinsic to the poem's presentation). Much of the work that I do by way of demonstration will show how the devices employed by Charles Williams, Micheal O'Siadhail, and Geoffrey Hill achieve the kind of engagement I have highlighted in a way that other forms of theological articulation do not, and to some extent cannot. But there is more to such a demonstration than creative rhetorical advantages, lest it be remarked that my project only confirms the biases I have noted—that poetry merely enhances theological ideas. Poetry does enhance speech, and in many ways induces pleasure, as well as provocation. As such, it represents a valuable resource for communication; and when that communication directs attention to Christian concerns and the implications of the gospel specifically, its value to the witnessing Church is evident. But there is a difference between emphasizing that a mode of creative articulation suits the needs of Christianity's expressive interests and claiming that it also constitutes a specifically *Christian* mode of expression.

---

48. The Christian theologian, for example, may appropriately argue that God's acts in the world are in some sense unique (particularly God's speech acts), and so do not lend themselves *too hastily* to the validation of seemingly analogous activities on the part of human beings, such as the writing of verse.

Through my discussion of these three poets and my close readings of their select poems, I seek to advance both claims. For this purpose, in the concluding sections of each chapter I have included the commentary and insights of Christian thinkers who contemplate the distinctively Christian nature of formal performance—as *conversation partners* with the poets. Also for the purpose of establishing both claims, and as a further refraction of my close reading of these poems, I incorporate the poets' own arguments and Christian sense about the formal nature of their craft. In Williams' "Arthuriad," for example, I focus on what he calls "the development of images and discovery of the rhythmic technique" as both a method of creative engagement with readers for whom Christian ideas have grown remote, and as an excursus into the Christian "way of images" (as he identifies it). In Micheal O'Siadhail's *The Gossamer Wall*, I demonstrate how poetic structure and the manipulation of rhythm and rhyme patterns provide a compelling method of historical redress, and how this method supplies a Christian ethical model for witness as it seeks to include within its own testimony sensitivity to the testimonies of others about their experiences. Then, lastly, in my analysis of Geoffrey Hill's *The Triumph of Love*, I bring together many of these same elements as I find them in this poem, showing how Hill achieves "pitch of attention" and a form of "poetic kenosis" through these same devices, and, of special applicability to his art, through the manipulation of syntax and points of view.

In a sense, my treatment of Hill represents the climax of my argument. Through Hill's critical ideas and their manifestation in *The Triumph of Love* I show how a proper view of Christian poetics and theology of language must include an account of linguistic performance: as a phenomenon characterized by Christian ethical concerns and specific to a biblical and even christological vision. Regarding ethical concerns, in all three main chapters I develop the claim that accuracy and the careful study and use of language comprise theological virtues, given language's inherent susceptibility to corruption (its "fallenness," as Hill declares it). In this light, I advance the argument that poetry provides a critical site both for exposing these conditions and for negotiating the tensions that arise from them, in the interest of public accountability and, ultimately, of truth telling. Regarding poetry's interaction with biblical texts and motifs, I show how its capacity for intensity and innovation sets up a mutually illuminating exchange not only for readers of either the Bible or of poetry, but for potential "readers" of *Christianity* in contemporary late-modern societies. Then, significantly, as forms of Christian expression I show how the poems I have selected manifest a unique ability to transfigure the humanly familiar into meditations on christological themes, and do so along the lines of what I call an Incarnational *style*—that is, a style that features ways of re-inscribing the very manner of God's presentation of his purposes in Christ. There are ethical issues at hand here also, as style converges with the virtue of humility in particular, a view Hill encapsulates in the phrase "poetic kenosis." In all of these aspects, the "peculiar advantages" of poetry and the poetic craft emerge as formal properties of a reflective theology. Moreover, such advantages prove effective to engage disaffected audiences in terms demanded by faith's "deposit" in the gospel; and in the gospel's deposition by Christian witnesses these poems convey the "unexpected light" of that message as an eminently viable vision today.

Lastly, by placing the formal elements at the fore of my discussion I give due emphasis to my own method of demonstration through close reading and my focus on style and form as significant theological categories. By this arrangement I also preserve the integrity of the poems, which demand that they be read in their own terms and in regard to what they enact before deriving application to theology and to the task of Christian witness specifically.

The claim, therefore, that poetry *matters* to Christian theology and to Christian witness in this age along the lines I have emphasized stands or falls depending on the methods employed by poetry's theological interpreters. If demonstration of this claim in its many aspects is forthcoming, we must hear the poets and their poems first. Hence, to this task I now turn.

2

"From the Exposition of Grace to the Place of Images"

Incarnational Witness and "the Way of Images" in Charles Williams' Arthuriad

The Place of Images[1] within Christian Theology and Its Late-Modern Cultural Setting

I HAVE TAKEN THE TITLE PHRASE FOR THIS CHAPTER FROM WILLIAMS' poem "The Vision of the Empire," found in the first series of his "Arthuriad," *Taliessin Through Logres*.[2] In this poem, Williams depicts the visit of his protagonist and soon to be "king's poet" Taliessin to the Empire's capital city Byzantium. Having arrived in the Imperial city, the poem continues,

> Taliessin walked through the hither angels,
> from the exposition of grace to the place of images.[3]

---

1. The concept of "image," of the "imagistic" or "figurative," is subject to numerous technical and connotative definitions. I am using the word *image* because it was Williams' preferred idiom as well as a term he specified. See, e.g., his discussion of Dante's Beatrice as "image" in *Figure of Beatrice* (*Figure*), 7.

2. Although Williams wrote other Arthurian poems, including fragments for his proposed third book of the Taliessin cycle, we will restrict our study to his two completed works *Taliessin Through Logres* (1938), and *The Region of the Summer Stars* (1944). The texts used here and their page references come from the Eerdman's reprint with notes, and will be designated as follows: references to *Taliessin Through Logres* will appear as *TTL* and references to *The Region of the Summer Stars* as *RSS*. In addition, references to Williams' unfinished *Arthurian Torso* and to C. S. Lewis's notes on the cycle will appear under the heading *AT*.

3. *TTL*, 24.

Several questions arise immediately from this brief description of his protagonist's movements. What is meant by "*the exposition of grace*" and "*the place of images*," as well as the relationship of the one to the other? Does the former represent a particular mode of reflection, as the word "exposition" connotes, whereas the latter refers to a physical location only (a "place" within the imagined world of the poem), or does it too signify a mode of reflection, and of perception? Does Taliessin's passage from the one to the other, then, mark a break in states of perception, which also signals a shift in method, or does it entail a continuity of sorts? If the latter meaning, are we then to understand from this poem that a Christian concept such as grace is susceptible of diverse modes of contemplation and expression, including the imagistic as well as the expository?

Taken together, such questions begin to disclose some of the larger issues that Williams' Arthuriad addresses as they emerge from the verse, and in turn help to direct our theological interests in his achievement. Among these issues, the matter of rhetorical modes—as modes of both interpretation and expression—represents one supervening area of consideration as we examine Williams' poetry and thought. In the context of this poem, for example, we cannot justifiably conclude that "*the exposition of grace*" represents a form of analytical prose readily contrasted with an imagistic manner of presentation. Assuming that the first two stanzas of "Vision" represent Taliessin's initial glimpse of Byzantium, the "exposition of grace" he encounters and from which he proceeds is in fact a scene of Imperial order dramatized:

> The organic body sang together;
> dialects of the world sprang in Byzantium;
> back they rang to sing in Byzantium;
> the streets repeat the sound of the Throne.[4]

If this scene "exposits" grace, then it is grace understood as a phenomenon of animated relational harmony, a view reinforced aurally by the pattern of rhythm and internal rhyme that extends and embodies it. Exposition, therefore, assumes the character of "exposure," as grace is given amplitude surpassing conceptual denotation: as God's abiding initiative in the world it is perceptible, and so presentable, in terms of its operation and effects.

4. *TTL*, 24.

For Williams, this is true of all of God's activity as human beings perceive it. In his notes on the cycle, for example, Williams explains that in the myth of the poem the Emperor signifies "operative Providence,"[5] and represents "God as active, God as known in Church and State, God as ruling men."[6] Hence, Williams here offers to our imagination, as throughout the Arthuriad, what we may call *metaphysics in motion*, reified in his presentation of Byzantium as a pattern of "God-in-operation or God-as-known-by-Man."[7] Accordingly, the Imperial city is a place teeming with activity. Though it is activity of a unique and idealized character, Williams gives it a dynamic quality through the use of poetic devices, which heighten this impression of vitality (for example, the frequent use of interior rhymes and alliteration). In addition, the variegated metre, line length, punctuation and enjambments modulate the tempo, quickening and slowing the pace interchangeably like a syncopated pulse. In effect, what risks flattening into a staid depiction of order is lifted by the poetry into a dynamic portrayal of order-in-action, a patterning of providence as a vital interpenetration of thought and act realized in speech. Notably, then, the Empire is also itself a world of the word ("the Word") in motion: of the ringing out of "*dialects of the world,*" the "*translating [of] the Greek minuscula,*" the "*bearing of missives through the area of empire*"; even the household "*inscribes the Acts of the Emperor.*"[8] The poem *portrays* speech as the movement of tongues toward action and instantiation, not as something prior to action or reflecting upon it but as itself the activity of the world, as the poem is itself the activity of portraying a world.

Furthermore, in his own gloss on the text Williams informs us that in this initial encounter Taliessin stands in the direct presence of the Emperor, and so witnesses the perfect realization of the Emperor's will in the Imperial city. In terms of the theological symbolism in play here, Taliessin's movement from that space to the "outer world, which is precisely a place of images," also signifies a progression "from 'God in

---

5. Preface to *RSS*, 117.

6. "The Making of Taliessin," *Image of the City* (*Image*), 181.

7. From his "Notes on the Arthurian Myth" (*Image*, 178), where he also elaborates that "The Empire is the pattern; Logres the experiment" (ibid.).

8. *TTL*, 24.

Himself' to 'God in His creatures'";[9] in other words, from an experience of the immediate to one of mediated capacities. The latter aptly describes the operation of images and of figurative speech in general—in this context given a particular theological demeanor as it also describes the manner of the Incarnation.

At the level of the poem as we read it, however, what Williams renders in *both* instances aims at depiction. The portrayal of the Empire's inner sanctum as the "exposition of grace" and a vision of "God in Himself" offers an image of one kind—that is, of grace dramatized. What Taliessin then "sees" extends the figuration of grace towards its corporeal manifestation: "*the identities imaged in a sapphire sea*"[10] taking creaturely, indeed fleshly, form as the far reaches of the Empire appear to him.[11] The harmony of the Empire's "organic body" materializes in a symphony of images, commingling the conceptual with the concrete, the cosmic with the creaturely, and infusing the ordinary phenomena of the human with the operations of a providential order. By this means, Williams introduces us to a world that also conveys an image of our own world as he would have us understand it: always itself in the substance of its own particulars, while invested with the creative, providential and incarnated activity of God.

With regard to the poetic drama, the great challenge for Taliessin as the bearer of this vision to Logres becomes the endeavor to realize its further extension (i.e., to "re-incarnate" it) through the establishment of Arthur's kingdom. In terms of our reception of the Arthuriad as its readers, our task involves the discovery of how this work of the imagination also speaks meaningfully to our own situation. Read theologically, a central problematic emerges as a theme developed within the cycle and as a topic directing our analysis of it: What is the *place* of images within Christian theological discourse and its contemporary public expression?

On the one hand, no focus of attention is more appropriate to the study of poetry than its images and imagistic methods. A poet's use of

---

9. Quoted from King, *Pattern in the Web*, 26. Williams develops this distinction through images in his "Prelude" to *RSS* (120–21).

10. *TTL*, 25.

11. As we discover in his theological aesthetics, for Williams the human body offers an "index" for the divine as its human locus. See, e.g., his essay "The Index of the Body" in *Image*, 80–87; cf. *Figure*, 64–65.

symbols, tropes, metaphors, similes and all variety of figural presentation is germane to the craft of poetry, and an obvious category when inspecting the method, content and effects of poems. On the other hand, to pursue theological studies under the rubric of image and images seems an undertaking fraught with hazards. Such a topic lands us in a centuries-long history of theological debate, calling up associations with iconoclastic controversies, deliberations over how best to understand and articulate the nature of God-incarnate, and ongoing debates about the meaning and methods of Christian hermeneutical, liturgical and devotional practices. In addition, largely due to the proliferation of electronic media in nearly every sphere of late-modern life, the very idea of image has undergone enormous shifts in perspective and attitude, leading to no less vigorous debates about the status and use of images within the culture at large as well as the Church. Discussions about *image*, in all of its theoretical and phenomenal formulations, churn with innumerable points of contention.

Yet, for all of the debates, it must still be asserted that Christianity cannot think its own beliefs and praxis without the category of *image*. Christians are bound to uphold such fundamental convictions as humans are made in the image of God, that God assumed that same image as the consummate act of self-disclosure within the world (John 1:18; Heb 1:1–3), and that their sacred texts and liturgical practices depend in no small measure upon the use of images and figurative speech to convey the meaning of their faith—to themselves as well as the world around them. What remains, of course, and what has stood at the center of the Church's longstanding exploration of the topic of image, is to discern what implications can be drawn from these assertions. More precisely, what does the central phenomenon of Christ the consummate image of God—what Hans Urs von Balthasar called God's "arch-image"—indicate about the role and value of images to Christian reflection and expression?

Even more radically, do imagistic presentations and figurative discourses such as we find in the Arthuriad entail a method of *doing* theology, as one way of re-formulating Christian doctrine and of showing-forth Christian beliefs? (In our concluding section, we will return to this question in light of more recent studies in figurative discourse, specifically that of Janet Soskice.) In this vein, how do features of late-modern societies and the sensibilities they exhibit make the matter of images a priority for theology's public tasks? In an "age of the image," and particularly in cultural contexts wherein the native meaning of Christianity's central imagistic concepts—Kingdom of God, Incarnation, revelation, the Cross—appear remote or alien to many, the role of images in the Church's witness seems a topic in serious need of re-examination on the part of Christian thinkers. Hence, a cardinal concern that directs our study of Charles Williams' "place of images" depicted in his Arthurian poetry regards the Church's need to recover and renew the significance of its own images on behalf of an uncommitted public. Put broadly, we ask: How can the work(s) of God in the world be portrayed in such a way that knowledge of God is further disclosed, or at least brought closer to the capacity of human perception, and how does the Arthuriad serve this endeavor?[12]

Williams was acutely aware of the historical and theological issues surrounding questions about images, and sought with vigor to advance his own theology of the image and "the way of images" as an appropriate and indeed central focus for Christian theological reflection and expression. Moreover, his *Christian habit of mind* was alert to the challenges of rendering a Christian vision of life to contemporary audiences, and his Arthurian cycle represents the crowning demonstration of that sensitivity. Williams understood, however, that the issue here is not merely a matter of competing for attention; that at its heart, whatever uses of images the Church employs in its practices it can only follow and achieve its most potent expression from deeply held convictions about the nature and value of images themselves. In this regard, he advanced what he called "The Way of the Affirmation of Images."

The Ways of the Images and the Enactment of an Incarnational Theology

By the "Affirmation of Images" Williams meant generally our esteem for material manifestations or representations—of ideas, actions, states of affairs, essences or various modes of "substantial being"—and our recognition that images of innumerable variety can be vehicles for conveying meaning beyond their immediate referents.[13] The affirmation of

---

12. Or as Austin Farrer asks succinctly, how is it that "images are able to signify divine realities" (*Glass of Vision*, 57)?

13. Cf. n.1. Like faith, the Affirmation of Images comprises a principle of action in human life that issues in Christ-likeness. Williams writes, "Justice, charity, union; these

images, therefore, involves an operation of both the senses and the intellect. When converted into acts of re-presentation, the results are apprehensible to the rational mind, but also manifestly felt in the emotions.[14] In its broadest purview any phenomenon in the world may provide an occasion for this affirmation and insight—whether the object of our attention is a creaturely fact, the relationships between creatures, or a manner of life. It is also, significantly, a way of apprehending God which God initiated through Creation and, consummately, the assumption of humanity by Christ. As Williams declares in his gloss on the Athanasian Creed, it

> produces a phrase which is the very maxim of the Affirmative Way: "Not by conversion of the Godhead into flesh but by taking of the Manhood into God." And not only of the particular religious Way, but of all progress of all affirmations: it is the actual manhood which is to be carried on, and not the height which is to be brought down. All images are, in their degree, to be carried on; mind is never to put off matter; all experience is to be gathered in.[15]

Read one way, these comments imply a natural theology of images, a principle attributable, as Williams says, to "all progress of all affirmations," and similar in approach to Karl Rahner's "ontology of the symbol."[16] To elaborate Williams' thought here, images disclose something beyond their surface appearance only by virtue of their actuality or substantial fact-ness, whether the image is "natural" or an artifact of the human imagination. (Here, too, we find his criterion for a "successful" image.[17]) For Williams, however, such a universally discoverable principle receives its ultimate clarification, legitimacy, and potency

---

are the three degrees of the Way of the Affirmation of Images, and all of us are to be the images affirmed" (*Image*, 158).

14. In speaking of Dante, for example, Williams writes, "when we talk of Dante setting the experience of beatitude in intellectual knowledge, we have to remember that it was the intellect of poetry; that is, that it had a much greater emotional sensitiveness about it than thought for us usually has" (*Figure*, 66).

15. Williams, *Descent of the Dove* (*Descent*), 59.

16. Rahner, *Theological Investigations*, Vol. IV, 222–35.

17. In Williams' commentary on *Othello*, e.g., he writes, "The symbols are so intensely themselves that they are enabled to be symbols: stability and innocence and destructiveness are defined as philosophical elements by the force of their mortal exactness. It is the great gift of poetry" (*Reason and Beauty* [*RB*], 132).

in the Incarnation of Christ. As he declares elsewhere, "It is a result of the Incarnation that opened all potentialities of the knowledge of the Kingdom of Heaven in and through matter. 'My covenant shall be in your flesh.'"[18] The insight proffered, he insisted, is unique, "allowing to matter a significance and power which (of all the religions and philosophies) only Christianity has affirmed."[19] Accordingly, the faith of Christians is "a faith in the interchange of the kingdom operating in matter as out of matter,"[20] and that faith extends logically and forcefully to a wider affirmation of images, which likewise may serve as material vehicles for the "signification of divine reality." In sum, Williams insisted that although this pattern is observable throughout the natural world, only by the Incarnation does it receive its fullest expression and its final validity.[21]

In this respect, on the one hand God's self-disclosure in Christ serves as the central apology for the method of images (or, as he puts it, "the approach to God through . . . images"[22]), the application of which has broad implications for the value of a variety of Christian imagistic practices. On the other hand, it is neither the case that all images serve the purpose of divine disclosure, nor do images comprehend all that can be known of God. Thus, the necessary complement to the Way of Affirmation is what Williams called the "Way of the Rejection of Images," or the "Negative Way."[23] Williams encapsulates the dynamic relationship between these two approaches in his famous dictum, "*This also is Thou; neither is this Thou.*" The first assertion describes the emphasis of those Christians who sought to render Christian faith and life as a positive declaration of the goodness of material existence,

18. Williams, *He Came Down from Heaven* (*HCDH*), 101.

19. Ibid., 106.

20. Ibid., 128.

21. As he writes in his postscript to *Descent*, "By an act of substitution he [Christ] reconciled the natural world with the world of the kingdom of heaven, sensuality with substance. He restored substitution and co-inherence everywhere. . . . It is supernatural, but also it is natural. . . . It is the image everywhere of supernatural charity, and the measure of this or of the refusal of this is the cause of all the images" (235).

22. *Figure*, 9.

23. Williams speaks of the Crucifixion and the Resurrection as a blending of both "ways," writing, "The Crucifixion and the Death are rejection and affirmation at once, for they affirm death only to reject death; . . . and beyond that physical rejection of earth lies the re-affirmation of earth which is called the Resurrection" (*Figure*, 10).

reconfirming God's own esteem for creation made consummate in the Incarnation and Resurrection.[24] The second terminus—"neither is this Thou"—insists upon the ultimate limitation of human comprehension, finding its characteristic expression among those Christians who provided the "profound mystical documents of the soul, the records of the great psychological masters of Christendom."[25] Together these two ways form the "web" or "pattern" of the cosmos and the divine "glory"[26] in its earthly and human manifestation: "The one Way was to affirm all things orderly until all the universe throbbed with vitality; the other to reject all things until there was nothing anywhere but He."[27] In other words, to evoke another of Williams' famous categories, the two ways "co-inhere" in a harmony of comprehension and expression,[28] as two ways of knowing and of showing the divine within the limitations of human experience and creativity.

The poem "The Departure of Dindrane" portrays this dialectical unity of the two ways through the figures of the poet Taliessin and the saintly novice Dindrane. As Taliessin leads her away from Camelot to the convent where she will confirm her vows, we read:

>   the two great vocations,
> the Rejection of all images before the unimaged,
> the Affirmation of all images before the all-imaged,
> the Rejection affirming, the Affirmation rejecting ...[29]

Both ways, therefore, depict the way of images in its positive and negative manifestation, and both reciprocate a testimony to the nature and character of the Christian God as he is in his own unfathomable being and as humans comprehend him in their (and his!) finitude. It is within

---

24. This is the category into which fall the doctors of the Church along with all those Christians who "develop[ed] great art and romantic love and marriage and philosophy and social justice" (*Descent*, 58).

25. Ibid.

26. The "web of glory" was one of Williams' preferred characterizations of this reality. As an image, it captured both strands of his formula. See, e.g., *HCDH*, 39, 146.

27. *Descent*, 58. Williams elaborates this point in *Figure*, writing, "As above, so below; as in him, so in us. The tangle of affirmation and rejection which is in each of us has to be drawn into some kind of pattern, and has so been drawn by all men who have ever lived" (10).

28. *Descent*, 57.

29. *RSS*, 150.

this interplay of "This also is Thou; neither is this Thou" that Williams situates the distinctive vocation of the poet, principally as a purveyor of the way of affirmation, but, as we shall see, also as a witness to human limitation.

In varying degrees, Williams believed that all poets are affirmers of the way of images in his Christian sense of that way (as he attributes to the king's poet Taliessin—the central image of poetry and the poetic genius in the Arthuriad—even in his "pre-converted" state; see *RSS* 124). Poets, he asserted, are unifiers—of form and substance, of matter and spirit—and their poetry constitutes the union of such dualities. In this respect, poets image Christ in their work, albeit analogously, as a native function of the poetic genius. It is, again, the doctrine of God-incarnate which provides the discoverable template and the consummate legitimization for this unifying tendency, whether recognized or not by the poet at work.[30]

More striking than this general analogy, however, in the Arthuriad Williams' "Affirmative Way" demonstrates a *conversion of Christian thought into images* within a drama of human experience; and it is here that we find his most distinctive contribution to Christian theology and witness. Specifically, the poet's development of images does not merely embellish Incarnational themes but *enacts an Incarnational theology*, both recapitulating the Incarnation's own mode of disclosure as a "knowledge of the Kingdom of heaven in and through matter" and re-presenting various strains of an Incarnational, or christological, vision of life. This crucial distinction regarding what the poetry does, central to my thesis as well as to the poet's sense about the intrinsic relationship between form and the vision it seeks to articulate, will govern our closer readings of select poems.

In this regard, we can read Taliessin's passage from the exposition of grace to the place of images as itself an image of Williams' entire project to explore human experiences and the works of God in the world by *showing* rather than merely talking about this dynamic interplay. It is this quality of display that Williams hails in Dante's figure of Beatrice, who "aids our faith" in a way distinct from philosophy because what

---

30. Writing of Spenser, Williams asserts, "whether the doctrine of the Resurrection be true or not [a concession to his audience, and not a statement of his own skepticism], it seems only by some such resurrection of the earth in their reconciled minds that the poets can justly find union" (*RB*, 62).

philosophy does by reason, "she does . . . through vision."³¹ And it is a quality he finds in Wordsworth's poetry—a "visionary power," which brings to fullest capacity this union of form and substance: "*the turnings intricate of verse*," as *Prelude* V renders it, presenting forms and substances "*as objects recognized/ In flashes, and with glory not their own.*"³² Citing other verses from this same passage from *Prelude*, Williams comments:

> Visionary power again attends on the viewless winds which belong to that Nature, but here it is embodied in words. And there—in those words—are recognized forms and substances; the soul knows not merely *how* but *what* she felt.³³

Williams' word for this achievement in verse is *passion*, a "passion [that] . . . sees into the life of things,"³⁴ and which reciprocates a new intellectual and emotional intensity regarding the objects of contemplation, as well as a new possibility for our identification with them. In creating a poem, Williams argues, poets offer "a living thing to our apprehension,"³⁵ and elsewhere (sounding a note we will find in Soskice) he adds that theirs is "the creation of something with a new life of its own. . . . It is the entering-in, through the senses and through the mind, of another existence. So much is true of the shortest and simplest lyric."³⁶ Here we find a description of the poetic process as well as its result, a formulation that construes the nature and effect of imagistic speech generally: an "entering-in through the senses and through the mind," which in the Arthuriad yields a fresh display, or enactment, of *Christian* forms and substances.

Williams develops this connection between form and the vision which shapes it, and so, between the task of the poet and a Christian sense of that vocation, in his development of the figure of Taliessin. Rather than stating this principle, he dramatizes it as a conversion of one man's

---

31. *Figure*, 63.
32. Wordsworth, *Prelude* V, 603–05, *Works*, 674.
33. *RB*, 22.
34. Ibid., 29.
35. Williams, *Poetry at Present* (*PP*), 176.
36. Ibid., 159. In *Figure* Williams states further: "The poem is an image with many relevancies, . . . is itself the expression of the relevancy of its own images each to the other. The poem . . . is the existing thing, the image we have to deal with; the meanings assist and enrich the line; they do not replace it" (45).

sensibilities. From his commission in the wood of Broceliande where, for all his poetic endowments, Taliessin is still *"lacking the formulae and the grand backing of the Empire,"*[37] to his new role as the king's poet and "the founder of the company" whose *"cult was the Trinity and the Flesh-taking,"*[38] the poet progresses from a condition of possessing evident talent and deep poetic instinct, but without understanding, to a state of sanctified perception and sense of enlightened purpose for his art. The poem "The Calling of Taliessin" recapitulates this crisis of conversion, which, significantly, advances by the operation of images.

Whether awake or asleep in that wood of *"secret-swayed Broceliande,"*[39] by the prompting of Merlin and Brisen Taliessin hears as in a dream *"an image springing from a tangle of names,"* and *"was caught by a pulse of truth in the image.*[40] Visual images accompany voices as the poem's portrayal of Taliessin's awakening sensibility unfolds in the rarefied atmosphere of the mystical. Allusions to Paul's revelation in the "third heaven" reported in 2 Corinthians 12, to Dante's development of images in the *Paradiso*, and to Wordsworth's *Prelude*—complete with the *"humming"* of *"the feeling intellect"* and *"the far humming of the spiritual intellect"*[41]—generate this climate. Williams' mingling of these references also pays tribute to the vocation of poets, suggesting a continuity of visionary insight between poetry and the apostolic mission. Like the Apostle, but unlike Dante-pilgrim, Williams' poet returns from this state of reverie, now able *"to share in the doctrine of largesse"* (Williams' phrase for the expansive love of God),[42] and so endowed to "fulfill his errand" in Logres. As Taliessin manifests Williams' image of poetry, so this episode images the transformation of the poet's mind and genius into its fuller capacity. By this means, Williams implies a critique of the modern notion that poetic genius and personality alone suffice to produce art of the most exalted quality. A Christian poet, at least, is bound by more than a private vision. Accordingly, in another aspect we may view Taliessin's journey through Logres and participation

---

37. *RSS*, 124.
38. Ibid., 154.
39. Ibid., 127.
40. Ibid., 131.
41. Ibid., 132.
42. Ibid., 134.

in the drama of Camelot and the Grail quest as Williams' effort to trace the progression of a Christian theological poetics, not as a theoretical subtext for the cycle but as the unfolding drama of the Christian imagination in pursuit of a vision of "largesse."

Despite the supernormal quality of his conversion, Taliessin, like the other characters in the Arthuriad, remains flesh and blood. As one who stands in submission to a greater glory Taliessin's experience images the limitations of "*the grand art*," in keeping with Williams' own formula of the way of images, "This also is Thou; neither is this Thou." Confronted by this supernal vision, we are told,

> The weight of poetry could not then sink
> into the full depth of the weight of glory.[43]

Thus, as the spell of vision reaches its point of most sublime intensity, with the dreamscape now drenched in the magisterial colour of porphyry, before giving way to a less lofty manifestation of Logres-Britain, the question arises: " (*beyond body and spirit,/ could the art of the king's poet in the court of Camelot,/ after his journeys, find words for body or spirit*)"?[44] By bracketing the poet's prospects in parentheses, Williams illustrates graphically the idea that poetry inevitably faces limitations beyond which it cannot extend (or plumb, to stay with the image of depth and "the weight of glory"). Moreover, by placing this parenthesis within a final movement towards the un-presentable—"*the entire point of the thrice co-inherent Trinity/ when every crown and every choir is vanished*"[45]—Williams insinuates what "the way of rejection" affirms. Finding words for body and spirit the poet can do; but beyond both he falls silent in that place where "there is nothing anywhere but He." Hence, for all of its potency, the poet's affirmation of images *in* images remains but an "*approach* to God through images." In this way, Williams amplifies a further element in his theological poetics, reflective of his Christian doctrinal convictions: that human comprehension of ultimate reality is ultimately limited. That very limitation, however, Williams believed poetry could also show.

---

43. Ibid., 133.
44. Ibid., 134.
45. Ibid.

Williams makes a case for this opinion in his essay "The Ostentation of Verse."[46] In this short but insightful piece, he contends that because we can distinguish poetry (designated as "verse") from prose by virtue of its measured lines, we are made aware of a limitation intrinsic to our human nature. Whereas prose, he elaborates, "conceals its human limitations," pretending "to subdue its own methods" and persuading us "that we can trust our natures to know things as they are,"[47] poetry, by virtue of its "rhythmical form," makes us aware that all human ways of knowing begin with a pattern conditioned by our choosing. The "ostentation of verse," then, consists of drawing attention to this fact about human knowing as pattern-making, hence showing in its form "that man only apprehends his experiences according to his own nature."[48] At the same time, Williams rescues poetry from possible debilitation as a vehicle able to express "visionary power," clarifying that, "The ostentatious pattern is an expansion and a limitation at once"—"is in itself a further enlargement" because as a "fact in the nature of writing" it mirrors "the nature of experience itself."[49] Thus, he surmises, "it is precisely a fuller experience; it takes man's limitation and makes that a part of his total sensation."[50]

The creation of such experiences as a distinct property of poetic effect, adds Williams, proves especially advantageous for the effort to capture the sensation of "the eternal present." While it is true, he insists, "we have not yet discovered any way of writing poetry in time which shall include all the experiences of time,"[51] we can *approach* that experience in verse. He writes, "The nearest we can get to eternity is either

---

46. Published as the first chapter in *RB*.

47. Ibid., 8, 7, 10.

48. Ibid., 8. Williams seeks to substantiate this claim by noting at the outset "in verse the reader is deliberately referred to a chosen measure; in prose he is not so referred. That reference ... is made known to him by the verse itself, and is ostentatiously insisted upon by the verse itself" (3). Furthermore, he elaborates, "One is, in prose, conditioned, but one is not by any means so intensely aware of the pattern of that conditioning ..." (4), whereas in verse the manner of arrangement is integral to the presentation, its patterned method "being known as a primary condition of our reading" (9).

49. Ibid., 7, 9.

50. Ibid., 9. He adds, "the magnificence of its [the poetic pattern's] assertion is made magnificent by its own limitation, and we know at once what we know, how we know it, and that we cannot know it outside our own nature" (10).

51. Ibid., 14.

all moments or one moment. But then the one moment must, in that aspect, be felt as entirely self-contained";[52] that is, compressed in the moment of the poem as that experience which it "catches" with "the sharpest poignancy of some experience, a sharpness which even in life we so often hardly realize."[53] By that very compression, however, which verse so uniquely achieves, we are enabled to "look forward to some other moment"; the poetic moment being "complete with the awareness of something else."[54] Poetry, by virtue of its composition, generates this dynamic interplay of compression and expansion, the former creating the condition, indeed the possibility for the latter.

Williams' theory about the ostentation of verse may be debated as an accurate account of poetry's advantages over prose. But its premise resonates with a Christian account of the human apprehension of God, as does Williams' identification of the central challenge of giving expression to the experience or the presence of the eternal in time. By this route, we come to the issue of history, which arises as a problematic in the shape of a *formal* challenge that goes to the heart of the intersection of poetry and theology. In his *Short History of the Holy Spirit in the Church*, Williams brings this challenge to the fore as a way of demarcating the nature not of the poetic task, but more broadly, of the *theological* task. He writes,

> The beginning of Christendom is, strictly, at a point out of time. A metaphysical trigonometry finds it among the spiritual Secrets, at the meeting of two heavenward lines, one drawn from Bethany along the Ascent of Messias, the other from Jerusalem against the Descent of the Paraclete. That measurement, the measurement of eternity in operation, of the bright cloud and the rushing wind, is, in effect, theology.[55]

However eccentric (or illuminating) theologians may find Williams' poetic idiom here, he nonetheless seizes upon a central dynamic governing all accounts of the works of God in the world through Christ. In whatever form articulated, the "knowledge of the Kingdom of Heaven in and through matter," central to christology and extended to doctrines

---

52. Ibid.
53. Ibid., 12.
54. Ibid., 15.
55. *Descent*, 1.

of the Holy Spirit and the Church, comprises a "measurement of eternity in operation." How Williams displays this dynamic in images represents one of the compelling features of his poetic witness to the Incarnation.

History, Myth, and the Drama of Glory Incarnate

Williams' own description of his Arthurian cycle provides a fitting entry point for our discussion of this topic, and helps to refine our focus on poetry as a form of theological discourse. He summarized the "history of Taliessin" as "a history . . . of the development of the Images," and "the discovery of the rhythmical technique."[56] Which "history" and what notion of history, however, does the poet have in mind? To be clear, on the one hand he meant to indicate the artistic challenges he sought to engage in his Arthuriad, and so the history of his own authorship as well as the appropriation of material with a longstanding literary tradition. In this respect, what Williams observed through his own study of Arthurian literature is the gradual discovery and then loss of the Christian meaning of the legend as its poetic and dramatic center—principally in the figure of Galahad and in the Grail quest—and which he sought to recover in his Arthuriad.[57] On the other hand, as we find elsewhere in his critical thought, Williams was keen to interpret the history of the Christian church and the unfolding of Christian thought as itself a development of images, beginning with its central image the "in-Godding of Man" in Christ. Not surprisingly, Williams weaves this same progression into his Christian myth of Arthur, as one of his principal means for locating his re-interpretation of the Arthurian narrative within a Christian historical-interpretative framework.

Some, of course, may question whether the history of Christianity, or even the very notion of history as Christians understand it, can be thought and explicated along these lines. One obvious difficulty lies with Williams's use of myth as a vehicle to explore Christian themes. Because Williams in broad terms understood myth as a product of the human imagination, however, the more relevant question here regards the use of a particular literary genre as a method of Christian interpretation and re-presentation. In this regard, myth serves as a means for

---

56. *Image*, 180.

57. Williams is careful to qualify that this development began as a *poetic*, not as a theological, discovery (see *AT*, 250–51; cf. 246).

structuring an imaginative whole and as a method for dramatizing a pattern of Christian meaning. Thus, we can to some extent agree with Charles Moorman that for Williams the benefit of deploying a "mythopoetic vehicle" such as the Arthurian legend lay in its ability "to give full and ordered expression to [Williams'] conception of the relationship of civilization and religion"—not as an escape from the present world but as a grand image of its own condition and prospect for redemption.[58]

Charles Williams understood that myth possesses this capacity, and so we may view the Arthuriad in part as an attempt to retrieve myth's ordering function and advantage. But he also recognized that his culture had undergone a fundamental change in the imagination such that, in its broadest sense, myth—as it once had been received—no longer served to frame modern people's conception of a meaningful universe. Asserting, for example, that with Hopkins' death came "the close of the myths" as a framing vehicle for literature, including "that greatest of the myths . . . Christianity,"[59] the use of mythic material for the modern mindset became indexed to subjective states of consciousness, in keeping with that parallel movement in the modern sensibility. The "real change" after Hopkins, he argues, was therefore "deeper than the mere disuse of myth; it was in the *new use*, not merely of myth but of metaphor and all knowledge."[60] As he had written earlier of W. B. Yeats' "new mythology,"

> ...for us all strangeness, most adventure, and in a growing sense all space, must be found within. It is rather in ideas of the world than in the world that novelty and familiarity must lie, and it is by *the recognition of the inner in the outer* that most of us find satisfaction....[61]

This last sentence, I think, signals both the challenge Williams believed he faced and the means by which he sought to meet that challenge in his Arthurian poetry. It goes to the heart of his motivation not only for his use of myth but for his method of interpreting it in images as well. The satisfaction achieved "by the recognition of the inner in the outer" represented a modern sensibility (as Charles Taylor confirms),

---

58. Moorman, *Arthurian Triptych*, 99.
59. Introduction to *New Book of English Verse* (*NBEV*), 16.
60. Ibid., 17; my italics.
61. *PP*, 60–1; my italics.

which Williams, himself a modern, saw, and approved.[62] But he would not abandon the higher demand he felt towards his own Christian convictions, a faith that extended immeasurably beyond the boundaries of a private vision towards an all-embracing "largesse." His "business" as a poet "to express his imagination of the universe"[63] was expressly that of portraying a *Christian* universe.

In light of this tension, we may pose the following question as Williams' own: How is one to re-present a Christian visionary landscape to an audience for whom its concepts and conception of the cosmos lie distant from their sensibility, and for whom the inner life has supplanted an external order, or *mythos*, as a more "satisfying" interpretive framework for existence? In the poet's own terms, when in the Preface to *RSS* he concludes his summary of the narrative elements in the cycle with the comment, "Logres is overthrown and afterwards becomes the historical Britain, *in which the myth of its origin remains*,"[64] we may interpret his poetic project as the endeavor to resurrect that myth in order to bring to light its enduring resonances. Thus, although his selection of the Arthurian myth did provide a way of ordering his themes in an otherwise disorderly world (as Moorman contends), his manner of developing that material imagistically enabled something further. The relationship between civilization and religion that the Arthuriad explores as one of its themes in fact unfolds as a critique of the former under the auspices of the latter, and argues for the subordination of any one individual's personal ambitions to a larger vision. In Williams' vocabulary of redemption, it is the response of his characters to the doctrines of "substitutionary love," "co-inherence" and "the way of exchange" as extensive features of Incarnational "largesse" that determine their fate as well as the fate of Logres.

One striking [negative] example will help to illustrate Williams' method in this regard: the nonsuccess of Arthur, captured poignantly

---

62. He praised Yeats along these very lines, concluding that "he has renewed in us the sense of great interior possibilities" (ibid., 69). And as he affirms elsewhere, "in the end anything that means anything to man has to be in terms of something remotely significant to man" (*HCDH*, 41).

63. *PP*, 32. As he declares in his study in Dante, "private vision is a very important thing, but it is not, for all its greatness, ultimate; all that is ultimate is duty and the proper order, the right co-inherence of things" (*Figure*, 141).

64. *RSS*, 118; my italics.

in two poems from the cycle. Arthur's failure to fulfill his kingdom's potential consists of the rejection of his true function as a servant of his people and a steward of the mystery of exchange signified by the Grail. The seed of that failure, we are told, is present already at his coronation when Arthur stands "*to look on his city,*" and ponders (as if negotiable) the question: "*the king made for the kingdom, or the kingdom made for the king?*"[65] In subsequent episodes Arthur reveals his tragic answer, poignantly evident in his quest to make himself the center of his domain, for instance in the minting of coins which bear his face and his family crest (tellingly the figure of a dragon). It is Bors (in "Bors to Elayne: on the Kings Coins") who first detects the corruption in this enterprise. While meditating on the doctrine of exchange as embodied by his wife Elayne, herself an image of "*Christ the City*" and "*the sole figure of the organic salvation of our good,*"[66] Bors imagines the dispersal of Arthur's "*small dragons*" throughout Logres as a stark contrast to that image:

> He has struck coins ; his dragon's loins
> germinate a crowded creaturely brood
> to scuttle and scurry between towns and towns,
> to furnish dishes and flagons with change of food;
> small crowns, small dragons, hurry to the markets
> under the king's smile, or flat in houses squat.
> The long file of their snouts crosses the empire....[67]

Williams' diction here, particularly the alliterated "*scuttle*"-"*scurry*"-"*squat,*" delivers the exact judgment sought. "*Organic salvation*" has given way to *infestation*, resulting in the displacement of a natural order of exchange—whose sustenance depends upon transactions of goods and services between people—by an artificial means that serve only to promote the king's ambitions. That subversion leads Bors to lament: "*I saw that this was the true end of our making*" (ibid.).

It is Taliessin who then seals this judgment. As a poet, he brings an additional insight to the matter, one which conveys Williams' own belief that inattention to the power of images leads to significant social and spiritual consequences. Accordingly, the king's poet rebuffs the

---

65. "The Crowning of Arthur," *TTL*, 39.
66. *TTL*, 61.
67. Ibid.

confidence of the king's steward Sir Kay that "*Money is* the *medium of exchange*" (my emph.), telling him,

> 'Sir, if you made verse you would doubt symbols.
> I am afraid of the little loosed dragons.
> When the means are autonomous, they are deadly ; when words
> escape from verse they hurry to rape souls ;
> when sensation slips from intellect, expect the tyrant ;
> the brood of carriers levels the good they carry.
> We have taught our images to be free ; are we glad?
> are we glad to have brought convenient heresy to Logres?'[68]

Taliessin's point is not so much an argument for poetry as it is a principle that can be learned *from* it, and which reverberates with implications for society. What poets bring to speech, this passage asserts, is not mere decorum but discipline. As such, their craft is itself an image of the circumspect mind, alert to the dangers of autonomous means pursued for the sake of convenience or self-promotion, and of the tyranny waiting to exploit those for whom sensation has been severed from intellect. For this reason, as Taliessin emphasizes in his rebuke, poets who understand the need for restraint and carefully measured expression in their art know to "doubt symbols," and fear them when they are set "free" from the rigours of *measured* reflection.

By giving free reign to his aspirations, Arthur takes himself and Logres a further step towards dissolution and away from the true nature of exchange, which a third protagonist, the Archbishop Dubric, eloquently summarizes:

> this abides—
> that the everlasting house the soul discovers
> is always another's ; we must lose our own ends ;
> we must always live in the habitation of our lovers,
> my friend's shelter for me, mine for him.
>
> ... the wealth of the self is the health of the self exchanged.'[69]

Dubric's words capture the range of references Williams includes under "the way of exchange," references that encompass human interactions as

---

68. Ibid., 62.
69. *TTL*, 62–63.

well as the interaction between heaven and earth, and which together form a reciprocal economy comprehensible in terms of images. That is, the images of exchange we find in human interactions point towards the consummate example of exchange in Christ, and "Christ the City" provides the ultimate image by which we can read and assay the world of human interactions in terms of what does or does not reflect the vision of life he manifests by his supreme example of "substitutionary love."

Our next poem in the cycle, "The Star of Percivale," takes up this motif directly, once more applying this economy of exchange to the plight of Arthur. Its controlling thought occurs in the line, "More than the voice is the vision, the kingdom than the king."[70] It is a signature statement not only for this episode but for the entire drama of Logres; and with this, for poetry, statecraft, and, by implication, for all else that civilization encompasses. We recall in this regard Williams' epigraph for the cycle taken from Dante's *De Monarchia* and translated as: "Hence it is that the proper operation [or function] does not exist for the sake of the essence, but the essence has its being for the sake of the operation."[71] Williams interpreted this "great sentence" as a universal principle denoting a Christian understanding of vocation, which he also relates to his own sense of the way of images. He writes, "Almighty God did not first create Dante and then find something for him to do"; rather, he continues, it is "the primal law of all images, of whatever kind; they were created for their working and in order to work."[72] Viewed in terms of a critique of culture, for Williams Dante's maxim comprised a call to serve a higher purpose than one's own ambitions, as "the definition of the Way."[73] Thus, Williams, who admitted the value of a poetry able to satisfy us with "sensuous apprehension" and of the "new use" of myth, metaphor and knowledge in the modern temperament, nevertheless would not hold with any form of presumptive autonomy, whether for poets or kings: "*more than the voice is the vision.*"

---

70. *TTL*, 64.

71. C. S. Lewis offers this helpful gloss, particularly in light of Arthur's "fatal flaw" to resolve the question "the king made for the kingdom, or the kingdom made for the king?" He writes, "Lovers exist for the sake of love, poets for the sake of poetry, kings for the sake of kingdoms: not vice versa" (*AT*, 296).

72. *Figure*, 40.

73. Ibid., 51.

Arthur, and with him Camelot, fail to venerate the higher vision of exchange, and do so poignantly on the occasion when the opportunity to do otherwise is most available: at Mass. As "The Star of Percivale" builds to its expected climax in a chain of imagistic moments figuring the way of exchange, with the arrival of the king and his court that chain is broken. In the concluding lines we find the king's household kneeling; but the posture belies the spiritual state of the presumed worshippers: Balin is restless with his "*causeless vigil of anger*," Lancelot is preoccupied only with thoughts of Guinevere, and Arthur, the civil head of Logres, is, ironically, possessed only of himself: "*the king in the elevation beheld and loved himself crowned.*"[74]

As with the account of the king's coins in the previous poem, this further account of Arthur's pride and spiritual callousness tells a familiar story, as do the inevitable consequences of his fall. This is not, however, merely a moral tale, but one that delivers real moral impact because the poet invests personality, and by extension society, with expansive theological dimensions. Arthur's failure is not mere folly, to an extent excusable in human terms. It is the rejection of a divine order of existence, and so has ramifications that subvert the prospect for creating a redemptive, "noble" *human* order of existence.[75] As Williams declares in his theological writings,

> Sin has many forms, but the work of all is the same—the preference of an immediately satisfying experience of things to the believed pattern of the universe; one may even say, the pattern of the glory.[76]

What Williams wanted was an effective vehicle for translating that conviction and that pattern into an idiom that would re-substantiate the vitality, indeed the *reality*, which the doctrines define. The Arthurian myth provided such a vehicle.[77]

Furthermore, Williams came upon an even more profound realization about the dynamics of the mythic imagination as a means to

---

74. *TTL*, 65.

75. In speaking of the "noble life," Williams comments: "authority is always a mutual act; . . . . Like pardon, it is a welding of wills, and an exchange of largesse," applying equally to those who rule as well as to those who obey (Ibid., 82).

76. *HCDH*, 42–43.

77. As Glen Cavaliero surmises, "To use doctrine as myth . . . is to put it to its proper use; it relates it to the responsive imagination" (*Poet of Theology*, 30).

re-present Christian themes, and which has a particular bearing on the relationship of Williams' poetry to Christian theology and the Christian sense of history. In addition to the commentary on history his cycle delivers, as the site of failed vision and the defeat of one form of redemptive promise (in terms of a political reality), a more subtle strain attempts the *intersection* of myth with history. In this endeavor Williams displays some of his greatest ingenuity as a Christian poet and interpreter.

As with his view of images, Williams' account of our relationship to history and to time, as well as to the eternal, arose not from a theoretical but from a biblical and liturgical provenance. Regarding the biblical record of divine and human action and the ongoing rehearsal of the same in the rituals of the Church, for example, he wrote:

> . . . all that did happen is a presentation of what is happening; all the historical events, especially of this category, are a pageant of the events of the human soul. But it is true also that Christendom has always held that the two are indissolubly connected; that the events in the human soul could not exist unless the historical events had existed.[78]

We note here his emphasis on the present reality of sacred history as Christians both receive and rehearse it—"all that did happen is a presentation of what *is* happening"—and his use of the term "pageant" to describe what he then calls "[t]he union of history and the individual."[79] The latter comprises the immanent and ongoing operation of God's activity in history on the consciousness of the human soul.

Williams admitted the narrative line that the Bible follows; but to his theo-poetic sensibility it was pageantry that best captured the commingling of the temporal with the eternal, the present with the ever-present, the exigencies of history with the expanse of heaven. As he writes later in this treatise on the Incarnation, "We operate, mostly, in sequence, but sequence is not all," a point he supports with the conviction that "Messias had brought all things into the pattern of the Atonement" to the effect that, "The laying down of the life is not confined, in the universal nature of the Sole-Begotten, to any points of space or time. It flashes and returns, in a joy, in a distress, and often without joy or distress. Along

---

78. *HCDH*, 6.
79. Ibid., 7.

such threads the glory runs..."[80] In evidence of this view as it pertains to the experience of believers, Williams cited the Church's evolving understanding of the Eucharist by which, "History and contemporaneity and futurity were joined; the Church had been reconciled to time only to reconcile time to its Cause."[81] Its dynamic effect, he states earlier, lay in its simultaneous movement in two directions: "the great Rite soared to its climax in the eternal, and yet communicated the eternal to time."[82] Such is the potency of pageant, of ceremony and ritual, to apprehend *in time* the "flash and return" of that which also exceeds time. We see this ceremonial or sacramental sensibility manifested throughout the Arthuriad,[83] and also in its very structure, which itself represents an attempt to "communicate the eternal to time."

Williams' base material of the Arthurian myth as it has developed in the literary imagination for centuries follows a familiar narrative line, and as an aid to the new reader C. S. Lewis attempted to reconstruct Williams' adaptation in these terms.[84] But as helpful as this may be at an introductory level, it misses a crucial point about Williams' imagistic vision. To be sure, the Arthuriad gives us many of the common elements of the plot, but it does not follow a strict chronological pattern. Why, we need to wonder (as did Lewis)? The answer, I believe, lies with the pattern that does emerge as Williams intended it. What we observe are two continuous cycles of interacting episodes that form a progression of interweaving images, or *imagistic rhythm*. Each poem in the cycle creates a field of reference taken up in other poems through repeated patterns of images, which collectively enact the cycle's principal themes; and the characters—themselves images and portrayed by images—interrelate in terms of these same imagistic coordinates. In short, what Williams renders is not plot but *pageantry*—a deeply textured parade of images.

---

80. Ibid., 130, 131. As it pertains to the Christian life specifically, he earlier contends, "The new life might still be sequential (in the order of time) but every instant was united to the Origin, and complete and absolute in itself" (81).

81. *Descent*, 115.

82. Ibid., 114.

83. Indeed, this mode accords with Williams' view of poetry in general: "The language of poetry," he writes in *NBEV*, "is bound to be ceremonial.... The progress of poetry has been the continual discovery of a variation in ceremony to manifest some new intensity of the complex life of imagination" (11).

84. *AT*, 280.

This pageant-like or ceremonial deportment yields an advantage more attainable by poetry than straight narrative or prose. It endows the Arthuriad with what we may describe as a *sacramental symmetry*: the interaction of time with timelessness, or the compression of the temporal and the eternal, such that the presence of the one is perceived, and *felt*, in the other (in a manner reminiscent of his argument in "The Ostentation of Verse").

The very structure of the cycle, therefore, images the Christian notion of time between the times, the "while" before the Second Coming towards which the promise of Logres-Britain inclines but ultimately fails to achieve in terms of an earthly reflection of that eschatological reality.[85] Williams' genius lay in his ability to reify that metaphysical economy in poetry that, again, enables us to *see* its operation—the "operation of eternity in time"—and so reinvigorates its potential as a way of exploring and interpreting our own age in these terms. And nowhere does this aim prove more formidable than in the presentation of one of the cycle's central visionary elements—one that has appeared already in the poems we have surveyed. I refer here to the "pattern of glory."

Perhaps more than any other Christian theme, the glory of God, its substantive reality, challenges form to rise to a new adequacy.[86] The key to its material re-presentation in images, which is also the key to, as well as the legitimization for, Williams' imagistic poetics in the Arthuriad, is the Incarnation. For all of the theological ink expended to define the nature of God-incarnate (not inappropriately), for the most part it has been artists who have exploited—if I may use such a term—the dramatic possibilities of the Incarnation;[87] and among poets and other interpreters, even fewer have sought to elaborate and disclose its import as the manifestation of glory.[88] And yet, the biblical testimony is that Christ is "the radiance of [God's] glory" (Heb 1:3), and Christ's first

85. *RSS*, 117–18.

86. This way of stating the matter was given to me by my thesis supervisor Ben Quash.

87. Williams' own view of an imbalance in christological reflection included as well what he felt was a neglect of Christ's humanity as an area in need of dramatic elaboration. He writes, "The doctrine of our Lord as God with its corollaries took centuries to work out.... The other doctrine of His Manhood, with its corollaries, has still to be worked out and put into action" (*Image*, 156).

88. Among theologians, one obvious exception is Hans Urs von Balthasar, particularly in his magisterial seven-volume treatment of this theme *The Glory of the Lord*.

witnesses declared summarily, "we beheld His glory" (John 1:14). The coming of glory, then, designates one overarching feature in the person and redemptive works of Christ, as integral to his eternal substance as it is to his manifestation of the divine in human form. Accordingly, what gives Williams' fusion of forms and substances in the imagery of the Arthuriad its distinct christological thrust, and with this its visionary power and persuasive force as a *Christian* work of the imagination, is his achievement in verse of a new statement of the glory of God as it was "made manifest" (1 John 1:2) in and through Christ. And this not only at those moments in the cycle of high contemplation; but in keeping with the Incarnational mode, in circumstances of a more ordinary variety Williams develops images precisely along these lines. In all, his Arthurian verse explores the dynamics of the Incarnation as occasions pregnant with the potential for glory, producing "more vivid forms of glory and grace"[89] that both re-interpret and re-describe the implications of God-incarnate in human experience.

The Two "Preludes": Incarnate Glory and the Landscapes of History

Taken together, the "Preludes" to the cycle establish Williams' interpretation of the Arthurian myth along the "thread of glory," meaning the convergence of historical and material existence with spiritual reality—each a substantial reality in its own right, and by virtue of the Incarnation, brought to a new substantial whole. To elaborate, in these poems the Incarnation is given its historical dimensionality as the operation of the divine within space and time, while, by virtue of this same operation, "history" as the phenomena of human events and experiences is elevated to a new potentiality. As we also discover in the first "Prelude," however, with the rejection of that possibility comes a re-interpretation of history as a failed landscape, wherein the permanent is diffused in the transitory. That failure, signaled, as we have seen, in the figure of Arthur, nonetheless gives rise to the expectation of a hope explored over the course of the cycle which looks towards another,

---

89. *HCDH*, 108. In a similar vein, he writes in *Descent*, "It is the more necessary . . . whenever possible to colour belief with the finest qualities, and not only with itself" (199).

"From the Exposition of Grace to the Place of Images"   51

eschatological horizon; a hope that emerges in the Arthuriad as a present promise for those faithful to the vision inspired by the Grail.

In the "Prelude" to *TTL*, Williams recapitulates the rise and fall of Logres-Britain, and in its larger purview, of Byzantium, portraying those movements in a series of three succinct, imagistic episodes that traces the appearance and loss of glory. It opens in a spirit of exaltation—"*the glory of the Emperor stretched to the ends of the world*"[90]—then resolves into an attitude of lament: "*lost is the light on the hills of Caucasia,/ glory of the Emperor, glory of substantial being.*"[91] Here, Williams transposes the events of medieval Europe carried out on a geo-political plane into an image of cosmic upheaval, the overthrow of one perceived order of existence by another. By this series of events, he establishes from the outset the lines of trajectory for the drama of Arthur: the struggle to found one kingdom serving as an instance in, and an image for, the larger drama of the conflict of kingdoms unfolding on a material as well as a spiritual plane.

In all three variations on the theme of glory, we note first that glory is not withdrawn from the world to a sphere of the numinous. It is portrayed here, like grace in "Taliessin's Vision of the Empire," as a dramatic force whose proper habitation is as much the world as that which lies beyond it. It is "the glory *of* substantial being," made manifest in its extended forms as in its Origin, and for this reason assumes definitive shape:

> Carbonek, Camelot, Caucasia,
> were gates and containers, intermediations of light ;
> geography breathing geometry, the double-fledged Logos.[92]

Thus, glory is neither ethereal nor is it idealized, but in its earthly manifestation it bears the character of a precise spiritual intelligence and organic reality—"*geography breathing geometry.*" Glory, we therefore conclude from this passage, has a *pulse*, not vague in its manifestation but keenly perceptible. The imagery succinctly captures Williams' view expressed throughout his critical works, for example when he asserts, "The word glory, to English ears, usually means no more than a kind of mazy bright blur. But the maze should be, though it generally is not,

---

90. *TTL*, 19.
91. Ibid., 20.
92. Ibid., 19.

exact, and the brightness should be that of a geometrical pattern."[93] Appropriating Plato's dictum that "God always geometrizes," Williams elaborates the biblical notion of glory as a divine pattern made evident throughout Creation, but which is brought to its fullest expression in Christ. "'[T]he Son of Man,'" he writes, "is to be seen in the 'glory of his Father and with the holy angels', that is, in the swift and geometrical glory seen by Isaiah and Ezekiel." The earthly, material evidence of this is seen foremost in what Jesus *did*: "it is the acts of Messias which form the glory"; "The pattern of the glory is a pattern of acts."[94]

All of this becomes crucial to our appreciation of what Williams attempts in the Arthuriad—a dramatization of "Incarnate" glory in images. Because glory is made visible in the works of God in Christ, who is "the image of the glory of God," its appearance, its actuality, becomes the focal point for the concentration of images that develop this christological pattern into a recognizable identity. What we find striking in this "Prelude," however, and indeed throughout the Arthuriad, is the subtlety and "restraint"[95] with which Williams advances this aim. In this overture to the cycle the poet already gives us his summary of the "plot" in terms of the rise and fall of an immanent glory, specifying some of its properties but without any overtly familiar nomenclature. As a result, we are prompted to wonder where, and significantly, to *whom* will this poetic drama of Logres ultimately lead.

At this point, we are given certain clues about that progression and identity. Woven into this historical tableau of Logres and Byzantium, for example, we find only indirect allusions to Christ. References to wisdom and its embodiment in both time and space through the figure of Sophia summon traditional associations with Christ, and the phrase "*the immaculate conception of wisdom*" in line 6 points up this same association. In addition, the poem does not name Christ as such, but

93. HCDH, 39.

94. Ibid., 66, 136, 137. These acts, according to Williams, include especially "the way of exchange," made consummate in Christ, by whom, "The formula of the knowledge of this pattern on earth is disclosed" (ibid., 66).

95. At various points in his criticism Williams lauds poetry that shows "beauty in restraint" and "restraint and calm balance" (*PP*, 20, 30). By esteeming this quality Williams emphasized that successful poetry does not make obvious designs on the reader's beliefs, but performs its work subtly *as* poetry. So he writes in praise of W. H. Davies, "he has communicated his wonder rather than indoctrinated us with the gospel" (ibid., 75).

instead offers innovative pseudonyms for him: "*the double-fledged Logos*" (L. 9), "*the lord of charity*" (L. 17), "*the sole flash of the Emperor's glory*" (L. 18), "*the glory of substantial being*" (L. 27), all provide figurative designations that arouse our interest and open up fresh interpretations of Christ's nature.

Furthermore, the poem's varying musical structure and "rhythmical technique" show a similar subtlety as a means of developing the cycle's interpretation of history within this paradigm of glory. So, for instance, in the first strophe the frequent use of hard consonants—punctuated by the three accented verbs "*heard*," "*sprang*" and "*stretched*"—gives the lines a sharp, declaratory edge, adding pitch to the manifestations of wisdom and glory. In the following strophe, however, that impression softens abruptly with the more fluid phrases "*In the season of midmost Sophia*" and "*they sang in Sophia the immaculate conception of wisdom*." The theme of glory-incarnate suffers no diminishment as a consequence of this shift in mood, but instead acquires greater affective range. In addition, the heraldic rhythm (achieved by the clipped phrasing and repeated use of semi-colons) facilitates a certain quality of control for the theme of glory, giving the images of glory's appearance and of the consequences issuing from its rejection an authoritative (even prophetic) register. By modulating the rhythm and metre (in three- and five-foot lines), and varying the diction—hence generating shifts in mood and attitude—the intersection of glory with history also takes on an appropriately dramatic character. Williams' poetic technique gives glory its dignity while creating suspense over the floundering prospects of its consummation in the world (reminiscent of Paul's discussion of the "triumph" of glory and the vicissitudes of its reception).[96]

In effect, the poem advances through its prosodic form the view that glory has real dramatic force in the world because it faces actual, historical risk. It remains a possibility that Williams' Galahad—being "*Quickened in the Mercy*"—recovers towards an alternative redemptive promise. The appearance of glory, in other words, does not resolve tension, but heightens it, as cosmic agency confronts contingency, and so becomes vulnerable to the vagaries of human response. And here, with subtle but salient force, the multiple allusions to Christ gather into a portrayal of the Incarnation as both the emerging center of a drama

---

96. Cf. 2 Cor 3:18; 4:3–4.

of glory, and, manifestly, the demonstration of God's willing vulnerability. In this manner, poetic form materializes and enacts theological substance.

The second "Prelude," providing the "overture" to *The Region of the Summer Stars*, further discloses and refines the Incarnational dimensions of the cycle. In marked contrast to the highly compressed style of the previous poem, in this piece Williams creates a flowing, narrative surface for the poetry. The more plotted and at times discursive presentation in turn places peculiar demands on the Incarnational imagery to rise above this surface as the focusing energy for the whole.

As in the first "Prelude," the subject involves the intersection of history and glory; only here the poem presents this dynamic as the activity of human speech and reflective discourse. Specifically, this poem interprets the drama of glory as the struggle to find words to articulate adequately its earthly manifestation, as the operation of a redemptive providence in time. The first line, indeed the first word, of the poem establishes this linguistic interest: "*IRONY was the Fortune of Athens.*"[97] Irony, which it is inherently a function of speech to express, marks one terminus in the struggle to articulate the meaning of existence. At the other, though not precisely opposite, end of the spectrum is *faith*. Accordingly, after surveying the early formulations of Christendom, the poem concludes in the last section,

> that in the stuff of the Empire the quality of irony
> flickered and faded before the capacity of faith;
> all the peoples awaited the Parousia . . .[98]

The word "*stuff*" registers the appropriate sense for what the poem asserts throughout, and succinctly captures the nature of the clash between the ironic fatalism of Greco-Roman philosophy and the Incarnational metaphysics of Christianity. For, standing between these termini of irony and faith as the center of negotiations is the flesh-bound appearance of God. In that time of expectancy in which "*the Empire . . . awaited the Second Coming/ of the Union,*"[99] a new pressure emerges as the challenge to assimilate, however incompletely, this new pattern[ing] of meaning. That pressure, this "Prelude" argues, consists of a new

---

97. *RSS*, 119.
98. Ibid., 122.
99. Ibid., 120–21.

rhetorical demand—the endeavor to find the speech for this instauration of glory that will establish its distinctiveness with the peculiar language of Incarnational faith.

Accordingly, the poem portrays Paul's evangelistic mission among the Greeks as a stance "*against their defensive inflections of verb and voice,/ their accents of presaged frustration.*"[100] Paul meets this demand in kind, depicted here as that moment when the "*thorned-in-the-flesh*" Apostle "*named in its twyfold Nature the Golden Ambiguity.*" Two implications arise: first, the "summing up of all things" in Christ includes speech, as an obvious implication of the advent of the Word. Second, the "summing up" of language and speech in Christ consequently summons his witnesses to translate his appearance in the world into a faithful idiom. Hence, the poem continues,

> Then for the creature he [Paul] invented the vocabulary of faith;
> he defined in speech the physiological glory
> and began to teach the terms of the work of glory.[101]

The phrase "he *defined* in speech the physiological glory" expands this second implication. In seeking a faithful idiom Christ's witnesses are to aim at precision, and so avoid the very forms of rhetorical distortion that this poem imagines Paul confronting in Greece—in sum, "a false style of words," which Williams traced as far back as Cain's attempt to deflect guilt over the murder of his brother.[102] So Williams declares in his commentary on the *Inferno*, "accuracy is fruitfulness—it is the first law of the spiritual life,"[103] and so he admonished the Church in his own age: "Accuracy, accuracy, and again accuracy! accuracy of mind and accuracy of emotion."[104] The "physiological glory" and "mathematical splendour" of Christ, this poem adduces, demands no less of Christians then as now; and for Williams it is poets especially who sustain this ethos as crafters of speech. Thus, the "*young poets*" of Camelot—"*Breathless

---

100. Ibid., 119.

101. Ibid. Williams writes of Paul, "To call him a poet would be perhaps improper. . . . But he used words as poets do; he regenerated them. And by St. Paul's regeneration of words he gave theology first to the Christian Church" (*Descent*, 8).

102. See *HCDH*, 116.

103. *Figure*, 133.

104. *Image*, 157.

explorers of the image"—*"studied precision"*;[105] and so Palomides saw in Iseult's arm *"how curves of golden life define/ the straightness of a perfect line"*[106] and later sought *"the accurate flash of her eyes."*[107] In this light, when the "Prelude" then represents *"the orthodox imagination"* as the preserver of orthodox *doctrine*,[108] it accords with this virtue of accuracy as that which the circumspect poetic imagination is distinctly suited to convey. Specifically, the claim champions the endeavor to render "the physiological glory" of God-incarnate in *images* that accurately convey the "commingling" of spirit and flesh in a union of the timeless with time—*"there, for a day,/ beyond history, holding history at bay."*[109] By this method Williams weds the vocation of the poet with that of the Apostle and of all Christ's witnesses, as "Affirmers" of the "Way of Images."

The poem elaborates and extends this last connection by drawing a seamless narrative line from the instauration of the witnessing Church to the "history" of the Grail (and so, to the setting of the Arthuriad), thus situating the poet's own project within the tradition of the orthodox imagination. The cycle, too, will attempt to "define the physiological glory," which this poem achieves by punctuating that linear progression with moments of acute figurative amplitude, creating a further *"zone/ of visionary powers."*[110] So, for example, in the rebuttal of "heresiarchs" who wrongly asserted that *"flesh [was] too queasy to bear the main of spirit,"*[111] the poem continues:

> Professing only a moral union, they fled
> from the new-spread bounty; they found a quarrel with the Empire
> and the sustenance of Empire, with the ground of faith and earth,
> the golden and rose-creamed flesh of the grand Ambiguity.[112]

The re-description of the Incarnation in this last phrase fills our verbal palate with a flourish of sensuous imagery. Coupled with images of feast

---

105. *TTL*, 48.
106. Ibid., 52–53.
107. Ibid., 82.
108. *RSS*, 120.
109. Ibid.
110. Ibid.
111. Ibid., 119.
112. Ibid., 120.

and harvest, hinted earlier in the words "*breakfasted*" and "*handfasted*,"[113] the passage also invokes the Eucharist. Only here, the Eucharistic theme is given a provocative ambience as we are prompted to imagine the body of Christ as not only "*sustenance*" but as well a delectable offering of "*golden and rose-creamed flesh*." Image has now assumed and amplified the force of the earlier assertion regarding the Apostle's language of "physiological glory." What Paul originally "defined in speech," but which, this "Prelude" argues, subsequent "*converted doctors*" undermined through lack of courage, the poetry endeavors to recover by its own elaborate re-presentation of that material-spiritual reality. In effect, Williams' Eucharistic imagery, interjected at this point in the *poem's* discourse, doubles as commentary on the history of Christian discourse: that is, the Church's discursive quest to articulate its most basic, Incarnational assertions.

Furthermore, what the "great Rite" displays through figurative *action*, the poem re-interprets in figurative *speech* that achieves a similar presentational effect, or "sensuous apprehension." The words "*new-spread bounty*," "*sustenance*," "*golden and rose-creamed flesh*" operate sensuously on the more abstract "*the ground of faith and earth*" and "*the grand Ambiguity*," giving an evocative range to these already inventive restatements of the Incarnation. This confluence of the conceptual and the concrete registers a forceful rebuttal to the notion that Christ forged "*only a moral union*" between God and humanity. It does so, however, by a display in words which advances that conclusion as a function of poetic form. The poem's Incarnational speech, in other words, reifies the decisive nature of the phenomenon it re-presents, as unequivocally "Word made flesh."

Williams' method here once more focuses attention on the kind of expressive task the Incarnation demands. The affirmation of *that* image, this Prelude both suggests and puts on offer, involves what imagistic speech itself proves uniquely suited to achieve: verbal acts of "fleshing out" meaning. His re-interpretation of the Arthurian material, which he aligns with a tradition of figurative discourse inaugurated by Paul and other exemplars of the orthodox imagination, assumes this quality as an expansion of such an "approach to God through images." In the process, as we saw in the Prelude to *TTL*, Williams re-excavates the import of

---

113. Ibid., 119.

Incarnational doctrine and, as a result of the drama of Incarnate glory he produces, generates an *atmosphere of disclosure rather than of closure*. Close readings of two other poems from the cycle will demonstrate further how the Arthuriad amplifies this disclosive capacity of the way of images, and provides a subtle but compelling testimony to the import we derive from the "in-Godding of man" in Christ.

"Bors to Elayne: The Fish of Broceliande": Incarnation and the Natural Order

"The Fish of Broceliande" is a love poem delivered in the lyric mode. In it, we depart from the more rarefied atmosphere of universal history to a domestic space, and from the use of a sweep of images for world-portrayal to the development of one concrete image born of local and familial province. The use of a more traditional form of rhyming tercets and modulated iambic pentameter suits this shift to a more contained, domestic field of attention, although the imagery remains as layered and complex as we find in the two "Prelude" poems.

Its central figure is "the King's servant" Bors. Though he will participate in the Grail quest and will accompany the High Prince Galahad and Percivale on "The Last Voyage" for Sarras,[114] his principal role in the cycle is to serve as an image of "the ordinary man, married, with children," as well as "the spiritual intellect concerned, as it must be, with earthly things."[115] As a tribute to the theological significance Williams placed on marriage and domestic life, the poem is told from Bors' point of view, as a loving husband's meditation upon his wife. Its inspiration, however, arises from the king's poet's song of the mystical wood of Broceliande:

> In the great hall's glow
> Taliessin sang of the sea-rooted western wood;
> his song meant all things to all men, and you to me.[116]

Although a poet may provide the impetus (and insight) for romantic love between a man and a woman, however, only the lovers involved understand its depth and personal emotion. It is from that passion—

---

114. *TTL*, 102–6.
115. "Notes," *Image*, 177.
116. *TTL*, 42.

the natural "human capacity" for romantic love in its marital form, which, Williams argued, is "partly at least, a recovery of matter"[117]—that this poem progresses towards its meditation on the Incarnation.

We note first that the poem's central image of the fish *travels* in the manner of a metaphysical conceit, spanning a variety of referents beginning in the local and immediate then expanding towards a broader theological horizon. At the same time, Williams sustains its particularity as a concrete image throughout, thus maintaining its vitality as a *living* symbol. Its energy derives first from its propinquity to the "*sea-rooted western wood*" of Broceliande—"*I plucked a fish from a stream that flowed to that sea*"[118]—which functions as an image for the power of the imagination to transmute substances into material forms.[119] The poem makes this relationship of the fish to the sea-wood immediately complex, however, as Broceliande is evoked not from Bors' own experience but, again, by the memory of Taliessin's memorial to it. Thus, from the outset we are deep within the world of images and their interrelationships: the sung image of the wood transports Bors to that unvisited province of the untamed creative spirit, and from that visionary state he conjures, or *discovers*, a relationship between the wood and his wife: "*was it of you?*" he asks.

But to Bors, Elayne is not merely an object of his imagination; she is his beloved; she is "*substantial flesh.*"[120] Accordingly, the image of the fish "*plucked*" by Bors on its journey through Broceliande is connected to Elayne and to his relationship with her. Was it, he asks further, "*from you? for you?*" Is she, in other words, its inspiration and the fish her figural embodiment, or is it a thing applied to her as an interpretation of her nature? Here the status of an image is itself called implicitly into question. What, the poem prompts us to ask, is an image's relationship to the original?[121] Is it an image born of the substance it signifies ("*from*

---

117. *Figure*, 51 n. 1. "Marriage," adds Williams, "is the great example . . . of the Way of Affirmation. The intention of fidelity is the safeguard of romanticism; the turning of something like the vision of an eternal state into an experiment towards that state" (ibid.).

118. *TTL*, 42.

119. See "Notes," 179.

120. *TTL*, 44.

121. It is a question Williams believed lay at the heart of Dante's prolonged meditation on the image of Beatrice, her voice "the sign of the salutation of love." He writes,

you?"), or is it applied to that substance as its [poetic] interpretation (*"for you?"*); or is it, in some sense, both? Moreover, do images provide a means of illumination leading to identification, or are they an imposition that displaces meaning and obscures recognition? The poem follows this line of inquiry through its development of dramatic images, and weaves into this progression an evolving meditation on the Incarnation.

Bors continues,

> shall I drop the fish in your hand?
> in your hand's pool? a bright-scaled, red-tailed fish
> to dart and drive up the channel of your arm?
> the channel of your arm, the piercing entry to a land
> where, no matter how lordly at home is set the dish,
> no net can catch it, nor hook nor gaff harm?[122]

The fish displays the particularity of its kind—*"bright-scaled, red-tailed"*—while Elayne's presence compresses into two focal points, the *"pool"* of her hand and the *"channel of* [her] *arm."* Both characterizations are necessary in order for these respective images to convey the larger signification the poem grants them: as a *"piercing entry to a land"* that lies, ultimately, beyond nomination.

From this third tercet pair the poem does more with these images than specify their immediate and individual referents, however. Elayne's body and the fish fuse into a new composite whole, together occupying the same figural space:

> but it darts up the muscles of the arm, to swim
> round the clear boulder of the shoulder, stung with spray,
> and down the cataract of the backed spine leaps
>
> into bottomed waters at once clear and dim,
> where nets are fingered and flung on many a day;[123]

By virtue of this "consubstantial" movement, the poem begins to signal its Incarnational arc. The corporeal, so physically manifest and

---

"The whole of Dante's life and work had been to achieve that distinction and to understand it. . . . Was so long, so beautiful, so horrible, so tedious, a Way necessary? It seems so, if indeed he was rightly to understand image and original" (*Figure*, 219–20).

122. *TTL*, 42.
123. Ibid., 43.

"From the Exposition of Grace to the Place of Images" 61

so vibrantly displayed as the fish figure courses over the landscape of Elayne's body, becomes suffused with the mental and the mysterious: "*yet it slides through the mesh of the mind and sweeps/ back to its haunt in a fathomless bottomless pool.*"[124]

This in turn gives rise to a question as intransigent as it is inevitable:

> is there a name then, an anagram of spirit and sense,
> that Nimue the mistress of the wood could call it by ?
>
> None but a zany, none but the earth's worst fool,
> could suppose he knows ;[125]

Naming is made synonymous with the discovery of "*an anagram of spirit and sense*"; but neither cooperates with the other to yield a definitive identification. Moreover, the urge to find and affix a name to the emergent image not only amounts to the presumption of lunacy. As the poem unfolds it also becomes clear that a move to pin down meaning in such manner would foreclose the very possibility that the imagery propels. There is at this point, nevertheless, a crisis of signification that demands resolution of some kind. By invoking Nimue, the personification of the "untamed" imagination, the poem underscores the nature of a different challenge which now erupts in earnest. Bors' meditation points to something unconstrained, something ultimately incapable of full delineation, which is "*at once clear and dim.*" It is a complex interplay, which makes for a hazardous undertaking. Are his associations between his wife and the fish appropriate? Bors seems to ask. Will he, in effect, give himself over to the imagination, and if so, to what end?

Bors does not resist this impulse, however; nor, perhaps, can he. Once released, the traveling image of the fish, having entwined the body of his beloved, is given its full figurative head: "*no net can catch it . . ./ but it darts up the muscles of the arm.*" It is the freedom but also the danger of images to bear such power, a theme Williams explores directly, as we have observed, in the second Bors poem "on the King's Coins." Something of this same concern lurks in "The Fish of Broceliande," although this poem directs our attention to another problematic feature of imagistic speech. As the fish imagery literally traverses the text of

124. Ibid.
125. Ibid.

the poem, more than the danger of images to distort truth, the poem here indicates the risk that images will not prove adequate to the task of disclosing the truth they purport to signify.

The crisis of signification created by the imagery, however, is one that in its own fashion imagery also resolves. The poem continues, "*no name was thrown thence*," and no name is proffered here. Rather, Bors recalls something else that his entire meditation has stirred in his mind: "*some say a twy-nature only can utter the cry*." Still, resolution of one kind does not follow from this further prospect. The clause "*some say*" leaves the appeal ambiguous, and "*a twy-nature*" is not presented as an answer but the agency by which a new possibility is advanced. The next tercet heightens this tension. The bracketed questions " (*what? how?*)" end abruptly with "*and if—*," issuing only in a further extension of the fish image: "*inhumanly flashing a sudden scale,/ aboriginally shaking the aboriginal main*."[126] Once more, the relationship of an image to the original is brought to the fore, though here the word "*aboriginal*" connotes a deeper provenance. The fish, which had returned to "*its haunt in a fathomless bottomless pool*," resurfaces in a "sudden flash" (we have heard such words before); only now its appearance is tied to the prospect that the utterance of "a twy-nature" can "*bring it from the stirred stream*." But because the issue of such a cry leads only to the return of an image now "*flashing*" in Bors' mind as well as on the surface of the poetic text, we are in turn led to surmise that an image, therefore, provides a more (perhaps the only) fitting reply to the perplexity over meaning that images tend to provoke.

To elaborate, more than mere contrivance or decorum, images instantiate a reserve of meaning that additional images are more suited to clarify. *Images*, in other words, *beget images* as their further, and commensurate, embodiment. Does the poem, then, assert, the autonomy of images? In response, we might say rather that it asserts the unique *adequacy* of images. Though images—because they create new wholes—are in a sense independent, when successful they integrate the familiar with the unfamiliar such that additional resonances accumulate for a subject. Furthermore, images open a fluid and expansive field of reference, such that—to read these lines one way—to resolve the suspense of meaning (though not a *suspension* of meaning) which an image

---

126. Ibid.

provokes by affixing a name to it would constrict an image's evocative force. The entire momentum of Bors' meditation accumulates in the opposite direction, towards disclosure, and with a vivacity made tangible by the energy of the fish image itself. Hence, when the poem breaks off the urge towards naming, and instead gives way to a further development of images, the crisis of signification, which acknowledges one kind of limitation, is ingeniously converted into an occasion to open up towards a wider horizon of meaning. "The Fish of Broceliande" sets in motion this dynamic, and by virtue of its manner of presentation advances the idea that form and substance can "co-inhere" in one locus—an image and the indication of an identity through the image. The development of the image of Elayne testifies to Williams' conviction about matter, about bodies (the female body in particular) and their capacity to disclose a "largesse of spirit."[127] For Bors, this same *discourse* of largesse emerges from his meditation on Elayne's form.

We, like Bors, see the form. What, however, is the substance to which this poem leads us, what "great diagrams are perceived,"[128] which its imagery embodies and clarifies? Bors discovers a unity of one kind, which his awakened imagination pursues but then loses as the image of Elayne "*slides through the mesh of the mind*" and eludes his ability to name. In his struggle to bring the passion aroused by his wife to more decisive recognition, however, another discoverable precedent occurs to him. It is his *union* with Elayne, itself a "*twy-nature*," that offers the disclosive properties pre-figured in his meditation on her body. Not one body only, therefore, but two bodies in union comprise an "*anagram of spirit and sense*," an "arch-natural" image[129] that overcomes the impasse he feels.

But even here the poem has not completed its trajectory. Something as deep as it is apparent is called for in order to supply the very notion of a "twy-nature" with an ultimate grounding. Once more, it is the fish image that enables that progression. Only now, Bors projects its appearance as a vision shared with Elayne. Having erupted in a sudden flash "*shaking the aboriginal main*," he now imagines:

127. See *Figure*, 61; cf. 64.
128. Ibid., 44.
129. Williams applies the phrase "arch-natural" as a means of designating images that show "[t]hat great sense of exchanged derivation" made manifest in Christ and the Christian vision. See Williams, *Letters to Evelyn Underhill*, 38; cf. *Figure*, 102.

> Double tracks then their dazzled eyes seem
> to follow : one, where the forked dominant tail
> flicks, beats, reddens the smooth plane
>
> of the happy flesh ; one, where the Catacomb's stone
> holds its diagram over the happy dead
> who flashed in living will through the liquid wish.[130]

The words "dazzled" and "flashed" renew the cycle's interest in glory, and recall the idea of "stupor" that Williams explores in his commentary on Dante especially.[131] It is the state of the lover when beholding the beloved and a paradigm of "Romantic Theology," which comprehends the divine "romance" in terms familiar to human experience. Other lovers are brought to remembrance here, however: "*the happy dead/ who flashed in living will through the liquid wish.*" Hence, the one "track" returns Bors to the contemplation of Elayne, the "*happy flesh*" of her body and of his union with her which the fish image conveys; the second opens a vista towards another union, also figured by the [unspoken] image of a fish: the symbol of Christ chosen by the early Church which served as an "anagram" for her Incarnational affirmation and the basis of her "*liquid wish*" (or "living hope") in their own bodily resurrection. In bringing these several, diverse images of unity together under one symbol, the poem consummates the passion it has evoked in a single moment of recognition. The "happy flesh" of lovers and the will and wish of "the happy dead" inhabit the same affective and "arch-natural" figural space, and receive their ultimate legitimacy from a common source: the twy-natured, God-man Christ.

The fish-image then undergoes its final transmutation. Having plunged to the depths and resurfaced now within a distinctive christological register, it appears as a transformed and transforming vitality:

> Will you open your hand now to catch your own
> *nova creatura* ? through stream and cataract sped,
> through shallow and depth ? *accipe*, take the fish.[132]

The image has completed its "journey," and a decision *about* it, rather than a definition of it, is called for. Bors thus answers his earlier

---

130. *TTL*, 43.
131. *Figure*, 7; cf. 232; also "The Coming of Love," *AT*, 239.
132. *TTL*, 43.

question: the fish is both "from you" *and* "for you": "*accipe, take the fish.*" The very image that Elayne inspires returns to her as an image of what she requires, in union with her husband and in union with her God—both unions deriving their substance from the Incarnation. The image of the body of a woman has evolved to signify the image of the body of God, as wholly human, wholly natural manifestations, as familiar and accessible as the passion a man feels for his beloved. Simultaneous with this movement, the development of images pursued here displays the conditions by which the unfamiliar, the ultimately supra-natural, both gains a footing in our experience and bears the power to transform experience—literally to create a *nova creatura*.

This reciprocity is crucial to the potential thus disclosed, depending as it does throughout the poem upon the reality of physical bodies, which the fish imagery brings to such dramatic vitality and visual consistency. By weaving the fish imagery throughout the poem (as it were, *entwining* the text as its fixed but fluid mode of presentation), Williams supports and sustains this acute physicality, without which the very basis for the transformation advanced as a possibility and a choice also would be undermined. That is, in its theological import, without the Incarnation of God-in-flesh there can be no transformation of the flesh into God, no *nova creatura*, no new life. The contemplation of Elayne's real body, then, which summons the appeal to a twy-nature also materially constituted, signifies a pattern which is thoroughly Incarnational. The drama of Incarnate glory is, and must remain, a drama of bodies. This is Williams' "true Romanticism," the critique of the Romantic impulse as well as its extension towards a consummate legitimacy and substantiation, which sees bodies and the various unities they manifest as sites of revelation, but whose significatory power not only captures but exceeds even the most profound human passion.[133]

The poem ends on this revelatory note as Bors, empowered by the imagination and the insight it has engendered, once more regards the body of Elayne. Though he has not been to the wood, he has "*seen the branches of Broceliande*," and perceives that by its "*probing*" "*everywhere through the frontier of head and hand*,"

---

133. See "Natural Goodness," *Image*, 75–80; also *Descent*, 69–70.

> everywhere the light through the great leaves is blown
> on your substantial flesh, and everywhere your glory frames.[134]

It is in and through the "substantial flesh" of his beloved that Bors comes finally to perceive the thrice-repeated "everywhere" of the vision she has inspired. As the complex image of a "blown" light settles on Elayne, she in her "mortal exactness"[135] becomes the instance that harbors the capacity to show an expansive glory, and in this guise manifests a familiar but translucent image of the Incarnation. It is an illuminating power, however, also predicated upon the command to "*Take*" which stands at the head of this passage. Only by opening her hand "*now*" to accept ("*accipe*") that image of herself which reflects a more consummate union will she realize the potential her very body instantiates. The word "*Take*" also echoes the "*tolle*" of Augustine's *Confessions*, the moment of his conversion when he hears the command to "take, and read" Paul's text. Elayne, too, along with Bors, is to perform an act of reading, though their "text" consists of bodies, and of *a* Body. By this means, the poem issues a veiled but poignant invitation to its readers: will we take this *poetic* text, and by its illumination also open our hand to catch our own *nova creatura*, thereby joining the body of "the happy dead" whose "living will" and "liquid wish" bore testimony to the light refracted by the one Body (i.e., the body of the "One")?

We conclude with two observations and a final, but provisional, comment about this poem's merits. First, we note that Williams' treatment of his subject in "The Fish of Broceliande" neither abandons nor subverts a natural order. Rather, the poem subsumes the natural within an Incarnational order, granting the phenomena of bodies, romantic passion and marriage their validation as well as their potential as sites of revelation. As Williams contended, the possibility that the Holy Spirit could reveal "the Christ-hood of two individuals each to other . . . is possible only because of the Incarnation, because 'matter is capable of salvation,' because the *anthropos* is united with the *theos*, and because the natural and the supernatural are one in Christ."[136] It is a "both-and" formulation that accords well with the view expressed throughout the Arthuriad, that the Incarnation of the Son represents a consummation

---

134. *TTL*, 44.
135. See n. 17.
136. *Descent*, 131.

of the order of Creation, not a departure from it: the union of spirit and matter summarized by Williams as "The presidency of the Holy Spirit over the "holy and glorious flesh" ("*la carne gloriosa e santa*")."[137] In addition, this poem makes claim to the power of the imagination—of images and figurative speech—to bring that assertion to recognition and to prompt a response in kind to the claim upon *us*, which the Incarnation calls forth. That the development of images in this poem begins and ends with reference to Broceliande as both the source and the energy of its unfolding makes this claim emphatic.

In "The Fish of Broceliande," therefore, Williams does more than merely entertain the hypothesis that the Incarnation can be thought in images. He demonstrates how the fully human and bodily phenomenon of God-incarnate can be *clarified* through images—as a method of interpretation appropriate to Christ's nature, who is the "form of God" made visible in the "likeness of a man" (Phil 2:5ff.), and as a means of making that same assertion recognizable in terms familiar to our own experience. His poem, in other words, presents a visual account of that which has become visible, and which therefore cannot be apprehended as such in any other way. Hence, the formula "images beget images," which constitutes the poem's progression as successive tercets expand the fish image towards its christological resonances, is itself a portrayal of this basic Incarnational affirmation: it reprises the process of becoming visible. Because the imagery is freighted with a natural, physical density—a fish negotiating a stream, a woman's body, the "happy flesh" of marital union—what comes to visibility through these images in the form of God-incarnate smacks of the familiar, even as we are alerted to the possibility of something more, something uncontained, inhabiting this natural space.

The visionary power of poetry thus appears as the visual power of the Incarnational imagination in "The Fish of Broceliande." In our final poem, the poetic imagination itself takes center stage as a nexus for Incarnational themes.

---

137. Ibid., xiii.

"Taliessin's Song of the Unicorn": Incarnation, the Poetic Imagination and a "passion that sees into the life of things"

"Taliessin's Song of the Unicorn" stands out in the Arthuriad as one of only two poems having no immediate setting within the narrative of Logres and the Grail, other than their declared author.[138] Although it makes significant reference to familiar places—Broceliande, Caucasia, "the City"—and echoes imagery found elsewhere (*"Shouldering shapes,"* *"flesh"* and *"blood,"* human anatomy), as a poem within a poem it remains a curiosity. Its very peculiarity, however, mirrors one of its prominent themes: the estranged status of the poet and his art within the natural concourse of human society and experience. In this respect, it provides a counterpoint to "The Fish of Broceliande," which it also precedes in the sequence of the cycle,[139] as well as a companion piece to that poem—a connection reprised in "The Calling of Taliessin" when the king's poet opines,

> It is a doubt if my body is flesh or fish,
> therefore no woman will ever wish to bed me
> and no man make true love without me.[140]

"Taliessin's Song," too, is a love poem; only the image of love it develops from the perspective of the estranged figure of the poet-unicorn reveals a strikingly different facet of the way of exchange, one that unfolds, ultimately, under the signs of Incarnational faith. As we have seen, the thrust of "The Fish of Broceliande" accumulates in the direction of the ordinary as the figural habitation of the extraordinary. Here, the direction is reversed, as the extraordinary—in this case the poetic genius cast in the shape of the alien and mythic—is rebuffed in the realm of the ordinary. Hence, the poet's role in love, as Taliessin laments in the "Rose-Garden" piece,[141] comprehends exchange as a "bitter brew" in that the sensitivity of poets issues a return to others but not themselves:

---

138. *TTL*, 40–41; the other is "Taliessin on the Death of Virgil" (ibid., 49–50).

139. Perhaps Taliessin's song is in fact the very one recalled by Bors as the source of his own inspiration for his love poem to Elayne.

140. *RSS*, 125; cf. 128.

141. Ibid., 139–46.

"*[we] see everywhere the hint,/ ... we bid for a purchase;/ the purchase flies to its aim in the heart of another.*"[142]

Yet, as we shall see, the passion of poets in "Taliessin's Song" ends not in lament but triumph—directing us towards a further aspect of Christian, "Incarnational" love. Like our previous poem, a moment of conversion occurs, and by it the convergence of the natural with the supra-natural, and of the sensual with the spiritual. In this poem, however, it is the figure of the poet under the pressure of poetic longing that brings this theological interest into focus and gives it its dramatic force. Also similar to the "Bors" poem is the formalistic style, but here too the comparison gives way to a significant difference. "Taliessin's Song" consists of a single weave of rhyming quatrains without stanzaic break, often employing enjambment to generate a feeling of earnestness, which creates a dynamic tension that enlivens the traditional form. And most striking of all with respect to the prosody, the entire poem comprises only one long sentence, sustained for thirty-six lines. As a result, we feel nearly breathless in our reading of it, enabled to feel within ourselves the plight of "*the quick panting unicorn*" (L.5) as the poem's images accumulate towards a revelatory climax.

The word *climax* does double duty as an appropriate description of this poem's dramatic progression. It denotes the ascent towards disclosure captured summarily in the last word "*unclosed*," and it indicates the sensual, erotic atmosphere that prevails throughout as sexual yearning commingles with poetic longing, then subsequently emerges as an expression of Incarnational passion. This dual impulse of disclosure and desire propels the development of the unicorn image, which progresses quickly from its initial emblematic stature ("*lordlier for verse is the crest/ of the unicorn*," Lines 4–5) to the figure of a frustrated would-be lover, then finally becoming the locus and "paramour" (L. 36) of a transforming vision that is at once sensuous and spiritual. How the poem, then, elaborates the figure of the unicorn—the *primus inter pares* of the "shouldering shapes" and image of the poetic spirit—proves central to its latent argument on behalf of the poetic imagination as that unique capacity to reveal (when embraced) the contours of a world now infused with the presence of God-incarnate.

---

142. Ibid., 141.

The poem unfolds, roughly, in four movements. The first, and briefest, begins in a mythic register:

> Shouldering shapes of the skies of Broceliande
>   are rumours in the flesh of Caucasia ; they raid the west,
>   clattering with shining hooves, in myth scanned — (Lines 1-3)

These lines evoke a sense of timelessness and the mystery of origins, reiterated again when we are told that the unicorn has "*galloped from a dusky horizon it has no voice/ to explain*" (Lines 10-11). The concatenation of Broceliande and Caucasia provides certain coordinates, however, and forms the broader context for what follows—the merging of the spirit of creativity with the "place of images" in the figural geography of the cycle. This, then, is the space of poetry and the emergence of the poetic genius (its "creation myth," so to speak), bringing form to the world even as it evades any final explanation as to its origin.[143]

As the mythic shapes summoned from the sky take on physical attributes, raiding the west and "*clattering with shining hooves*," the singled-out figure of the unicorn quickly assumes sensuous properties: "*quick panting*," it approaches a girl, drawn by her "*crooked finger or the sharp smell/ of her clear flesh*" (Lines 6-7). At the very outset of this second movement, however, the unicorn is abruptly repelled— "*to her no good*"; its "*snorting alien love*" (L. 9) failing to offer what her blood craves. Furthermore, in this initial encounter it is a creature both mute and impotent, a grotesque and "*ghostly*" figure with "*no voice*"; its "*silver horn pirouetting above/ her bosom*" possessing the shape but not the substance "*to rejoice/ in released satiation*" (Lines 11-13). Its advances misunderstood, the girl who seeks only one form of delight feels "*chill-curdled*" at the touch of the unicorn's "*gruesome horn*"—the hyphenated word perfectly capturing the dual sense of horror and repulsion the beast provokes. No, the poem continues, her freedom will come by another man, the "*gay hunter*." His "*flesh-hued*" spear (the intended ambiguity here, as with the unicorn's horn, is obvious) both satisfies the maid and proves the literal and metaphorical weapon that slays the unicorn, leaving its "*spoiled head*" displayed above the lovers' couch, and so returning it to the status of a voiceless emblem. The poem passes no condemnation on this outcome, however. Rather, the episode de-

---

143. Taliessin voices this sense of mystery attendant upon the poetic genius in "The Calling of Taliessin," declaring, "*I am a wonder whose origin is not known*" (RSS, 124).

picts the "*right*" tale of "*a true man*" and his maid, the familiarity of which Williams underscores by the concluding words, "*such, west from Caucasia, is the will of every maid*" (L. 20).

At the same time, the graphic language and provocative mood that so poignantly evokes the sultry reality of flesh and fleshly desire, also intensifies the feeling of loss which accompanies the unicorn's unsurprising but violent fate. As a personification of the poetic genius, its plea for a union with bodies, rejected under one set of conditions—the natural affections and desires of human beings—reappears as an urgent plea for that same kind of satisfaction under a new set of conditions and a different order of affections. That effect prepares us for the third movement, which begins as a moment of disjunction: "*yet, if any . . .*" (L. 21). The inevitability of the unicorn's rejection and demise gives way to an alternative possibility, from which emerges the invocation of an equally poignant passion:

> yet, if any, having the cunning to call the grand beast,
>   the animal which is but a shade till it starts to run,
>   should set palms on the point, twisting from the least
>   to feel the sharper impress, for the thrust to stun
> her arteries into channels of tears beyond blood (Lines 21–5)

The development of the unicorn from a vague mythic shape to its fleshly embodiment is thus reprised along a new axis, called to life by "*cunning*," being "*but a shade till it starts to run.*" The effect of that cunning suggests the operation of a poetic sensibility and insight, as "*grand beast*" echoes "*grand art*"—the Arthuriad's nomenclature for poetry. Only here, it is not a *poet's* cunning but that of an ardent attendant, whose identity and character will emerge in the final movement, not by a name but by association with another "maid." Williams' use of the word "cunning" also has theological overtones, which we will examine presently.

The dominant motif in these lines is that of stigmata, here made tangible as an experience of acute physical and emotional sensation: "*palms on the point,*" "*twisting,*" "*sharper,*" "*thrust,*" "*stun,*" "*channels of tears beyond blood.*" The ecstasy of lovers and the agony of rejection so manifestly projected in the second movement now reappear with these same evocative proportions, but in a surprising inversion. Love is now in agony, and its ecstasy consists of pain. It is a masterful invocation of the Crucifixion as a spectacle conjoining these remarkably dissonant elements within a single act. The next line advances the allusion by direct reference: "*(O twy-fount, crystal in crimson, of the Word's side)*," the brackets rendering a visual reminder of the Crucifixion's exclusive-inclusive character. The phrase "*crystal in crimson*" gives an iconic sheen to the image of water mixed with blood, though the poem resists its idealization (the outflow has, after all, spilled from the "side" of a real man). Rather, the description further refracts the recurrent theme of Incarnate glory, directing our attention to another of its facets: the suffering of "the Word." The brackets set this act apart—not imposing it over the text, but "piercing" it, so to speak, with sudden historical and theological pertinence, even as the surrounding imagistic environment absorbs the declaration as an integral element in its composite weave. Christ has appeared in an image of his passion, while images of passion—fleshly, erotic, poetic—coalesce towards an image of Christ: incarnational poetics evolve into a poetry of the Incarnation. With our attention thus temporarily arrested and directed towards one focal point, the poem then gathers up all of the evocative force produced by its images of passion, pain and blood and presses that energy towards its most innovative, and alarming, moment.

The maid who has dared to summon and receive the advances of the "grand beast" is subsequently ravished by it:

> and she to a background of dark bark, where the wood
>   becomes one giant tree, were pinned, and plied
> through hands to heart by the horn's longing . . . (Lines 27–9)

In short, she is crucified, pierced by the desire of another as its willing victim . . . but to what end? The images of Eros and crucifixion are so intertwined that each becomes radically disoriented. The fourth movement only exacerbates that effect, opening with the declaration,

>   O she
> translucent, planted with virtues, lit by throes,
> should be called the Mother of the Unicorn's Voice, . . .
> (Lines 29–31)

The unicorn, by his "*horn's longing*," has *impregnated* the maid, who consequently undergoes further transformation. Having been identified with Christ-crucified, she now assumes a Marian role—not a Theotokos, but a kind of "*Poetokos*" who bodies forth the "Voice" which would otherwise remain the incomprehensible "snorting" of a creature perceived only as grotesque. The conditions for the unicorn's "incarnation," in other words, have been met by her act of yielding, thus fulfilling the grand beast's desire which, together with her own submission, is cast in a virtuous light—"*O she translucent, planted with virtues, lit by throes.*" And the unicorn now takes on a commensurate role, identified with the Holy Spirit as that agency which unites spirit with flesh, and brings the invisible to visibility.

But what are we to make of the provocative confluence of associations that accompany this sequence of images, depicting the emergence of poetry in a seemingly bizarre appropriation of the Incarnation and Passion of Christ? Has not one perception of the grotesque given way to the assertion of an even more grotesque kind of *dis*figurement—through this disorienting blend of the sacred and the seductive and the mutant transformation of the maid? The poet certainly has our attention; but again, to what does this development of images point?

Viewed in one aspect, images of erotic passion as well as pregnancy and birth are appropriate enough to the poetic imagination. But, to my knowledge, nowhere in European poetry have these same images been given such radical christological shape. Williams' invocation of the passion of Christ on the cross, and subsequently the conception of Jesus in the womb of Mary, through the confluence of human sexuality and poetic yearning stands out as a unique expansion of the kinds of visceral connections others have made between the human and the divine, and between human romance and the *amor dei*. Once more, the poet's understanding of the Incarnation undergirds this move.

In Williams's reading, the Church erred when it deprecated sexual passion, upholding the prescription of marriage while refusing romance the "dynamic of divine things."[144] Against this tendency, he observed (characteristically) that it was the poets—he cites Dante and Wordsworth especially—who recovered passion to "Reason" and to an Incarnational theology.[145] Commenting on the Gryphon moment from the *Purgatorio* (Canto XXXI), for example, Williams remarks: "with such a dramatic moment of common human experience of sex were the high dogmas there united. Christ was *anthropos* and *theos*; so, after its kind,

---

144. *Descent*, 129.
145. See, e.g., *RB*, 22–23.

is human and romantic love."[146] Mention of the gryphon in "Taliessin's Song" as one of the "shouldering shapes" (L. 4) signals the connection with Dante's insight. Only for Williams, who argues in *Figure* that by virtue of "the Incarnacy" humanity as a whole has been "in-Godded,"[147] it became his purpose to draw out the implications of this conviction to encompass *all* that this doctrine allows. That is, what Dante emphasized by his attention to the body and to human passion, Williams meant to extend through his own chosen figure of the unicorn.[148] In his idiom, the underlying premise is the universality of "co-inherence," such that he asserts with full Christian conviction, "The value of the sexual act itself is a kind of co-inherence," manifesting as it does "this business of 'living from others.'"[149] By this derivation, the movement in the opposite direction is validated, that is the reference to these human phenomena as images that point to the all-encompassing reality of Christ who "reconciled all things to himself" (Col 1:20).

Accordingly, Williams aimed to go *deeper* into this fullness of God-incarnate, that is, deeper into the *flesh* of humanity as that place where all flesh finds its redemption and restoration through the "Word made flesh." Again, for him Dante heralded this movement; and we see in Williams' own recovery project his imitation of a strategy Dante also exemplified: that is, "taking every advantage of a doctrine"[150]—here, the doctrine of the Incarnation in all of its scope—in order to fashion a poetic statement that *shows* that doctrine's implications and import. Or as Williams said of Dante's achievement, his poetry has "*turned the formulae of belief into an operation of faith.*"[151] "Taliessin's Song" discloses through its dramatic images this integral connection between human sexuality and Incarnational conviction.

Yet, a further question arises, the response to which the poem not only presents, but also provokes by that same mode of presentation. To borrow Williams' language, what "operation of faith," and faith in *what*, come to the fore here? Because the figure of the unicorn-poet is drawn

---

146. *Descent*, 134.

147. Op. cit., 222, 223.

148. Williams comments: "Dante himself did not go far in the analysis of the human body itself; much there remains to be done" (ibid., 64).

149. *Image*, 150.

150. Cf. *Figure*, 111.

151. *Descent*, 123; my italics.

through the vehicle of the maid into such close proximity (indeed is juxtaposed) with the works of God in Christ, we are incited to wonder which is given precedence, poetry or Christ.

The final lines only reinforce this ambiguity. In bearing the light of the unicorn's virtuous seed, the maid turned *"Mother of the Unicorn's Voice"* is brought to full stature, along with, and as the refracted light of, the issue of her "womb":

> men see
> her with awe, her son the new sound that goes
> surrounding the City's reach, the sound of enskied
> shouldering shapes, and there each science disposed,
> horn-sharp, blood-deep, ocean and lightning wide,
> in her paramour's song, by intellectual nuptials unclosed.
> (Lines 31–6)

She has joined the company of a once distant, "alien" glory, now made manifest in *"her son the new sound,"* an immanent, world-shaping force *"surrounding the City's reach"* as a permeable border line with the transcendent. As the drama of the poem comes full circle, what animated a cloudscape of Broceliande felt only as *"rumours in the flesh"* now defines a cityscape, fully invested with the corporeal while simultaneously expansive in its dimensions—*"horn-sharp, blood-deep, ocean and lightning wide."* In the figurative constitution of the poem, imagination and myth converge then erupt in a new vision, not as the introduction of a new element but the re-creation of a world, materialized in the image of the "City" as the embodiment of co-inherence and the way of exchange.[152] The neologism *"enskied"* encapsulates the nature and force of this transformation. The "shouldering shapes," which first appear in a sky, now *compose* the sky! And by the illumination made available in this penumbra of commingled sight and sound—*"the sound of enskied/ shouldering shapes"*—knowledge itself is set in order—*"and there each science disposed."*[153] The harmonization of passion and intellect, of feel-

---

152. Space does not permit a full treatment of the metaphor of the City, which for Williams was a signature image for these doctrines and for the eschatological horizon of Christian faith. His classic treatments of this view are found in the essays "The Image of the City in English Verse" and "The Redeemed City," in *Image*, 92–109, as well as in HCDH, 134–47) and in numerous passages in *Figure*.

153. Comments from *Descent* suggest that the "sciences" Williams has in mind here include especially the dogmas of the Christian faith. In a manner reflective of the imagery we find, he says of the dogmas of the Medieval Church that they were "as broad

ing and thought, is brought to full bloom "*in her paramour's song, by intellectual nuptials unclosed.*"

It is an image replete with Incarnational significances, remarkable for its economy of presentation as a display of the "taking up" of humanity into God and of "all things" into Christ, and returning to the world the capacity for redemptive understanding. But is it a vision of world re-creation and reaffirmation that poetry uniquely achieves, or one which poetry serves? Once more, at issue in "Taliessin's Song," as throughout the Arthurian cycle, is the status of images as vehicles of disclosure. At the center of this poem's figural economy—and the *crux* of its christological affirmation—we indeed find a study in images, but (perhaps contrary to our expectations) not one which makes either poetry or the poetic genius paramount. To elaborate this contention, we need to retrace our steps briefly.

The progression of images from the erotic to those of sacrifice and birth, and the thick weave of both, follows one determinate course: that of giving voice to, of bringing to speech, a new song. What accelerates that progression and makes this outcome possible is passion, but passion of an extraordinary kind. Whereas the passion of the unicorn was rejected when [mis-]perceived exclusively in erotic terms, the introduction of a different will (unlike the "*the will of every maid*," L. 20) opens up the new horizon that culminates in the final lines of the poem. Significantly, however, it is the passion of the *maid* and not the unicorn which occasions the turning point. This transference is critical to our assessment of Williams' christocentric interest. Had Williams sought merely to appropriate images of the Crucifixion in order to elevate the passion of poets and the capacity of poetic genius, he would have placed the unicorn, figuratively, on the cross. Instead, by making the second maid the crucified one Williams advances a "true Romantic Way,"[154] bringing *faith* to the fore as the locus for a transforming passion. In this light, her transformation from a Christ-like figure to an image of Mary makes sense, as each manifestation conveys a quality of faith demonstrated by Christian faith's great exemplars: the faith of the Son of God, made evident in his submission to the Father by "becoming obedient

---

as creation, as high as the topmost movement of the soul, as deep as the genesis of the blood, and as remote as Adam and the Day of Judgment. Such . . . the principles of Christendom must always be" (128).

154. See *Figure*, 145ff.

"From the Exposition of Grace to the Place of Images" 77

unto death, even death on a cross" (Phil 2:8; cf. Heb 5:7–8; 12:2), and the faith of his mother who made herself the servant of God by submitting to the disturbing annunciation of God's angelic messenger.

The maid's *"cunning"* (L. 21), however, which initiates the series of transformations that follow, seems contrary to the spirit of faith I have described. To be sure, Williams' choice of this word serves the continuity of the poem. It both carries forward the eroticism of the second movement (connoting a kind of seductiveness) and furthers the development of the unicorn image as manifestly a creature of the poetic imagination which, figuratively, *"starts to run"* (L. 22) only when summoned by the "cunning" (in a second sense of the word) of one possessing the quality of insight that can see past its gruesomeness to its grandeur. But can we also say that faith itself involves a kind of cunning?

Here, Williams pursues an idea in an image, and indeed in a word ("cunning"), which reverberates with theological import. That idea he found expressed by Ignatius of Antioch, who declared at the brink of martyrdom "My Eros is crucified." Williams believed that this "greatest epigram of all" encapsulated the union of the physical and the spiritual made consummate in Christ: "he who is *Theos* is *Anthropos*, and all the images of *anthropos* are in him."[155] And not only is this union declared, but by it the transfiguration of love itself appears to the imagination— *under the sign of faith*. Williams continues, "The Eros that is crucified lives again and the Eros lives *after a new style*: this was the discovery of the operation of faith"; and by this appearance of Eros crucified "the great Romantic vision approached" and "the great doctrines of interchange, of the City, approached."[156] "'My love is crucified'; 'My Love is crucified'; 'My love for my Love is crucified'; 'My Love in my love is crucified'": so Williams revels in its multifaceted implications. The thought itself is provocative, but Williams' transformation of it into the image of a crucified maid who is subsequently transfigured into a Marian figure is stunning. And she, like a Beatrice summoning Dante, calls forth the image that she herself becomes—an image, however, wholly derivative of its christological moorings.[157]

---

155. *Descent*, 46.

156. Ibid.; my italics.

157. "All the principles of derivation," wrote Williams, "lie in the Incarnacy, but the Incarnacy in its person" (*Figure*, 222).

In this regard, the order of this development of images is also significant, proceeding as well under the sign of Incarnational faith. The "cunning" of the maid refracts a mode of perception Williams believed was integral to faith demonstrated in the celebration of the Eucharist (allusions to which are also evoked by the imagery), and which recalls the matter of time and time's redemption in Christ. We find a clue to this connection also in his "history of the Holy Spirit":

> As the Church accommodated herself to time in her dealing with the world so she also receded out of time in her union with her Victim and her Way. He had commanded her to command him, and she did; there, in the *here and now* of each particular Rite, the holy exchange was perfected. She communicated and she adored.[158]

Is the maid, therefore, a maid only? Is she a Beatrice figure? or a figure of Mary, even of Christ? Is she, as these last comments indicate, an image of the Church? In the complex weave of the images she embodies the maid may signify all of these. Her "cunning" expresses not only an artistic sensitivity but the "command" of faith, and her contrition the humility of faith to obey the command to summon the One who summoned her. And by means of this exchange, the very heart of the Romantic impulse, that kernel of so much of the world's poetry—variously expressed in the passion of Eros, the union of bodies in sex, the longing of lovers, all displayed with such intensity in this poem—is transfigured by the force of Williams' imagery into this "new style" of faith. The manifest form of the imagery, which composes the thought "My Eros is crucified" gathers love into this distinctively christocentric ambit. As a critique of our notions of romance, it is a *coup de grace* in a quite literal sense of the phrase.

Having addressed the issue of the maid and the riddle of her cunning, what, finally, are we then to surmise about the unicorn-poet and the contribution of its development to theological insight? Even with the strength of the preceding analysis, it may still be argued that the power of the poetic imagination emerges as the supervening interest of "Taliessin's Song"—that Williams has only reinvented a familiar brand of Romanticism, giving a high view of poetry more explicit Christian features which, in the end, induces belief in poetry rather than

---

158. *Descent*, 77.

inspiring faith in Christ.[159] That Taliessin pays tribute to this power is obvious, and has been noted. But is the question of precedence—poetry or Christ?—although incited by the poem and appropriate to our theological reading of it, conducive to an adequate account for what we find here? *Because* the images of poetry and Christ are so integrated it seems our question needs reformulation. We might better ask: How, in enacting this relationship, does "Taliessin's Song" resolve questions of priority; and, more significant with regard to poetic effect, what role does the poetic imagination assume as the poem reaches towards its ultimate visionary statement? Both questions return us to the final lines of the fourth movement.

From the abrupt switch in verb tense in Line 31 (from "*should be called*" to "*men see*")—a shift unjustified by the comma where a colon would fit—two further disorienting effects ensue. In the lines that follow, the syntax becomes disjointed and the imagery clotted with paradox and discordant sensory impressions—shapes made manifest in sound, "*intellectual nuptials*," a vista characterized as "*horn-sharp, blood-deep, ocean and lightning wide*." It is as if the poem, now at the zenith of its statement, struggles to capture what it has unleashed, but which cannot finally be composed in any easy harmony—remaining, as the last word emphasizes, "*unclosed*." It is an early stirring in the cycle of an assertion Williams brings to explicit recognition in "The Calling of Taliessin," the afore quoted lines, "*The weight of poetry could not then sink/ into the full depth of the weight of glory*."[160] There, it is glory's depth that eludes consummate expression in poetry, plunging like the fish in the Bors poem into "*a fathomless bottomless pool*"; here it is glory's height which poetry seems unable to surmount. The poetic composition once more generates the attitude appropriate to the poem's implicit commentary. In this case, the fissures in its syntactical flow create an impression of fragmentation, as if the poem were breaking apart in its ascent, unable to withstand the atmospheric pressure generated by paradox and the

---

159. I am cautious about my choice of categories and terms here. The issue of poetic "belief" or "assent," or "belief in the poetry" (the latter being, as Williams himself insisted, all that a poem can achieve), is a troublesome matter when speaking in terms of how and to what effect a poem persuades us. In regard to "Taliessin's Song," by referring to a "belief *in poetry*" as a generic category, I am highlighting an issue the poem itself suggests and makes problematic: as a presumption set within (and in some sense against) the context of Christian faith.

160. *RSS*, 133.

emergence of an expansive vision. Or, in keeping with the motif of pregnancy, we may say from the strained speech that the poem itself is "lit by throes," suffering the labor pains of the "new sound" it has struggled to birth. As noted above, a definite Incarnational shape emerges from these lines, but the poem seems to set a question mark against its own ability to embody it.

At the same time, the disharmonious effect of the syntax and the straining of speech to indicate a vision it cannot fully articulate remain within the harmony of a sustained form. This combination of continuity and discontinuity releases a peculiar energy flowing from the statement "*men see her with awe*," which in turn brings to culmination the passion that the poem has evoked throughout. The poem becomes a "container" (to borrow the idiom of the first "Prelude") of the uncontained, as well as the uncontainable: the "*paramour's song*" of the unicorn-poet presses through the disorienting effects produced by these final lines and the transmutation of the maid to create a *re*orientation of focus. To elaborate our previous analysis, on the one hand the images of human sexuality and the images of Christ's crucifixion and advent—each familiar in its own right—are made unfamiliar by virtue of their figurative entanglement, thereby subverting our habits of association. On the other hand, and as a result of their fusion, new light is shed on both phenomena—romantic passion and sexual union become images of divine passion and the union of God and man respectively, and the Incarnation confers dignity, indeed sanctity, upon these deeply human and creaturely experiences.

This effect, again, highlights a central facet of an Incarnational theology, which the poem enacts: the assumption of the creaturely by the Creator (in "all things") has resulted in a boundless interpenetration of the human and the divine. The one Union "takes up" all unions into itself; an assertion "Taliessin's Song" brings to fresh intensity by virtue of its dramatic figural display. Indeed, the very activity of its images mirrors this operation of "taking up" or gathering into new wholes, to the effect that the entire poem signifies an Incarnational deportment, which its continuity of form serves to reiterate and sustain. And integral to this development, we observe that the poetic imagination—dramatized through the figure of the unicorn as the yearning for form—has (both literally and metaphorically) prised open the potential of natural phenomena to signify a larger reality by bringing these into union with the "arch-natural" image of the Incarnate Word. Moreover, this very movement towards disclosure is itself an image: one that depicts the role that poetry and the poetic imagination perform. But as the poem reaches its climax and begins to unravel, another image of poetry emerges that resists any presumption of autonomy.

In being wholly wed to images of the crucifixion and advent of Christ, and proceeding under the signs of faith exemplified in these events, the figures of the poetic, like the images of Eros, are subsumed under this new nexus of theological images. As a result, poetic *initiative* is displaced as the animating force of the vision that emerges. What begins as the mythic imagination seeking form, but which fails in that ambition, evolves into the *discovery* of a substantial precedent that finally brings about the birth of the unicorn's voice (in this respect mirroring the development of images displayed in "The Fish of Broceliande"). As that voice swells to encompass the City (the "Redeemed City"?) in expression of an alien love finding form in the world, it is comprehended already as the product of this synergy of imagination and Incarnation. The power of the imagination, in other words, is derivative of the Incarnation, though the movement between them does not remain unilateral. When read in regard to theology's public expression, Williams' poem also bears witness to the power of the poetic imagination to create the conditions by which the Incarnation is given further amplitude through the figural union of sensuality and thought—"*by intellectual nuptials unclosed*"[161]—even as poetry itself appears at the limits of its capacity. What this interchange invites is a subtle but provocative form of assent as we are led through a series of figural transmutations to "believe" in the images presented on condition that we also accept the underlying premise that governs their eventual consumption. That premise is an Incarnational faith, which affirms the power of images to disclose meaning, a faith whose vision of life is at once recognizable and expansive—"*horn-sharp, blood-deep, ocean and lightning wide.*"

Viewed in this light, "Taliessin's Song of the Unicorn" reprises Williams' entire reading of the Arthurian tradition as a discovery of Christian significances in a myth, and which he recovers and elaborates in his own reinterpretation of that myth. "Taliessin's Song" gives us a

---

161. In his essay "Sensuality and Substance" Williams states, "Poetry is sensual and intellectual—like sex" (*Image*, 72), a description that clearly resonates with, and which likely informed, this image.

microcosm of the figural world he invents in his Arthuriad to effect that recovery. In so doing, Williams also reinvigorates something of greater significance to Christian theology, and which this poem offers as one of the poet's most masterful statements in this regard. The confluence of poetic imagination and Incarnation, here cast as a drama of intermingling passions, reciprocates an implicit but equally passionate plea for the rebirth of the Christian imagination. What is at risk for the unicorn-poet—impotent and mute until set free to "run" with the full vigour of its voice—figuratively exposes the stakes involved not only for poets and poetry, but also for the witnessing Church. The poem, in other words, manifests a "cunning" of its own—not as a form of persuasion that manipulates our thoughts and emotions by distorting the "formulae of belief," but a form that translates the manifest implications of dogma into a persuasive concourse of "sensuality and substance," of a passionate intelligence that "sees into the life of things."

Conclusion—Figurative Discourse and the Witness of Incarnational Faith

Charles Williams' Arthuriad, like its literary predecessors to which it continually alludes (Dante's *Commedia*, Wordsworth's *Prelude*), is to a significant degree a cycle of poems about poetry. As Williams has insisted, although "Poetry, one way or another, is 'about' human experiences," it remains poetry and is not the experiences themselves.[162] At the same time, he adds, "good poetry does something more than allude to its subject; it is related to it, and it relates us to it," and "by its style awakes a certain faculty for that experience."[163] It is this awakened faculty of "relating"—akin to what I called "resonance" and "recognition" in my Introduction—that serves to direct some final comments about the contribution of the Arthuriad to Christian insight and witness.

Williams the literary critic once stated that "the question we always desire to put to a poet is how he has enlarged the experiences of English verse."[164] We may concede this achievement to him in his Arthuriad. Our question of Charles Williams the "artist in theology,"[165]

162. Williams, *English Poetic Mind*, 3.
163. Ibid.
164. *PP*, 146.
165. Cavaliero, viii.

however, is *how has he enlarged the experiences of Christian faith*, and this not only for a Christian audience but for an unbelieving, even skeptical public as well? Our answer, in sum, has been that the Arthuriad's "conversion of Christian thought into images" and "enactment" of an Incarnational theology re-envisions ways of perceiving the significance of God-incarnate and, as a result, awakens new possibilities of recognition. Put otherwise, the pageant-like drama of immanent glory and Incarnational vision that the cycle depicts (and indeed, embodies as a whole) transfigures history and myth into a human drama of redemptive possibility—of perceiving the extraordinary [of the divine] in the ordinary commerce of human existence, derivative of the Incarnational doctrine which undergirds it.

We have also observed Williams' skill as a poet of images, conjuring scenes and moments supported by his diction and prosody that are conspicuous for their intellectual and emotional vigour. Freighted as well with a Christian interpretation of the world, the Incarnational imagery nonetheless makes no overt demands upon the reader to assent to this poet's "imagination of the universe." Rather, in keeping with the character of figurative speech, it proceeds with "subtlety and restraint" to create a disclosive atmosphere that insinuates rather than imposes christological meaning. C. S. Lewis perhaps expressed this effect best when he commented in his notes on the "*Arthuriana*" that as a "book of wisdom" it is "unequalled in modern imaginative literature," not merely because, he insists, "many of Williams's doctrines appear to me to be true," but because "*he has re-stated to my imagination the very questions to which the doctrines are answers.*"[166] As with Lewis, Williams' "vivid forms of glory and grace" animate us to explore the substance of the vision his poetry re-embodies. It is by the poet's indirect but compelling style of relating human experience to the manifold relationship of the human and the divine consummated in Christ that his imagistic language of Incarnational faith acquires such persuasive power.

Williams himself made a connection of this kind in his appraisal of Dante's advantages as a poet of vision, drawing the "moral" from his presentation of Paradise "that it is not only Apologetics, but the *style* of Apologetics that matters. A thousand preachers have said all that Dante says and left their hearers discontented; why does Dante

---

166. *AT*, 375; my italics.

content? because an Image of profundity is there."[167] The production of images of profundity naturally marks the ambition of poets. To expand its application, because such images "content" in a way other forms of expression often do not their creation commends a similar ambition to the witnessing Church. From "exposition to the place of images" in this sense designates a timely movement for a Church on a quest to renew its speech—and indeed the vitality of its own images—in the public squares of the disaffected. To prompt, to awaken and arouse, to convey a passion that sees into the life of things in order to compel the attention of those for whom Christian concepts no longer hold meaning or sway—all are crucial ingredients in the public task of a Church that would bring the gospel to bear on the consciousness of uncommitted people. Written foremost for the sake of producing good poetry, for this very reason as "a statement to our imagination" his Arthurian cycle yields a style of Apologetics that instructs about how fresh, concrete images re-interpret an Incarnational faith in ways that constitute an innovative witness to Christ.

Still, Williams' contribution to *Christian* theology lies in more than his poetry's communicative power. As we have observed, Williams—who held that "an increased attention to style would at times have done Religion all the good in the world"[168]—insisted nonetheless that "the Way of the Affirmation of Images" principally comprised a theological insight rooted in biblical doctrine. In consequence, his view assigns to matters of style and rhetoric perennial urgency in any endeavor to "realize the meaning" (Alter) of Christ on behalf of the Church's diverse publics. On this analysis, expressive forms, figurative speech, are more than accessories to theological reflection; they reflect a concern integral to a theological discourse that seeks to renew the public intelligibility of a gospel that itself comprises the intersection of substance and form, of a "word made flesh." Williams does not stand alone in this conviction, nor do his Arthuriad and his "way of images" represent statements peripheral to the public tasks of theology, as many recent interpreters avow. In recent decades we have seen renewed interest on the part of some theological thinkers to consider the place of images and figurative speech, as well as rhetoric and style, within Christian theology's

---

167. *Figure*, 212.
168. *Descent*, 194.

priorities. Among these, the work of philosophical theologian Janet Soskice in the area of "figurative discourse" offers an account that augments our assessment of Williams' art and thought. In these final comments, by bringing to the table her reflections on this topic we find further confirmation of the insights that have emerged through our close readings of Williams' poems.

Although she does not ground her analysis in an Incarnational theology as such, Soskice's lucid study of metaphor in terms of a philosophy of religious language—titled, appropriately, *Metaphor and Religious Language*[169]—confirms Williams' estimation of the "way of images" as integral to a language of Incarnational faith. In this book, Soskice aims to demonstrate the necessity and the utility of metaphor in religious language, stating at the outset that, "despite [the Christian's] utter inability to comprehend God, he is justified in speaking of God and . . . metaphor is the principal means by which he does so."[170] She elaborates that Christians do in fact refer to God in their metaphoric speech, and do so comprehensibly if not comprehensively—a position she later refers to as a "cautious realism."[171] Because space does not permit a full treatment of her defense of this position, I will highlight two elements that have direct bearing on our study in Williams. First, with Williams Soskice challenges the view that metaphors merely elaborate previously identified or "literal" meanings. Echoing Paul Ricoeur,[172] she contends that they are better understood as vehicles for creating new meanings and new fields of reference, as "complete utterances" in and of themselves.[173] Metaphors, in other words, are not dressed up ideas or ornaments for speech.[174] Sounding much like Williams, she writes, "A good metaphor may not simply be an oblique reference to a predetermined subject but a new vision, . . . a new referential access. A strong metaphor

---

169. Page references to this work will be indicated in parentheses within my text.

170. Soskice, *Metaphor*, x. She defines metaphor as "*that figure of speech whereby we speak about one thing in terms which are seen to be suggestive of another*" (15). Regarding the issue of reference to God specifically, she concludes that the "separation of referring and defining is at the very heart of metaphorical speaking and is what makes it not only possible but necessary that in our stammering after a transcendent God we must speak, for the most part, metaphorically or not at all" (140).

171. Ibid., 136.

172. See, e.g., Ricoeur, *Rule of Metaphor*, 188–90, 197, 199, 230–31, 291, etc.

173. Soskice, *Metaphor*, 45, 53, 84.

174. Ibid., 63.

compels new possibilities of vision."[175] As such, she adds, "Metaphors become not only part of language but also part of the way in which we interpret our world."[176] In this respect, metaphors are both irreplaceable and irreducible: they are not "reducible to a "literal equivalent" without consequent loss of content,"[177] but constitute "an embodiment of a new insight."[178]

In a similar vein, Soskice points out that metaphors also cannot be restricted to emotive speech. They have that advantage over other forms of discourse (as Williams insisted), but at essence they are also "cognitively unique."[179] They consist, she clarifies, of "an intercourse of thoughts"[180] and are capable of producing "new and unique agents of meaning."[181] Summarily, metaphors consist of "networks of associations"[182] that have enormous evocative powers to state in a new way what has not been said, or cannot be said, in any other way.[183] In terms of Christian theology's contemporary expressive challenges, her formulation addresses the question: How do we speak intelligibly about God and about our experiences of, and faith in, God to those who stand remote from both?

From these brief observations of Soskice's work, we may summarize the many points of contact with Williams as a complementary account of figurative speech. While Soskice's philosophical-theological approach to metaphor lends credibility to the very notion of "figurative discourse" as a native category to Christian reflection and articulation, Williams' Incarnational theology of images supplies doctrinal warrant

---

175. Ibid., 57–58.

176. Ibid., 62.

177. Ibid., 95.

178. Ibid., 48. She later adds, "The interesting thing about metaphor, or at least about some metaphors, is that they are used not to redescribe but to *disclose* for the first time" (89; my emphasis).

179. Ibid., 44.

180. Ibid., 45.

181. Ibid., 31.

182. Ibid., 49, 57.

183. Soskice's category for such speech is *catachresis*: "the supplying of a term where one is lacking in the vocabulary" (ibid., 61). It is also a form of what Soskice calls "reality depiction" (see, e.g., 132, 137 for explicit uses of this term). Hence, she clarifies, when catachresis assumes the form of metaphor we have not departed from the realm of the actual but have found a new way of speaking about it (cf. 70).

"*From the Exposition of Grace to the Place of Images*" 87

and insight for this same assertion. At the center of their convergence, which is the center-piece of my own discussion of Williams, stands the Arthuriad—as a material realization of their shared interests reflecting a common motive for their respective projects. When Soskice, for example, notes the familiar judgment that "in the twentieth century we have lost the living sense of the biblical metaphors which our forefathers had,"[184] she voices a concern that animated Williams in his quest to "discover more vivid forms of glory and grace." For Soskice, the further observation that "biblical imagery is lifeless to modern man"[185]—however accurate the description—reflects a condition she feels is due mainly to "the legacy of a literalism which equates religious truth with historical facts."[186] In other words, it is the anxiety over establishing the latter, whether by skeptics or apologists, that has prevented the Church from recognizing the character of its own sacred texts—as "chronicles of experience, armouries of metaphor, and purveyors of an interpretive tradition."[187] In this respect also Williams' assessment of the theo-poetic character of the biblical revelation (not wholly, but significantly), as well as the importance of style and the consequences of its neglect, resonates. Though I believe Soskice underestimates how deep the loss she describes has become in the modern consciousness—not in terms of quantity of people but in regard to the sensibilities of non-believers or uncommitted people—I think she rightly surmises at least one of its major causes to which Williams also would have subscribed.

Williams' penultimate answer to this dilemma in our age was a poem, which suffers no diminution but only ratification in light of Soskice's work. As Soskice declares towards the end of her book, "The great divine and the great poet have this in common: both use metaphor to say that which can be said in no other way but which, once said, can be *recognized* by many."[188] Here again, the categories of resonance and recognition emerge as attributes needed for the renewal of Christian speech—as that distinct operation of images which depict the reality of God and the experience of God in ways apprehensible to us. Williams

---

184. Ibid., 159.
185. Ibid., 160.
186. Ibid.
187. Ibid.
188. Ibid., 153; my emphasis.

eloquently conveyed this synergistic effect in his appraisal of Dante's images, by and through which, he said, the Italian poet "talked the language of our common blood."[189] We could appropriate the phrase as a signature statement for the contribution of poets to an Incarnational vision and its re-presentation, when it is a poet's purpose—as it was Williams'—to enact that theology through images at once sensuous and sublime.

Finally, in our own age of the image that has nonetheless seen the depredation of Christian images and "the loss of the living sense of the biblical metaphors," a recovery project such as we find in Williams' Arthurian cycle acquires cardinal importance as an effective response to this state of affairs. As I have sought to demonstrate through my method of close reading, Williams' reinterpretation of the myth of Arthur and the Grail bears witness to the power of images and figurative speech to transform Incarnational conviction into present communicative vitality. The poet's aim not to proselytize but to state a vision performs through the poem's "concentrated and piercing effect"[190] the crucial theological work of creating the conditions by which Christian persuasion becomes a renewed possibility, as the Church must seek to do in every age. In this respect, the "place of images" heralded and held forth in the Arthuriad commends a more vigorous attention to the way of images *within* Christian theology and witness. Indeed, as Williams' theology of images attests and as Janet Soskice's convincing advocacy of figurative discourse confirms, poetry of the quality Williams has produced instantiates a method of *doing* theology born of Christianity's own character and resources. Fruitful for the instruction of the Church in regard to her public, expressive task, his Arthuriad offers valuable instruction as a *primer* for the way of images.

On the strength of such convictions a whole field of creative expression opens up as fertile ground to be explored for the potential of the Christian imagination. Our next poet offers an example of just how diverse this field can become, and how far a Christian sense of the world must extend itself in order to speak meaningfully to our times, as we leave the mythic landscape of the Arthuriad to confront the tortured landscape of actual events in the recent past.

189. *Figure*, 179.
190. See *PP*, 83.

3

Poetry as Remembrance

The Poetics of Testimony and Historical Redress in Michael O'Siadhail's The Gossamer Wall

Introduction: Re-imagining Hope

THE DIFFERENCE IN LANDSCAPES WE FIND BETWEEN THE ARTHURIAN poetry of Charles Williams and the "*Poems in Witness to the Holocaust*" of Micheal O'Siadhail's *The Gossamer Wall* marks the distinct set of challenges these two poets undertook to address in their verse. Although in each sequence we find a portrayal of history as a "failed landscape," for Williams that feature of his cycle designated a clear counterpoint within a larger vision of glory, and one which is made to harmonize with that emergent vision by the logic of the Incarnation—as the summing up and reconciling of *all things* in Christ. For O'Siadhail, however, the horrors of human history comprise the central subject matter of his poetic sequence, which decidedly resists harmonization with a presiding intellectual framework—indeed, as a matter of principle. His *Gossamer Wall* does state a poetic vision in the literary tradition Williams upheld, and which also proves instructive for Christian theology and witness, but his focus of attention requires a radical adjustment of perception and artistic priorities.

The respective circumstances in which, and about which, these poets wrote serves up an irony that is itself notable in this regard. Williams completed and published his first books of Arthurian poetry during the same years in which the Nazis were carrying out their genocide of European Jews. On the surface, it seems no sharper contrast could be drawn than that between the mythic pageantry of a poem set in pre-medieval Britain and the coarse, grisly persecution and slaughtering of millions that raged in the undisclosed background of the poet's world. The obvious chaos of a world at war doubtless inspired Williams further to comprehend human existence in terms of a larger order; but we can only speculate how the full revelation of this more penetrating imbroglio of the Holocaust might have affected the expansion of his Arthurian project, had Williams lived longer.[1] In any case, I draw attention to this irony primarily to emphasize how the Holocaust has dramatically altered perception, so much so that the very notions of history as either a failed landscape or a site of redemptive possibility have become acutely problematic categories. So excessive was the diabolical nature of these events that the imagination of the West staggered at the prospect of assimilating them within a broader, meaningful context. And it is in part O'Siadhail's task in *The Gossamer Wall*—as a poet of a *post*-Holocaust world—to pronounce this difficulty.

By highlighting this comparison between the world of the poem and the world of the poet, however, I in no way mean to suggest a repudiation of Williams' poetic vision, as if it were now an untenable, even naïve, idealization. Indeed, the Holocaust evinces a litmus test for the enduring solvency of his vision—which, I would argue, the Arthuriad survives on the strength of its christological substance as well as its artistic merit. But this raises another issue crucial to our theological reading of O'Siadhail's poetry. For, whatever diminution the Arthuriad may suffer in its portrayal of a Christian order when assessed in the shadow of the devastating events of 1939–45, that valuation applies equally to the witness to hope held forth by the Christian church in the face of such unmitigated evil. For poets as well as "priests," the Holocaust raises severe challenges to the integrity of their respective vocations as speakers to their age. For poets of hope, of which Micheal O'Siadhail is one, this difficulty increases precipitously. How does one speak hope to a world pitted by such pitiless brutality? Moreover, to *whom*, and—particularly in light of the Holocaust—on *whose behalf* does one speak (should one dare to do so) a message of hope?

For the poet and the witnessing Church alike, the matter of form intersects with these questions with peculiar intensity. A substantive

---

1. Williams died only one week (May 15, 1945) after the official surrender of the Reich was declared, when public knowledge of the Holocaust in all of its scope was still quite limited.

theological poetics, which in Williams assumed the shape of "turning the formulae of belief into an operation of faith" through images, must with equal force deliver the same as an operation of *hope*. In regard to the question of how to speak hope, there is a general theological principle at hand, which we can approach from both the vantage points of biblical instruction and poetic practice. From the point of view of Christian theology, the *apologia* for hope includes the exhortation to "gentleness and reverence" (1 Pet 3:15b). *How* Christians say what they say, in other words, is as integral to their "defense" as *what* they say—as we saw emphasized by Williams in his appraisal of Dante's "apologetic." From the perspective of a poetry that adopts a similar ethos, such a stance requires a work of formal presentation suitable for conveying this attitude. Broadly speaking, then, and as an extension of my larger thesis, I hold that the formal demands on the poet obtain for the witnessing Church as well: that is, the search for suitable form entails a general obligation to virtue on the part of witnesses to hope. Specifically, I seek to demonstrate that in his *Gossamer* poems Micheal O'Siadhail fulfills this obligation; and by means of his *poetic craft* offers a model to the Church of how to speak hope to a broken world.

What, then, of the questions of "to whom" and "on whose behalf" does hope speak? *The Gossamer Wall* does not declare as its principal focus a witness to hope, but a "witness to the *Holocaust*." Here, the formal challenges faced by the poet become disturbingly complex. Because this is a topic arising out of O'Siadhail's poems, I reserve my more thorough elaboration of it for our close readings. But by way of introduction, some attention to two areas of concern will help to frame our analysis.

First, the Holocaust involved atrocities of such magnitude that any who address it in literature confront virtually intractable demands of presentation. To portray the experiences of its victims, as well as the calculated actions of its perpetrators, in such manner that human torment and the derangement of the ordinary become somehow accessible, or assimilable, requires a commensurate experiment in form. Holocaust scholar and literary critic Lawrence Langer underscores this difficulty for the genre he labels "the literature of atrocity," writing, "The art of atrocity is a stubbornly unsettling art, indifferent to the peace that passeth understanding and intent only on reclaiming for the present, not the experience of the horror itself . . . but a framework for responding to it, for making it *imaginatively* (if not literally) accessible."[2] Despite the note of hopelessness in Langer's comment, which I will take up presently, he rightly assesses the nature of the *aesthetic* challenge—an "aesthetics of atrocity"—when the ordering imagination seeks (even respectfully) to display a painfully *dis*ordered reality. He continues,

> The mind resists what it feels to be imaginatively valid but wants to disbelieve; and the task of the artist is to find a style and a form to present the atmosphere or landscape of atrocity, to make it compelling, to coax the reader into credulity—and ultimately, complicity.[3]

All of these aspects—the making compelling, the coaxing towards credulity and complicity—specify O'Siadhail's ambitions as a poet of witness. They also designate the demands upon his moral as well as his artistic integrity. To "find a style and a form" in order to speak on behalf of others' suffering (that of survivors as well as the silent dead), to make those experiences vivid without being voyeuristic, and so, to effect a *shock of recognition* on the part of his audience that enables them ultimately to recognize themselves in the midst of a drama remote from their own experience, places the poet at grave risk of presumption. When that same poetry also aims to convey hope, the risk may seem insurmountable.

The possibility of our own complicity in such evil raises one issue of ethical and theological import; but in the face of atrocities of this caliber in particular, the endeavor to express hope, even with "gentleness and reverence," strains against what for many is an irreconcilable discord. How O'Siadhail manages this tension is one of the most instructive features of *The Gossamer Wall*. Moreover, for him, as, again, for the witnessing Church, to refuse to speak hope is not an option. But to do so meets significant resistance. Hence, when Langer declares unequivocally that as an effect of the Holocaust, "For the first time in history human beings found themselves confronted with a situation totally incommensurate with their capacity for hope," he rightly assesses how these events radically disorient and problematize familiar

---

2. Langer, *Holocaust and Literary Imagination*, 12.

3. Ibid., 22. In Langer's estimation, this endeavor obligates the literary artist to various, cautiously nuanced forms of "realism." "The artist of atrocity," he writes, "is concerned with what 'really' happened . . ." (93), even when form assumes the shape of an "irrealism" (45).

categories of resolution.[4] In my opinion, however, despite Langer's otherwise sensitive and insightful analysis, on this score he over-determines what constitutes an "appropriate" response. O'Siadhail's contribution to this genre involves taking up this implied gauntlet, and demonstrating how, for all of the risk, one can both honor the memory of victims and speak hope to, and in the shadows of, that experience.

In broad terms O'Siadhail's response to this challenge involves a summons to hear (and to see) first, before advancing any summons to hope. The familiar biblical resonances of such a summons can be too hastily applied, but they signal further a vital connection between this poetry and Christian theological concerns. What O'Siadhail asks us to hear is foremost the voice of another (an "other"), and in so doing to allow these individual and corporate testimonies to precede and to shape our efforts at interpretation.[5] In other words, his summons in *The Gossamer Wall* has as its prerequisite a call to the reader (as well as to the poet himself) to heed the summons of the sufferer. Accordingly, any redress of these events in the form of critique and especially the offer of hope follows only from such acts of attention.

The theological implications of this order of priority for Christian witness are numerous, and will be raised. As a second framing comment, however, let me introduce at this point two categories that characterize the formal style of O'Siadhail's *Gossamer* poems as the embodiment of this attitude. I refer first to what has been called a "poetics of testimony." At times, but more directly in my conclusion, I will relate this practice to theological reflection, initiating another conversation with the philosophical theologian who coined the phrase and whose influence O'Siadhail admits—Paul Ricoeur. By way of advancing a general observation here, one further comparison with Williams' Arthuriad serves to distinguish O'Siadhail's "testimonial" approach. Whereas the tendency of Williams' richly imagistic style inclines towards a filling in and filling out, O'Siadhail's "poetics of testimony" inclines towards a clearing away

---

4. Ibid., 20–21. In a similar vein, in his book *Holocaust Testimonies* Langer adopts an attitude of suspicion towards any effort to address the experiences of Holocaust victims (including their *own* interpretation) with "bracing pieties like 'redeeming' and 'salvation.'" He argues, "Such accolades do not honor the painful complexities of the victims' narratives . . ." (2; cf. xi).

5. In this respect, he agrees with Langer who insists upon "making the role of witness prior to that of interpreter" (*Holocaust and Literary Imagination*, 184).

and an *emptying* out—a laying bare in order to disclose, made evident in his unadorned but sinewy phrasing, plain diction and, at times, almost journalistic mood.

Both approaches demonstrate disciplined speech, and each evokes a call to attention. But O'Siadhail's endeavor to expose layers of possible meaning through a persistent questioning of motives as well as methods, and in the process to strip away presumption—including any such attributable to his own authorial "witness"—enables the voice and experience of witnesses to these events to emerge, in some sense, in their own right. As a result, the confrontation with the past that the poet engineers becomes more immediate, and history is redrawn as the site of an enduring, and living, memory. This effect announces a second category integral to the poetics of testimony as its larger paradigm, and one equally susceptible of appropriation by Christian theology: poetry as an act of *remembrance*. As we begin our closer study of *The Gossamer Wall*, the elaboration of this guiding concept in regard to its historical and theological dimensions will enable us to situate these poems within a Christian understanding of witness.

History as Remembrance/Remembrance as Theology

> *Destruction turns all their presence into absence*
> *unless some testimony breaks their infinite silence.*
> *In remembrance resides the secret of our redemption.*[6]

In this passage from "Dust-veil" 9, Micheal O'Siadhail offers in summary form the motive and the promise of his endeavor to "distil" in verse the experiences of the Holocaust:[7] to "break silence" as a way to sustain the *presence* of its victims through acts of *remembrance*, and through such acts to heal as well as reveal. As noted, it is an ambitious (some would say audacious) undertaking for any who seek to redress the Holocaust, perhaps even more so for a non-Jewish Irish poet born in 1947 and

---

6. O'Siadhail, *Gossamer Wall*, 112. All subsequent references from this collection are taken from this edition and will be indicated in parentheses within my text.

7. In his essay "The Art of War," O'Siadhail describes his aim in these terms. He writes, "I have attempted to trace and distil the story of the Holocaust which had stirred me deeply.... I thought as a poet I too should try to remember. What those who died cried out for was that at the very least their lives would be recalled: Never, never again. Pleading remembrance" (*Insight*, 26).

writing six decades after it occurred. Hovering within a delicate balance between the risk of gross presumption, on the one hand, and that of *not* remembering on the other, the poet must also negotiate the danger of falsifying by artifice while holding forth the possibility of redeeming through art. O'Siadhail does not shy away from these moral intricacies in *The Gossamer Wall*, but invokes them explicitly: "*That any poem after Auschwitz is obscene?*"[8] the poem "Never" asks;

> Covenants of silence so broken between us
> Can we still promise or trust what we mean? (120)

The last line tells the difficulty of bearing witness to the past in any medium; but when that past is a horror and the medium used is aesthetic the risk of profaning rather than redeeming memory seems doubly pronounced. Who can tell the history of others and of the events which confronted them in a way that does justice to those experiences and reveals their enduring significance? Can poets?

Inevitably, the events of the Holocaust will fall to the province of history, at this time an even greater certainty as "*Last survivors fade and witnesses to witnesses/ Broker their first-hand words. Distilled memory.*"[9] Because history-keeping is not mere record-keeping but an interpretive enterprise, the question of suitable or adequate methods resurfaces. When "history" then takes the form of remembrance—of "distilled memory" as memorial or commemoration—the difficulty of choosing interpretive means grows more acute. With remembrance comes the notion of *living* memory and the effort to engender a *present* presence, such that the experiences of the past inhabit the shared consciousness of the contemporary (a point the sequence underscores by the habitual use of the first-person plural). Furthermore, in the case of the Holocaust there arises an urgency to impress the future with a promise fulfilled: "*Our promise to mend the earth? A healing trust?*" the poet asks in "Soon";[10] "*As never before we promise never again.*"[11] For history to take this shape of commemoration as enduring presence and future promise requires that room be made for the qualitatively human. Certainly, the sheer

---

8. The line refers to the challenge laid down by Adorno, whose words O'Siadhail reprises here.

9. "Soon," 123.

10. Ibid.

11. "Imagine," 119.

quantity of lives destroyed in the Holocaust does not fail to produce a qualitative effect. But the record of numbers can also have a numbing effect; and facts, as necessary as they are to history, are not transparent. Accordingly, this poem insists, for the sake of remembrance the bodies of "*six million dead*"[12] must also be recovered as "*The crying silence of six million faces.*"[13] History as remembrance bears this human face, and *The Gossamer Wall*'s poetry of remembrance aims to endow its account of the Holocaust experience with that faculty. It is for this reason that so much of its content has its source in personal testimony.

Still, we again may ask: Are poets able "brokers" of these testimonies? In the face not only of its victims but the vast complexities of this drama, can they somehow penetrate the "*bottomless puzzle*" of the Holocaust, with regard to which

> No matter how we rummage
> So much eludes us,
> So much remains hidden . . . ?[14]

We find O'Siadhail's ultimate reply to these questions in the *Gossamer* poems themselves, in evidence of claims he has made elsewhere—for example that, "Poetry has a special way to cut through history with images," and like all art it "can help us to remember" by adding "a different dimension to our remembrance."[15] Poetry *as* history, or as history in a "different dimension," and poetry as a suitable form of historical redress? How these possibilities emerge in *The Gossamer Wall* presents one set of issues revolving around remembrance as a means not only of expression but of interpretation as well.

To speak of remembrance in such terms also registers a theological field of reference. In Jewish-Christian theology especially, to remember involves obedience as well as reflection, or reflection on, and rehearsal of the past as itself an act of obedience. So Moses commands Israel at the ordinance of the Passover, "'Remember this day'" (Exod 13:3), and at the time of their entry into the Land, "'Remember the days of old'" (Deut 32:7); so Jesus inaugurates the *anamnēsis* of the Eucharist at the Last Supper, commanding his disciples, "'do this in remembrance of Me'"

---

12. "Numbers," 3, p. 13.
13. "Babel," 115.
14. "Entrance," 4, p. 24.
15. In a seminar discussion at Cambridge, 23 January 2003.

(Luke 22:19). In these instances, the aspects of reflection and obedience coalesce in forms of liturgical expression: in a word, remembrance in its biblical connotation comprises a form of sacramental recall, which also bears a distinctly public dimension in witness to the covenantal acts of God by the people of God. As with the *apologia* of hope, the formal element in remembrance proves integral to the act, and to the integrity of the act, inasmuch as form materializes the attitude of reverence that attends it. In the Hebrew Scriptures, the noun for this is *zikkaron*, translated "memorial" (cf. Exod 12:14), signifying an enduring, visible testimony intoned with the solemn as well as the celebratory. When in "Dust-veil" O'Siadhail speaks of testimony "breaking" silence, and writes, "*In remembrance resides the secret of our redemption*,"[16] he evokes this biblical motif and associates his own act of remembrance with it, imbuing his poetic narrative with a similar sense of traversing sacred space. But the evident symmetry here proves far from simplistic.

Viewed from one vantage point, to introduce theological interests into a discussion of this collection runs a risk of another kind—on our part, as interpreters of these poems. *The Gossamer Wall* represents neither a theological critique of the Holocaust (in the sense of attempting to comprehend it in terms of systematic doctrinal categories, whether Jewish or Christian), nor an effort to make sense of theistic claims in light of this tragedy (e.g., in the shape of a theodicy). Indeed, the sequence insists throughout upon the need to resist efforts to impose overarching structures of meaning on these experiences, though without abandoning the crucial element of interpretation such as all acts of witness and remembrance entail. To be clear, theological themes and concepts do appear throughout the sequence; however, they are introduced either to describe the experiences and *self*-reflections of victims, perpetrators, and sympathizers or to provide a vocabulary for the ongoing task of redressing these events as a human catastrophe with striking contemporary relevance. Notions of witness and testimony, remembrance, moral evil, forgiveness, redemption, trust, "facing," feasting all register a distinctly theological disposition towards the events, but they are not employed to encapsulate them within a particular theological framework. Indeed, at several crucial moments the appearance of such categories—particularly when a poem alludes to a scriptural theme or

---

16. A phrase taken, as the poet informed me, from the words of Baal Shem-Tov, the founder of Hasidism.

cites a biblical passage directly—is suffused with irony in a poignant critique of Christianity's manifest inconsistencies. In this respect we observe a further contrast with Williams' vision. Whereas for Williams irony is defeated by faith, in *The Gossamer Wall* irony is employed to prosecute faith's contradictions—both apparent and actual—as a provocative means of recalling faith to its own affirmations.[17]

At the same time, however, we rightly point out that poetry is itself an interpretive form—that is, a way of structuring meaning that seeks to interpret experience and give it material unity—and here not the experience of the poet but of *others* whose testimony ultimately exceeds all efforts at comprehension. In this vein, O'Siadhail's use of traditional poetic forms in *The Gossamer Wall* especially seems to jeopardize its integrity; that is, replacing one form of overarching structure with another and, again, aestheticizing his subject. That the poet intended to "trace and distil" his material in various poetic forms does indicate a possible advantage for poetry; and that he has by his own declaration sought to maintain an "impersonal stance" by "keeping my ego out of it"[18] does credit to his respect for Holocaust victims. But has O'Siadhail succeeded, and does poetry succeed, where, for example, more "rational" forms of discourse may fail or prove less adequate, when all the time his act of remembrance also comprises a method of organizing his material into a unified whole (which is literally what re-*membering* involves)? The burden of discovery that this question elicits, we rightly surmise, rests finally with the material itself, which, although itself diverse in form, collectively determines the stance of the poet-interpreter.

When the poem "Round-up" raises the question of "*how we can know/ The words to put in the mouth of another?*"[19] or when it is admitted in "Soon" that "*our second-hand/ Perspective*" amounts to "*a narrative struggling to understand*,"[20] the poet reiterates the sensitivity and restraint required on the part of all interpreters towards "the other." They are not to speak as though the story of others is readily accessible, or susceptible of being told simply in terms of one's own narrative framework. Hence, attention to the manner, or mode, of communica-

17. As his poem "Stretching" renders it, "*Our stories become labyrinths of irony that turn/ On irony*" (116).

18. Cambridge seminar.

19. "Round-up," 107.

20. "Soon," 123.

tion recognizes not only how form in part constitutes content (in regard to meaning), but also how the content (in regard to the subject-matter) dictates form. In this respect, O'Siadhail's stance in *The Gossamer Wall* implies a valuation about what material proves superior for the acts of remembrance he seeks to perform, and about which forms prove suitable to render that material faithfully and respectfully. The position he stakes out has distinct implications for a theology of remembrance, and it also indicates once more the "peculiar advantages" of poetry as one method of historical redress.

The title of the sequence provides an obvious point of departure for our consideration of the poet's attitude towards his subject. For example, by the words of the subtitle *Poems in Witness to the Holocaust* O'Siadhail evokes a range of connotations, all of which illuminate the nature of his poetic endeavor, as he understands it, as well as the challenges he faced in pursuing his task. First, the poet declares himself a witness, but one who, as noted, stands at multiple removes from the human experiences he explores. He might of course have created a poem about his own reactions, changing either of the prepositions "in" or "to" in the subtitle to "of." Had he done so, however, we would not then have an act of remembrance so much as an act of self-reflection: *their* story merely providing the occasion for telling *his* story, "in witness to" Micheal O'Siadhail's experience of contemplating these events. But the act of *witness* directs attention outwards, away from or beyond the person who witnesses towards that to which he or she bears witness,[21] and this seems doubly the case for one who "witnesses" to the witness of others. ("*Who witnesses a witness?*" the poem "Haunted" asks.)[22]

In addition, the title proper, *The Gossamer Wall* (an intricate image O'Siadhail borrows for his own elaboration)[23] reinforces this same sense of distance—of standing at a remove, only able to trace the outlines of what lies on the far side of, as it were, a veil of gossamer. Whatever can be discerned from this position, however, also constitutes a barrier to any definitive perception, a boundary area that marks what becomes over the course of the poem a hallowed space. At the same time, because

21. As Paul Ricoeur reaffirms in his essay "The Hermeneutics of Testimony" (1979), writing, "The witness testifies about something or someone which goes beyond him" (*Essays*, 146).

22. "Haunted," 89.

23. From Anne Michaels' novel *Fugitive Pieces*.

gossamer is also a flower, the image of a wall is rescued from the deadening effect that the word might connote. It is an image of life, which, in the context of the Holocaust, is born of the agony of the dying and the dead. Taken together, the title and subtitle thus introduce at the outset one defining aspect of the poet's stance with respect to his subject: that of a sensitive observer alert to the many complexities, and possibilities, of his undertaking; one who listens as *"Pleading remembrance/ Whispers through the gossamer wall."*[24] The material with which he has chosen to work, however, requires an even more refined sensitivity, and a sharpened attention to form.

The Poetics of Testimony: Recovering "fragments," "fugitive chronicles" and "spoors of memory"

There are, as we know, myriad witnesses *of* the Holocaust, most of whom did not survive to tell us about it:

> Neat millions of pairs of abandoned shoes
> Creased with mute presence of those whose
> Faces both stare and vanish....
> Each someone's fondled face. A named few.[25]

What they have left us are haunted relics of discarded lives, many (most?) unnamed, but *none* faceless. How can some meaningful account be given of their presence at this harrowing, of their *"thousand urgent stories forever unheard," "A muted dead* [who] *demand their debt of memory"*?[26] For those who did survive or who survived long enough to relate their experiences, what we have are testimonies; but these too defy any easy scheme of organization. There are the journals and diaries, but most exist in fragmentary form: *"fragments" "in milk cans and tin boxes...fugitive chronicles sealed into airtight/ Jars interred with rubble and sunk below/ Rebuilt houses"*;[27] "Cards flung from trains, spoors/ Of memory."[28] And there are also the testimonies of numbers stamped on the arms of camp victims—*"Telltale figures, eerie signatures*

---

24. "Repair," 121.
25. "Faces," 122.
26. "Summons," 63.
27. "Haunted," 89.
28. "Murmurs," 81.

*of violence."*²⁹ Last but not least, of keen urgency are the testimonies of living survivors, whose physical presence will soon vanish, compelling fresh acts of preservation

> Before the last attesting faces will retreat
> To echo-chambers of second-hand remembrance.³⁰

All of these testimonies refer, all signify, even in the case of those for whom little or no material record exists—"*Out of the cone of Vesuvius their lives rise/ To sky-write gaunt silences in the frozen air*";³¹ "*the hidden signatures of pain in the planet's hearth.*"³² This is the witness of the other, and to the other, with which rememberers and interpreters of the Holocaust have to grapple. How, then, to recover these testimonies, to preserve them without presumption, to order the fragments in acts of remembrance? Is such ordering even possible or appropriate, or *necessary*, and if so, which forms do justice to the scattered signs and the whispering silence?

A more apparent stance to take in this light is to refuse all efforts at organization and simply to publish the testimonies that do survive and let them speak for themselves. (Is not this history better told, if told at all, in a more "straightforward" fashion, some may ask?) The ethos of this approach clearly reflects O'Siadhail's commitment, and as one method it makes a critical contribution to remembrance. But in *The Gossamer Wall*, to put the matter somewhat crudely, he has determined to do more than present and embellish in verse a catalogue of testimonial archives. The poet himself speaks, albeit as much as possible in the voices of others. And in so doing, he shapes these testimonies into a poetic narrative that re-examines the complex factors which led to the Holocaust and the outcome of the "final solution," recounting the actions, attitudes and experiences of victims as well as their perpetrators and sympathizers. In short, O'Siadhail's memorial constitutes an historical commentary on the Holocaust, but one conveyed through recurrent images, free verse, blank verse, lyrics, sonnets, tercets and couplets.

Even to cite this list of poetic forms and devices as an approach to these events provokes the range of issues thus far indicated. We have,

29. "Numbers," 2, p. 12.
30. Ibid., 2, p. 13.
31. "Summons," 63.
32. "Signatures," 2, p. 22.

for one, noted the ethical difficulty of such an undertaking: the charge of aestheticizing the Holocaust. Although the tension over this matter abides, and does so as a feature of his poetic treatment, the attempt to re-imagine the Holocaust in order to confront contemporary audiences with the need to respond to their own age and future in terms of this past fulfills a necessary condition. As these events fade further from our conscious memory, we must to a significant degree rely upon the "productive imagination" (to borrow a concept used by Paul Ricoeur) in order to render them vital and relevant. Lawrence Langer admits this need, although he is scrupulous in his estimation of which forms of presentation actually satisfy it: "History provides the details—," he writes, "then abruptly stops. Literature seeks ways of exploring the implications and making them imaginatively available."[33] Accordingly, this conflux of history and the imagination becomes a site of conflicting interests in *The Gossamer Wall*, sounding further echoes with Williams' historical regard and returning us to those questions of interpretive form raised above. O'Siadhail's poetry of remembrance stages a collision of these two elements, and does so with the following premise in mind: Because the Holocaust itself defies any easy assimilation, the poetry which bears witness to it must accommodate this same problematic, while attempting to translate—or in the poet's words, to "distil" or "broker"—the qualitatively human material available into a compelling medium.

It is this dialectic between testimony and remembrance, cast imaginatively in a reconstituted form of historical investigation, which comprises the meaning of "redress" as I am applying it in this study. To clarify, by my use of this term I do not mean resolution, but again, redress as an effort at *recognition*, born of the poet's privileging of the voices of others. "*Can how we remember shape what we become?*" the poem "Waking" asks; and answers, "*A crisscross of testimonies in every medium.*"[34] Such form of recognition, then, also reconstitutes our relationship to the past, admitting that this past bears present and future consequences. At the same time, the prospect of recognition at the horizon of our experience—the shape of what *we* become—remains rooted in what defies understanding. "*There's no why here,*" the poem

---

33. Langer, *Holocaust and Literary Imagination*, 9. See also Paul Ricoeur's comment that "the past can only be reconstructed by the imagination" (*Time and Narrative*, Vol. 1, Part I, 82).

34. "Waking," 118; my emphasis.

"Here" recalls,[35] quoting Primo Levi's account of "life" in Auschwitz.[36] From that space of inscrutable horror, the experience of the irreconcilable must also be given a voice, as a feature to be recognized in the "crisscross of testimonies." In this [murky] light, O'Siadhail's uneasy negotiation of possible betrayal—that is, either betraying the memory of victims by relegating them to the past or by presuming to comprehend and explain what cannot be fully grasped—also, therefore, informs his act of remembrance as recognition.

Furthermore, by "redress" I do not mean restitution in the sense of paying back a debt of personal guilt. To be sure, the element of complicity takes on global proportions as O'Siadhail aims to impress upon his audience (and himself) the possibility that we, too, harbor the propensity for bigotry and violence that led to such inestimable destruction in mid-century Europe. But the "debt" O'Siadhail seeks to pay, and would prompt us to pay, is a *"debt of memory"* owed to *"A muted dead."*[37] Hence, his redress inculcates a resistance to time's potential indifference, an act of resistance that mirrors that of the Shoah's victims: *"Defiance/ Of record. Charged remembrance"*; *"a cache/ Of testimony, resistance of word,/ Troves of memory interred."*[38] In that this also involves a recovery of time *in time*, the biblical image of "redeeming the time" comes to mind in this regard, though to invoke it as a way to classify the forms of redress we find in *The Gossamer Wall* elicits a note of caution. O'Siadhail's vigilance to preserve the integrity of these testimonies and to honor the memory of victims encourages his equally determined resistance to ordering his account in terms of supervening categories of thought, theological as well as historical. Indeed, his own method of redress includes an interrogation of such approaches, inciting us to reprise our notions about appropriate forms of "discourse" in general.

In this vein, the personal face/voice of testimony as a record of history imposes a range of formal demands on the discursive and pries open new creative possibilities—and it is here that a responsive theology encounters in *The Gossamer Wall* a way of remembrance commensurate with the *summons* that testimonies invoke. As Rebecca Chopp avers in

---

35. Ibid., 67.
36. In Levi, *Survival in Auschwitz*, 29.
37. "Summons," 63.
38. "Recording," 85.

her essay "Theology and the Poetics of Testimony," with testimonies "we are summoned by a moral and theological imperative"—that is, the suffering and hope of the other—such that theoretical discourse is called upon "to attend to the practices of language," and in the process to revise its priorities and its methods of presentation.[39] What Chopp states in principle, Micheal O'Siadhail offers by way of demonstration: that is, he shows us what a witness to the other *looks like* when it is gathered into a responsive text. Thus, our theological reading of *The Gossamer Wall* inquires after not only the place of testimony and remembrance within the discourses of theology, but once again the role of the literary imagination as a means of *enacting* these theological interests as well. At issue for readers of these poems is our own capacity to be summoned to acts of attention and remembrance on behalf of the other, and to speak hope to a "post-Holocaust" world only as an outcome of revisiting the experiences O'Siadhail enables us to recover through his poetic journey. The structure of his sequence, his rhythm and rhyme patterns, and his images produce a range of effects that combine to create a highly refined but respectful proximity to these events. Included among those we will highlight are intensity, musicality and angularity, as well as a complex mood of invitation and interrogation, which together produce a thickly textured act of remembrance in *The Gossamer Wall* that embodies his urgent ethical—and as we shall see, his implicit theological—concerns.

Poetry as Remembrance: Structuring Discourses and the Ethics of Form

As a shorthand description of *The Gossamer Wall* I have referred to it as a sequence, but though there is progression at a number of levels we might better label it a *suite* of poems, or one long poem or series of poems constituting a unity that is at once verbal and musical.[40] The term

---

39. Chopp, "Theology and the Poetics of Testimony," *Converging on Culture*, 57, 63. Chopp clarifies her aim "to clear new spaces for the power and spirit of testimony in contemporary theology" (58) by directing her critique to issues of discursive practice. She writes, "Testimonies question the discursive practices of theory both in terms of what it frames or stages (whose voice gets counted) and *how it is represented*. Testimonies describe the real in ways that require people to see these events that reason and theory do not count, do not authorize, do not signify" (64; my italics).

40. Micheal O'Siadhail has himself used this vocabulary to describe the overall structure and intended effect of the collection (Cambridge seminar).

fits well with the musical themes and images that recur throughout, and as a formal description it reiterates the poet's belief that a linear presentation alone does not suffice to render all the complex strains of so labyrinthine and epochal an event as the Holocaust.[41]

O'Siadhail answers this challenge structurally by composing his poetic suite in the shape of a chiasmus. Its five sections begin with a broad depiction of the historical factors leading to the Holocaust ("Landscapes"), and end by opening out once more towards a broad horizon ("Prisoners of Hope"). As these two sections mirror one another, so too do the second and fourth sections ("Descent" and "Refusals"). The former proceeds along a downward spiral into the moral darkness and murderous actions of those who allowed or perpetrated the crimes of the Holocaust ("*Northeim*" and "*Battalion 101*"), the latter inclines upwards and against that darkness through poetic depictions of acts of resistance on the part of Jewish victims ("*Spoors*") as well as their sympathizers and defenders ("*Le Chambon*"). At the center of the suite and radiating in both directions is the series of fourteen fourteen-line sonnets titled "Figures." Herein lies the heart of the collection, and the section of gravest intensity, as O'Siadhail attempts to distil the experiences of victims as they suffered in concentration camps. In this section we also find evidence of mirroring, or better to call it "counterpoint," as the first poem in this series begins with a "summons" to "meditate" and to "*Imagine*" and the last poem ("Alone") ends with the word "*silence*."

Two further observations regarding the chiastic structure indicate some of the formal attributes of this collection as an instructive aid to historical-theological expression. The first rings familiar with any readers of the Christian as well as the Hebrew scriptures, which manifests this pattern in nearly every genre. What commentators point out with each instance of chiasmus is that its structure creates emphases through internal resonances that focus the reader/hearer's attention in a way that linear prose does not. Specifically, the form also embodies the meaning the author intends; or, we may say, the matter of form serves to highlight what matters—by organizing thought in such a way that added intensity accrues to the subject being addressed. Linear prose can achieve similar emphases, but it does not do so explicitly as a *function*

---

41. We recall that the same kind of distinction was necessary in order to describe adequately the character of Charles Williams' *Arthuriad*, referring to that cycle of poems as 'not plot, but pageantry'.

of its structure. To elaborate, the poetics of form calls attention to the *conditions* of meaning—that is, how meaning is conveyed constitutive of the form used.[42] Theologians reading the Bible carefully recognize all of these advantages; but the issue which intrigues is how this same chiastic structure may be employed in discourse *about* the Bible and its themes, even to the extent of conveying *moral* urgency about a subject, as does Micheal O'Siadhail in his *Gossamer* suite.

For him (as our second observation), the use of this pattern not only serves a distinct literary purpose as a way to provide unity and intensity of focus, but also serves to instantiate further his *ethical* concerns. That is, O'Siadhail's choice of this pattern, along with the whole range of prosodic and imagistic devices he deploys in the *Gossamer* poems, reflects his earnest desire to render the voice of the other in such a way that the other is not displaced. When chiasmus is used as a form of narrative structure the historical elements of the story—in this case principally testimonies of various kinds—are found first to reverberate with each other, and even against each other, in a polyphony of verbal and visual "events." Within this structure the appearance of these testimonial voices therefore marks a significant departure from traditional historical prose, following a pattern which privileges aural sense above chronological sequence. In this way, we can receive the testimonies of these witnesses in a manner that approximates their own historical singularity because we hear them first as they have been handed down to us and as they resound in relation to the broader witness of that period rather than as "data" that advances an ordered chronology. In effect, the unity achieved through chiasmus supports a diversity of voices and experiences without loss to their particular, and personal, character.

In this manner also the notion of "false witness" achieves further amplitude. The most extreme and reprehensible cases involve those who deny the crimes of the Holocaust.[43] But there is another form of false witness already alluded to that the poet himself feels at risk of committing, and which his chiastic structure in part seeks to overcome.

---

42. There is an expanding body of recent biblical commentary that develops this insight explicitly, including Robert Alter's works on the "arts" of biblical narrative and biblical poetry and Paul Ricoeur's three volume *Time and Narrative*. Two outstanding recent examples that focus on particular biblical texts are Walter Brueggeman's *The Prophetic Imagination* and Kenneth M. Craig's *The Poetics of Jonah*.

43. See "Remembrance," 14, L. 15.

The worry here consists of rendering the historical material as though the story could be told simply or "objectively"—for example as a mere chain of events that follows a blueprint of cause and effect—which risks effacing the individual, human quality that the testimonies of witnesses distinctively signify. More than a matter of stylistic preferences, then, *The Gossamer Wall*'s literary architecture seeks also to avert that tendency. By revising the traditional linear presentation, its chiastic structure holds in check the poet's own expository comments as conclusions derivative of an established plot. Accordingly, his task of bearing "true" witness involves exposing the *particulars* of these experiences and interrogating their implications rather than explaining their import—thus reacting to the central drama of human suffering instead of attempting, again, to recount the events of the Holocaust in a prescribed order, and arranging an interpretation of it in these terms.[44] His poetry thereby enables us as readers to maintain a similar priority "*to* try to look, to try to see," and to exercise comparable restraint in our reception of these experiences—chastening whatever tendency we may have to impose explanatory structures of meaning on them. O'Siadhail's strategy here is subtle but convincing, insofar as we feel left in suspense as to the explanation for "what happened" while drawn to the moral and spiritual significance of its consequences.

In other ways, however, the suite is more forceful and direct in its critique of form. Embedded within *The Gossamer Wall* we find an explicit critique of rational discourse itself, and of the sensibility that authorizes that form of speech in particular. In the poem "Entrance," found in the first section "Landscapes," where the poet attempts to give some account of what led up to the Holocaust, the question is raised, "*And how to contain this unbearable evil?*"[45] The word "contain" pronounces the ambivalence judiciously. Phenomenally, the evil of course was not contained, either in its occurrence or its extensiveness. Can it, then, be rationalized? The poem continues,

> Grails of theory, myths of explanation
> Struggle to pin down one psychic upheaval

---

44. By mention of the particular, a range of theological issues emerges in our reading of O'Siadhail's poem, and through it our 'reading' of the Holocaust, which I will take up directly in my conclusion. Among these issues, the matter of speaking truthfully in response to the pain of others especially surfaces.

45. "Entrance," Sec. 3, p. 24, L. 1.

> To make a make-up more easily understood. (3.2–4)

The effort to understand, to explain, to order such events in a way that makes them assimilable, may be "*Part compassion,*" and it may be

> Part consolation, craving for simple clear-cut
> Formulas, somehow to tame the untameable,
> Undo inexplicable tangles of this blackest knot. (3.13–15)

But "*Grails of theory, myths of explanation*" amount to what these images connote. Nonetheless, they reflect habits of the European mind, as the earlier poem "Hankerings"[46] iterates when it decries Europe's "*rage/ For everything certain and hierarchical*" (Ll. 3–4), her "*Rage for axioms, timeless abstractions*" and "hankering" "*after all things steady*" (Ll. 7–10). There is no Romantic "*blessed* rage for order," but only a *cursed* one (the subversion is intentional[47]), and one willing to select out and remove those who do not fit ideal patterns, whether philosophical, aesthetic or social:

> Outcastes, outsiders, freaks, beware
> Our tick-tock reason's overreach. (Ll. 17–18)

The word "tick-tock" is picked up again in the section "Prisoners of Hope" which mirrors "Landscapes." In a haunting series of couplets in the poem "Babel,"[48] the poem recapitulates the complicity of modern European philosophy and social outlook in the Holocaust:

> So sure we'd been of plot and *mis-en-scène*,
> A tick-tock dénouement, slow but certain.
>
> . . .
>
> Broken forever old spinning-jenny's thread,
> Our long and trusted dream of progress dead.
>
> *Bitumen for mortar*, they said, *brick for stone*.
> Paths of Auschwitz paved with ash and bone.

---

46. "Hankerings," 16.

47. As one review reports O'Siadhail's analysis of the Holocaust, "O'Siadhail believes the cause was Romanticism gone awry; the Romanticism that celebrated truth and beauty, beauty and truth, but forgot about the good. It was aesthetics gone wild, abandoning its cousin, ethics, to irrelevance" (McGarry, "Making a Plea for Memory," *Irish Times*, 14. O'Siadhail confirmed this interpretation of his view in a private conversation of 24 January 2003.

48. "Babel," 115.

> Still trembling in our galaxy's outer spaces
> The crying silence of six million faces. (Ll. 3–4, 7–12)

The line "*Our long and trusted dream of progress dead*" captures in a phrase the subversion of modern Europe's historical sense, a naïveté that the past can be departed from, whether forgotten or embalmed in categories of historical analysis. (Or in its even more inimical cast, that history can be idealized in terms of grand processes, as the faceless advance of irresistible forces or in terms of a naïve triumphalism.) Of equal significance to the conclusive statement of disrepute underscored by these lines, the passage demonstrates that carefully crafted rhythm and rhyme patterns can express a horror that transcends the "pleasure" of the musicality.[49] Indeed, the horror is made more intense by virtue of the paradox enacted between the mixture of clichés accompanied by a crisp musical pattern and the outcome addressed here. It is lyric in a self-critical mode, as efforts at idealization and reduction—whether philosophic or poetic—are themselves, by association, relegated to hapless clichés against the overpowering images of "*Paths of Auschwitz paved with ash and bone*" and "*the crying silence of six million faces*."

History is memory, but who gets remembered and, again, *how* they are remembered measures the aptitude of our sensitivity:

> And yet there's no Richter scale of tragedy.
> How to measure suffering? A calculus of pain?
> Behind each agony a name, a voice, a face.
> ("Signature" 3.1–3, p. 22);

> The hitches, the twists which ravel us into a plot
> Too intricate to comprehend. The eye tries
> To follow its loops but strays in baffles of a knot.
> ("Entrance" 1.6–8, p. 23)

---

49. In this vein, I object to the contention that poetry's foremost purpose is to produce pleasure. We might better say that what poetry achieves by virtue of its aesthetic effects is "satisfaction"; but as with this poem, what satisfies is not the music and the form for its own sake but how that form, even against itself and by intention, enacts a lament for the acts of inhumanity committed.

As Anne Michaels clarifies with poignancy in her Holocaust novel *Fugitive Pieces*, "History is amoral; events occurred. But memory is moral; what we consciously remember is what our conscience remembers."[50]

These passages, like those quoted above, intensify thematically the urgent need for a new sensibility and for alternative forms of engagement that eschew theoretical abstractions and romantic idealizations. They underscore as well the central preoccupation of *The Gossamer Wall*: human suffering has "*a name, a voice, a face*," whose features must be brought into focus through acts of remembrance that pronounce the sanctity of the human over and above any sanctioning of ideals *about* the human or our history. This poem's aim to redress the history of the Holocaust as an enduring witness to this esteem (as well as to its opposite) thus ultimately calls for *our* redemption—summoning us to heed a drama with "*twists which ravel us into a plot/ Too intricate to comprehend*," but which we cannot fail to enjoin. And within that summons there stands an element as integral to Christian faith as it is to O'Siadhail's poetic vision: the redemption of speech. As we turn to examine more closely several other poems from this suite, the endeavor to speak redemptively, already suggested in our discussion of structure, will recur explicitly and implicitly as both the site of tension and of potential transformation, which *The Gossamer Wall* advances through its carefully crafted composition.

The Rhythms of Remembrance and the Music of [Redemptive] Memory

We begin with close readings of two related poems, "Numbers" (12–13) and "Remembrance" (14). O'Siadhail establishes one theme in the former, the "overture" poem for the collection,[51] which "Remembrance" develops and amplifies: the problem of how to remember *in time*. The challenge these poems address consists of giving an account of experiences bound by time that releases them from the limits of time past into an ongoing meditation upon their contemporary and future significance.

"Numbers" considers this difficulty in three aspects or images: the arrival of a new century and new millennium ("*A year turning on the*

---

50. *Fugitive Pieces*, 138.
51. The poet's own description of this poem (Cambridge seminar).

axis of our numbers," 1.23), the prison numbers born on the *"stamped forearms of first witnesses"* (2.16), and the Psalmist's plea, *"Teach us . . . to number our days"* (3.10). Central to all three aspects is the theme of warning. There is first the *"lure"* of forgetfulness,[52] *"As though the digit shifts of centuries/ Disconnect what is from what has been,"* but which perpetuates the failure *"to recall . . . something not faced"* (1.1, 13).[53] There are the *"Indelible warnings"* of the numbers stamped on survivors' arms that *"this might happen again"* (2.17). And the poem issues a more veiled warning against the failure to fulfill the time-honored vocation of bearing witness—*"Have I not told you from old you're my witnesses?"* (3.13)—quoting God's exhortation to Israel from Isaiah 43:10.[54] "Numbers" thus brings the past, present and future within a shared space. The history of the Holocaust, the history of anti-Semitism in "Christian" Europe which promoted it, the sacred and the afflicted history of Jews, are all pressed toward a common horizon:

> An intersection, at once cadence and overture,
> Hinge and turning point, the moment when
> The pasts we shape begin to shape our future. (3.1–3)

The moment of that intersection, the Holocaust—*"the shaft of its* [the twentieth century's] *middle decade"* (1.6)—stands in the past but "haunts" (1.15) our present: *"Beware, beware a beast that slumbers"* (1.21). It endures in one sense as "cadence," caught up in the rhythm of time and the patterns of history, and in another as "overture," or the annunciation of themes and events that opens out towards subsequent movements. The passage also implies a question: How are we to give shape to things temporally situated but which, depending on the shape we give them, *"begin to shape our future"*? On the one hand, the poem as

---

52. Echoing one of the epigraphs to the collection, Arthur Miller's statement that "the Devil is known to lure people into forgetting precisely what is vital for them to remember. . . ."

53. O'Siadhail believes that the Holocaust is a tragedy that the world, Europe in particular, still has not fully *faced*, rightly worrying that the opportunity to do so effectively will only evaporate further with the fast-approaching disappearance of living witnesses (Cambridge seminar).

54. The citation bears a pregnant irony of its own, as this chapter from Isaiah reiterates God's covenant with Israel to be their savior and redeemer and their status as God's chosen people (vv. 1–7), while at the same time rebuking their indifference and calling upon them to "'Put Me in remembrance; let us argue our case together'" (v. 26).

a whole suggests the inevitable influence of the past, whether we hold it in regard or disregard. On the other hand, these lines insist that decisions are called for. This moment of shaping a moment that shapes us beckons responsibility. But where to begin and *how* to begin?

This third section of "Numbers" begins to indicate an answer to both questions. From the opening tercet it proceeds to invoke a name, "*Etty Hillesum*," the third name issued in the suite (the first two being "*Jew and Judas*," 1.19). The "moment" of the Holocaust is not an historical abstraction, but one populated by people; and naming the victims and witnesses, as well as perpetrators and sympathizers (even "nameless" ones—see "Nameless," 100), figures significantly in the effort to remember well.[55] Those who were reduced to numbers stamped on their forearms have personal identities, as the poem "Faces" in the mirroring final section emphasizes:

> Friedländer, Berenstein, Menasche, Blum.
> Each someone's fondled face. A named few.
> Did they hold hands the moment they knew? (122, Lines 8–10)

To name them overrides the indifferent brutality of their executioners, and instead solicits a plea to see persons sympathetically—in their dying as well as their living. In this passage, recalling names specifies and confirms the actuality, while the rhymed couplet that follows lends vitality—transporting us in a single line to a moment in time at once tender and terrifying: "*Did they hold hands the moment they knew?*" The poem "Numbers" raises that imaginative possibility rhetorically, the name Etty Hillesum both introducing the primary witness of testimonies and her story prompting a signature question for the entire suite: "*Is this the moment where testimony and story meet?*" (3.8). The question is bracketed by two biblical references, two half-rhymed lines that end in "*tears*" and "*forebears*." That reference and the resonance of those words apostrophize a history of suffering that the moment of Etty Hillesum's testimony signifies, and which the "moment" of O'Siadhail's long poem must somehow recover meaningfully. At issue is speech, and speaking—only in what mode? Can story convey this testimony of tears?

---

55. The reading of the names of victims, we recall, is also one of the principal practices on Holocaust Remembrance days, reflecting the long tradition of naming that extends back to the Hebrew Bible.

The poet's immediate response is to invoke further scriptural reference—"*Teach us, cries the psalmist, to number our days*" (3.10)—although with an uneasy appropriation of this appeal in light of "*The exile, the scattering, now the ovens and marches*" and the image of "*Isaiah's world still stumbling onwards in praise*" (3.11–12). To whose account, this juxtaposition implies, does the numbering of such days belong? The last tercet then repeats the pattern of the third; bringing into relief the middle line's gesture towards hope—"*The desert through which we pass will bloom again*" (3.14)—which is also bracketed by biblical quotations and lines ending in half-rhymed words ("*witnesses*" and "*darkness*"). The speaker in both instances is God, who interrogates his people and declares to them "I did not speak in secret in a land of darkness" (from Isaiah 45:19). Against the backdrop of the Holocaust, however, the statement rings with ambiguity in regard to the matter of speech. For witnesses of and to this nightmare, which is both like and unlike the longsuffering of the past, the difficulty of knowing what or whose words to speak that would dispel this new darkness proves acutely problematic. The example of God speaking openly "*in a land of darkness*" establishes the model to which he summons his people ("*my witnesses*"). But in the shadow of the Holocaust, to heed this example by speaking words of explanation and hope remains in fretful suspense.

The poem creates this tension subtly through its method of composition. Significantly, in both of these tercets we find the only instances of half-rhymes in this section, suggesting that even when reference is made to an acceptable larger context of meaning—in this case, the Bible[56]—we still have only begun to approach a discovery of this tragedy's import. It resists any easy application *on our part* of an interpretive scheme. In effect, through these passages the poem creates a pattern within the larger pattern of this tercet series, but in the process complicates the very idea that a pattern can readily be found and articulated to make sense of the events the suite explores. Thus, the "intersection of cadence and overture" in *The Gossamer Wall* itself forms an uneasy alliance with memory and witness: like the events on which these poems attempt to get some purchase, the cadence of measured lines and rhyme schemes cannot finally capture all of the extensive themes elicited. Accordingly, the poem places itself within the very perplexity

---

56. The title itself announces this referential context, appropriating the name for the fourth book of the Pentateuch.

over meaning and meaningful speech it invokes, refusing to stake out a position of superiority that definitively surpasses the ordering attempts of other forms of discourse.

At the same time, however, the poetry does achieve something of crucial significance for the redress of remembrance. By bringing a variety of particulars into focus it provokes our attention with an urgency that no simple statement about this perplexity could achieve and which would leave us with merely a vague declaration of abstract *ir*resolution. For the sake of the *wisdom* of remembrance (as the reference to Psalm 90 in 3.10 prompts us to consider)[57]—a manner of remembering that shapes the future by virtue of its scrupulous shaping of the past—more than vague uncertainty is needed. To remember well demands that the particulars of events, and of persons especially—their names, their stories, their testimonies—be brought to recognition. It demands as well what poetry can uniquely deliver in its witness to these: *precise emotion*. As we observed in our study of Charles Williams' imagery, in poetic speech form and substance cooperate in the production of articulate feelings, or more expansively, the "feeling intellect." In his *Gossamer* suite, O'Siadhail generates exacting emotional energy *through* his witness to the particular in order to enable people in one age to be brought into closer proximity, and sympathy, with the people and events of a previous one. In short, his poetry gives us drama, not of the poet's own invention but "distilled" for us by means of his prosody, diction and images, engendering a sharpened emotional pitch to *our* experience of others' past in "*a moment when testimony and story meet*" (2.18). The "time" of the poem, its *moment*, thereby becomes a fulcrum for resistance to time's receding faculty: recovery of the past becomes our present reawakening to its human significance.

Within the range of these emotions, we find included in "Numbers" an earnestness to preserve the testimonies of "*first witnesses*" (2.16)—"*Before the last attesting faces will retreat/ To echo chambers of second-hand remembrance*" (2.19–20). Here, too, the poem conveys the anxious plight of hope. To paraphrase (not the poetry but its effect), the prospect of hope does not emerge simply or naively—neither for us nor, markedly, for Holocaust survivors—but from a tangle of misgivings:

---

57. The prayer "Teach us to number our days" continues, "*in order that we may present to Thee a heart of wisdom*" (Ps 90:12).

> Obstinacy of survival, slowly reassembled life.
> Why was I one of those chosen to survive?
> For children, grandchildren? A demand to tell? (2.8–10)

To tell, yes, though the poet for his part will not put words in anyone's mouth. Rather, in re-presenting their testimonies to the past and to the present dilemma these create, his poetry offers a spectrum of possibilities that hovers over "*the long shadowed crux of that past:/ Remember too much, the Kapo laughs last,/ To forget breaks sacred promises to the gone*" (2.13–15). Poised within these alternatives is the possibility of hope with which this overture poem concludes: that "*The desert through which we pass will bloom again.*" O'Siadhail, however, leaves the gesture suspended in our minds as it is left suspended graphically on the page. The journey through this desert is necessary before that possibility can be substantively advanced—hope can only emerge with force out of the shadowy but substantial experiences of witnesses who have suffered what threatens to overwhelm it.

His next poem, "Remembrance" (14), engages this theme and the challenges it elicits directly, and with it the matter of time, representing a first response to the question about "the moment when/where testimony and story meet." The poem begins with two comparative images that disclose a possibility: "*A word . . ./ you think you've heard a million times over/ suddenly will sink further in*" (Ll. 1–3); a musical piece "*you begin learning note by note*" and practice in "*dreamlike repetition,*" but only years later "*re-awake to its music*" (Ll. 4–6). Both stanzas portray the habits of memory, and both also convey the possibility that *memory can deepen then re-emerge in a new vitality.* The clause "*dream-like repetition*" evokes a cautionary note, however. It embodies the suggestion of two horizons. The one is the twilight of the past towards which our sympathies may fade, because it has passed. The other is the dawn of a future that holds the threat of repeating the nightmare because we are neither awake nor alert to that startling prospect. The summons to remembrance stands at the juncture of these two horizons, in that tension which the phrase subtly asserts. Thus, from the outset the poem invokes the problems of memory and time as well as the possibilities for effective remembrance in time.

It then elaborates on such possibilities, though with equal sensitivity to the difficulties involved. The distance of years—clearly a restriction in one sense—nonetheless bears certain advantages. For example, new information surfaces when there is

> Time to find the chronicles below the debris
> of a cleansed ghetto, for piecemeal unearthings
> to air their testimony against false witness. (Ll. 13–15)

Such revelations confirm the accounts of eyewitnesses and refute various misrepresentations perpetrated by Holocaust deniers. The tension remains, however, because the ghettos have been *"cleansed"* (a word that reverberates with present as well as past signification), and the testimonies amount to only *"piecemeal unearthings."* In addition, more than the accumulation of archival evidence the distance of years also *facilitates* the endeavor to make sense of the Holocaust and to comprehend its relevance. Clarity of perspective may also improve over time,

> As though things can be too big for us close-up
> and need the slow-down of both time and distance;
> a wider angle, the gradual *adagio* of truth. (Ll. 7–9)

The last phrase, one of the most eloquent in the suite, provides a paradigm for the project of remembrance and expresses the mood as well as the mode in which *The Gossamer Wall* unfolds. It asserts, gently, that within time's contingencies truth acquires emergent properties, suggesting a process of discovery that is at once *"gradual"* and capable of harmonization—an *"adagio."* The compound words *"close-up"* and *"slow-down"* react to each other in a way that compliments this attitude, as does the internal rhyme pattern *"As though"*—*"slow-"*—*"adagio."* The combination of these elements registers a movement towards the events and the people who suffered, but as a search for meaning and perspective that does not insist upon a set interpretive framework. In this respect, *"the gradual adagio of truth"* supplies the medium by which the advantage of *"a wider angle"* can be explored. It is, in fact, the very medium that "Remembrance" and the suite of *Gossamer* poems enact: the musical prosody and imaginative engagement of poetry.

In the section mirroring this one ("Prisoners of Hope"), O'Siadhail recapitulates the dimensions of process and discovery as a proper mode for acts of remembrance on behalf of the other. The poem "Never" (120), for example—a companion piece to "Remembrance"—proposes

> A conversation so rich it knows it never arrives

> Or forecloses; in a buzz and cross-ruff of polity
> The restless subversive ragtime of what thrives. (Ll. 10–12)

The stiff and almost chatty tenor of the words "*buzz*" and "*cross-ruff*" set polity against the more vigorous mood associated with an open conversation, here depicted as "*rich,*" "*restless*" and "*subversive*" (the "r" sounds in accented beats reinforcing this distinction as they play off the flatter "z" in "buzz" and the unaccented "f" in "cross-ruff"). The "*ragtime of what thrives*" proves subversive not in itself but because it challenges the comparably disaffected banality of polity. In effect, the poetics activate the assertion that such a "musical" conversation provides a way of affirmation without emotional distance or [legislative] presumption, enabling acts of remembrance to span a future hope of life that answers the horror of a deadly past:

> Endless dialogues. The criss-cross of flourishings.
> Again and over again our complex yes.
> A raucous glory and the whole jazz of things. (Ll. 13–15)

It is "*our promise of never again*" (L. 18) sustained in the musical dynamics of "*Again and over again,*" the "*feast*" of "*a music's brimming let-go*" (L. 17). As such, "Never" enacts through its rhyming tercets, diction and musical imagery a response to the charge invoked in the first line: "*That any poem after Auschwitz is obscene?*" But is this naïve, or sentimental, perhaps betraying an impatience on the part of the poet to redress the tacit charge leveled against the poetry as it formulates a redress to the history that impelled it? To make music in verse of these experiences and to attempt to gather them within a musical paradigm places unique demands on a poetry of remembrance. Once more, the ethics of form emerges as an issue.

While preserving keen attention to the human quality of remembrance throughout as its necessary and abiding impulse, in the chiastically paired sections "Landscapes" and "Prisoners of Hope" O'Siadhail also strives to situate remembrance within the larger field of epoch, which careens along the continuum of past-present-future. What confounds that effort is the recognition, admitted by all, that the experiences of the Holocaust as they occurred and as they recur in historical reflection involve seemingly incorrigible *complexities*. The word proves crucial to O'Siadhail's poetic interpretation. He evokes it in "Never" with the provocative phrase "*our complex yes,*" echoing its first occurrence in

"Remembrance." In that earlier poem the phrase "*the gradual adagio of truth*" issues in both recognition and a further statement of possibility: To engage the process of discovery involves us in events

> So complex, so tangled as if we have to wait
> on some riff of imagination to refract detail,
> some fiction to shape elusive meanings of fact. (14, Ll. 10–12)

The "*as if*" of this stanza and the "*as though*" of the previous one (L. 7) convey the attitude of restraint that will emerge as reverence towards those remembered. Within time's contingencies all rememberers are bound to speak in such terms. But is it also possible to give a meaningful shape to this "complex" and "elusive" past?

In this tercet from "Remembrance" the poem puts forth the central *apologia* for the approach and technique of the whole: effective remembrance is an enterprise of the *imagination*. The effort to distil but not delimit, to shape but not shackle, the experiences of the Holocaust as a living memory with enduring valences depends, this poem asserts, upon an imaginative use of language. The "as if" and "as though" serve to register this theme generally, but the restraint they also convey indicates the quality of imaginative expression needed. It is not an imagination given free rein, but one subjected to the discipline of patience, when rememberers "*wait on some riff of imagination to refract detail*" and allow "*elusive meanings of fact*" to emerge gradually. O'Siadhail's recurrent geological imagery here serves to reiterate this attitude of patience and process:

> Just quiet moves and shifts in geological tempo,
> or the way climates show changes over decades
> of slow landscape ... (Ll. 16–18)[58]

And within that same mode the motif of music as paradigm returns as an instance of disciplined imaginative performance. Like the image of "*slow landscape*," music of the kind evoked here also proceeds gradually, but with one further advantage. It can materialize silence: "*In a rest between notes a music's bridled silence*" (L. 19). The model of music urges an attitude that writers may approximate when they leave out "*those

---

58. The image, along with many others (including the title of this suite), shows further the profound influence of Anne Michaels' *Fugitive Pieces*. See, e.g., 31, 48, 54, 77, 111, 112, 119, 138, 144, 161, 213, 221, 251 of that work.

things still best unsaid" (L. 20). This too involves discipline, often marking the difference between telling the story of others and *replacing* their story with one's own. Musical poise thus images a similarly desirable historical-discursive poise, and in both instances it is a function and capacity of the imagination to deliver that range of complex sensibilities in, as the geological image elaborates, "*A long redemption of time*" (L. 18).

O'Siadhail's *Gossamer* suite announces this view of the imagination, but the imaginative itself constitutes the mode of redress and remembrance attempted, performing this method by virtue of the poem's own "music." In the "time-art" of poetry, music is achieved in language principally through the interplay of metre, rhyme and verbal texture (the latter concerning the sounds of words chosen as well as their interaction with other words in the forms of assonance, consonance, and alliteration). The poet's own "complex yes" *in witness to the Holocaust* involves a similarly complex deployment of aural and prosodic elements, which invigorate acts of attention and elicit fresh proximity to these experiences. Poetry is artifice, but this does not mean that the attitudes it produces towards its subject-matter are artificial. O'Siadhail's use of traditional metres and stanzaic forms on the one hand emphasizes the artifactual. On the other hand, it exudes the discipline of imagination called for,[59] requiring the reader to be equally disciplined and attentive in the reception of the poetry. As a result, a *heightened* attentiveness, first demanded in the reading, affords a commensurately heightened *response* to the subject-matter. This effect in turn issues an *invitation* to inspect, to listen, and to imagine. As O'Siadhail has commented, "good poetry is not an argument but an invitation . . . into a world of images, into a worldview"; "a poet does take responsibility, but in an *interrogative mood.*"[60] This latter comment finds its corollary in contemporary approaches to theology, marking a vital connection between the na-

---

59. In the private conversation with the poet of 24 January 2003, O'Siadhail remarked that the deep ethical responsibility he felt in his treatment of the Holocaust found expression first in the process of writing in traditional forms. As he said of his use of sonnets in particular, "in the making of the poems the form and content develop together as a process of discovery that the form encourages." Because, he added, writing in such forms demands acute sensitivity to craft, the process itself involves "discovering how to speak as one wrestles with form as an act of attentiveness to language."

60. Ibid.; my emphasis.

tures of these respective enterprises.[61] *The Gossamer Wall* achieves this heightened effect and registers this invitation through the use of traditional forms; but what the poet does within these forms in terms of the interplay of images, rhyme patterns and verbal texture shows him at his most innovative.

We have observed some of this interplay already in the passages cited above. Further examination reveals further how the deep patterning of O'Siadhail's "verbal-musical" technique generates a new intensity about the experiences as well as a heightened sensitivity in the endeavor to remember them. To return once more to the poem "Remembrance," for example, we find here one of many instances of the poet's use of a "zigzag" rhyme scheme[62] buried within the pattern of regularly metred tercets. Taken in order of the stanzas in which they occur, we observe the rhymes and half-rhymes of *"word"*—*"heard"* (Stanza 1), *"note"*—*"rote"* (Stanza 2), *"as though"*—*"slow"*—*"adagio"* (Stanza 3), *"as if"*—*"riff"* and *"refract"*—*"fact"* (Stanza 4), *"below"*—*"ghetto"* then *"tempo"*—*"show"*—*"slow"* (Stanzas 5 and 6), *"rest"*—*"best"* and the final end-rhymed pair *"unsaid"*—*"dead"* (Stanza 7). When we trace the connotative strings of these matched words some are commonplace ("word"—"heard," "note"—"rote"), while others convey a harmony of evolving signification that the rhyme serves to reiterate (the assonance of "below"—"ghetto," "tempo"—"slow"—"show"). The final rhymed pair then takes this interplay of word meaning and aural evocation to a more urgent pitch as the plea for forgiveness is situated, as it were, within the shadows cast by "unsaid" and "dead." The musical climax is thus at once an interpretive climax and *anti*-climax as the problem of speaking memory once more surfaces; but that difficulty receives new force through the musical-conceptual accents articulated by the rhyme scheme. By virtue of that pattern, the promise of a "gradual *adagio* of truth" is thus itself chastened by this difficulty even as it is commended for its potential. The advantageous "wider angle" of historical perspective that adagio fills in can only be approached and explored indirectly, that is, *at an angle*; the zigzag pattern both reprises that necessity and *shows* that possibility, displaying the angular idea graphically as well as musically.

---

61. In *Self and Salvation*, David Ford avers, "Theology, like other intellectual disciplines, is pervaded by the interrogative mood" (2).

62. O'Siadhail's own term for this pattern.

There are, moreover, distinct rhetorical advantages made available through the poem's rhyme scheme, and which also display meaning in regard to the challenge of remembering in time. Because the zigzag pattern is embedded in the poem, the reader only discovers its presence gradually through a process of careful examination, of searching for and finding clues. The reader is invited to "enter in" to the poem's own methods of remembrance, and through this engagement with the poetry to enter in to the experiences that it reports. By formal analogy, then, the subtlety of the angular poetic pattern mirrors the pattern of remembrance commended. That is, the method of reading the poetry which the form demands images the method of reading the history which *it* demands, as a complex process of untangling the "*tangled*" events in order to "*shape elusive meanings of fact.*" Hence, the process of learning how to read in order to remember—which the formal pattern invokes as an invitation to seek for meaning—proceeds only in terms that the experiences themselves allow. No easy ordering of either the poetry or the experiences of the Holocaust would do justice to the latter's complexity. Here we see also how the regular metre and stanzaic form cooperate with the irregular rhyme scheme to preserve that ambiguity. The combination displays the presence of disorder within order, and vice-versa: both are captured within a verbal-musical harmony that manages to hold these diverse elements in a unified, dynamic tension. We hear it and *see* it, perceiving both strains simultaneously. When the *Gossamer* suite issues its ultimate note of affirmation—"*our complex yes*"—that same ambiguous-harmonious tension is maintained: "*The criss-cross of flourishings,*" "*The restless subversive ragtime of what thrives.*"[63]

The Summons to Remember [Well]

The poem following "Remembrance"—"Forebodings" (15)—employs a different rhyme scheme but one which elicits similar intensifying effects. Like the zigzag pattern it too is not readily detectable, and for that reason the reader is once more prompted to discover a pattern within a pattern, albeit elusively. Here also the spatial imagination of poetry finds full expression as poetic form mirrors and instantiates the meaning sought. The poem's subject-matter concerns the history of anti-Semitism that erupted in the Holocaust:

63. "Never," 120.

> Rumbles in bowels of myth. Again and again
> Eruptions, sulphurous gases of blame.
> An inwoven scapegoat down two millenniums. (Ll. 1–3)

Central to the exploration of this theme are the spatial images which give the history a multi-dimensionality: "*Bowels of myth*" (L. 1), "*Eruptions*" (L. 2), "*inwoven scapegoat*" (L. 3), "*poisoned wells*" (L. 8), "*Outsider inside*" and "*Love-hate's merry-go-round*" (L. 13), "*angular planes overlapping and awry*" (L. 16), "*Tragic fault line*" (L. 17), "*prejudice underground*" (L. 18). These images of depth, cycle and overlap interact with and play off the biblical references to the trial of Jesus, giving the *mis*application of that account an added historical dimension: a pattern of prejudicial motive "inwoven" in the European psyche, a "*Tragic fault line within us*"; text and tragedy enmeshed in a common conspiracy of *blame* with contemporary resonances.

The concept of blame emerges as the central problematic addressed in the poem, as it is a central motive in the history of the Holocaust. Along with the spatial imagery, the rhyme scheme forces the matter to the forefront of the reader's attention. As complex and interwoven as is the history of anti-Jewish prejudice—"*Those angular planes overlapping and awry*"—so too is the formal pattern of rhyme. To scan it in symbols, that pattern unfolds in stanzaic progression as a-b-c, d-e-a, c-e-d, f-g(d)-h, i-j-f, h-j-i. If we regard "g" ("*pitch*") as a half rhyme with "d" ("*it*" and "*spit*"), then only "b" emerges as the single, wholly unrhymed word in the poem. That word is "*blame*." We hear it with emphasis when it first appears, followed as it is by a full stop. We hear it again in the larger musical environment of the poem with even greater emphasis as it stands out in isolation from the other rhymed pairs. The assigning of blame is the problem, and the tendency to do so lies deep within the pattern of European prejudice even as the word itself rises and falls within the deep patterning of the poem.

Rather than merely pronouncing blame as both cause and verdict (by blaming those who blamed the Jews for their problems), however, the poem once more *invites* our inspection of this nefarious phenomenon. The spatial imagery engenders this attitude, suggesting the multi-dimensioned nature of blame and giving its history an emotional palpability that solicits the reader's engagement with the issue of blaming at a personal level. The rhyme scheme also works on our emotions, but its subtlety foregrounds again the issue of learning how to read intelligently. The endeavor to decipher the poetic text that the text itself promotes mirrors the process of unraveling the clues of the history which also consists of an enduring process of textual [mis-]interpretation. As parallel and overlapping movements within the poem, the issues of blame and blaming are not foreclosed, but opened up, which is precisely the interrogative attitude or mood that O'Siadhail strives to convey.

A great risk surfaces ominously in this approach to reading, however; a risk that our own interpretation of O'Siadhail's text may also arouse. Efforts to decipher, to search for clues, to unravel a mystery, can seem a form of amusement, creating distance rather than proximity, emotional laxity rather than sympathetic intensity. But the poem resists this profanation of historical memory at every turn. By punctuating the issue of blame through the rhyme pattern, the word as well as the idea permeates the entire poem (like "*sulphurous gases*"); or we may say it hovers over the poem as a searchlight that both illuminates and focuses every instance of anti-Semitism evoked. We hear blame in every material manifestation of Europe's treatment of Jews: "*An inwoven scapegoat down two millenniums*" (L. 3), "*Scatterings. Ghetto. Yellow badge. Pogroms*" (L. 7), "*Europe at fever pitch./ Crusades. Over again the Goyim's fall-guy*" (Ll. 11–12), "*Blood-baker, healer,* Jude Süss" (L. 14). And most disturbing of all, the matter of blame emerges in the references to the trial of Jesus, a text poignantly *woven* into the poetic text. No literate Christian or person familiar with Christian texts can miss the irony at work here. Christians, of all people, should recognize how to honor a scapegoat and to appreciate the significance of "*a waiting victim*" (L. 15); and yet it was "Christian" Europe which perverted that salvific principal as a mode of attacking the very people from whom their own scapegoat-Saviour had arisen.[64] "Christians" blaming Jews for their problems when it was a Jew who assumed the 'blame' and burden for their own transgressions.

The poem does not pronounce judgment in this regard, but forcefully indicates it through its formal strategy, and in such a way that the reader is now induced to "read" him– or herself in the history that the poem addresses. One simple shift in point of view underscores

---

64. The phrase, "*Our consummate scapegoat*" in "Wilderness" (p. 20, L. 35) achieves a similar irony with this same set of theological valences.

that movement. Where does fault lie? It lies along the "*Tragic fault line within us*" (L. 17; my emphasis). With this shift to the first person plural, the reader's historical stance is thereby thrust to the center of attention. The "searchlight" of blame has found a new object as the reader is called upon to contemplate his or her *own* complicity in the kind of prejudice that spawned the Holocaust. (There can be no easy economy of "us" and "them.") In this way, "Forebodings" bears witness to and uncovers a further historical dimension: the future of a civilization that will either learn from and redress its past as a present opportunity, or abandon that past, dull to its inevitable potential to repeat itself. In the present age, this poem provocatively insinuates, there remain "*Rumbles in bowels of myth*" and "*Moody engines of prejudice underground.*"

As *The Gossamer Wall* spirals towards its epicenter in the section "*Figures*," the summons to remembrance gains intensity. The poet deploys prosodic devices and images to create a thickly-tissued presentation, variously musical and angular—at times striking and eloquent, at others intentionally banal.[65] As elsewhere, the emotional proximity to bigoted destruction and human suffering achieved by the poetry in its resistance to time *in time* bears with it the complexities of discernment and of reading—ourselves as well as the actions and experiences of others. In "*Figures*" that challenge increases, and with it, the expectations of an ethics of form. Following the "descent" of Europe into the atrocities of the Holocaust in "*Northeim*" and "*Battalion 101*" (doing so, notably, in a most particularistic manner, by naming names without hesitation), and then pursuing a line of ascent out of that mire by tracing the acts of resistance performed by victims and their sympathizers in "*Spoors*" and "*Le Chambon*," the poem situates the experiences of the concentration camps in this poetic journey at the furthest remove from the margins.

Those experiences, of course, also stand at the furthest remove from the poet's experience, as well as that of most readers. For this reason, the effort to revisit the nightmarish landscape of those compounds places an enormous strain on the task of remembering well. The poet was not there; the majority of his readers were not there; but *there* is the place where the calculated energy of the Holocaust plummeted to its most sinister depth and depravity. For the purpose of remembrance, therefore, the history as well as the poetry urge us there; or as the fifth

---

65. In a letter of 1 April 2003, the author explained the intention of his "flat style" as an attempt to convey the "banality of evil."

poem of the sequence aims to situate us: "Here." But what form(s) can deliver the needed intensity without presumption, and issue a summons to remember that prepares readers for the possibility of hope's "complex yes," towards which the subsequent sections aim? The poet's unexpected answer to this need and this summons is the sonnet. Appropriately, the poem of that title—"Summons" (63)—introduces "Figures," and will be our final poem for close study.

The peculiar advantage of the sonnet consists of its capacity to compress a range of ideas and impressions into a concentrated expression of thought and feeling. Its structure and regulated metre and rhyme demand a discipline of expression that underscores and supports the intensity of poetic effect. Because of these advantages, it traditionally has been the form of choice for love poems, which itself serves up an irony in this context. As with the poems previously studied, however, how the poet handles this traditional form demonstrates its facility for the acts of attention and remembrance that he seeks to achieve. "Summons" delivers a poignant blend of temporal and spatial referents and images, variegated rhyme and verbal texture, all woven into the insistent plea of a witness to *imagine* what can only surpass our comprehension but which must not escape our present concern. It performs what O'Siadhail has himself announced as poetry's distinct advantage for remembrance and historical reflection: its "special way to cut through history with images."

The poem begins and ends with a similar plea: "Meditate that this came about. *Imagine*" (63, L. 1); "*A summons to* try to look, to try to see" (L. 13)[66]. Between this bracketing charge to the reader we find carefully choreographed shifts in perspective, verb tense and points of view that coalesce around four visual images. The first is told in the present tense, evoking an impression of the living-dead:

> Pyjama ghosts tramp the shadow of a chimney.
> Shorn and nameless. Desolation's mad machine (Ll. 2–3).

---

66. The line "*Meditate that this came about*" comes from Primo Levi's poetic epigraph to *Survival in Auschwitz*. O'Siadhail's addition of "Imagine" suggests his own project as well as the means by which we with him must seek to traverse the distance that separates us from Levi's own. The plea "to try to look, try to see" comes from Charlotte Delbo's *Aucun do nous viendra* (*None of Us Will Return*).

The word "*tramp*" in this context connotes a death march as these figures make their wraith-like appearance to our imagination, recalling Tony O'Malley's portrait *Concentration Camp* on the book's cover and the now familiar archival footage taken when these camps were liberated. The images are perhaps *too* familiar. The internal rhyme of "*Imagine*" (L. 1) with "*Desolation's*," the "*am*"—"*im*" half-rhymes, the assonance of "*ghosts*," "*shadow*" and "*Desolation's*," and the alliterated "*shadow*"—"*shorn*" and "*mad machine*" verbally animate these figures. The poetics supporting the image serve to re-summon the dead who are made to live again in our imagination. Though at one time "shorn and nameless," they still "tramp the shadow of a chimney." The reader, then, must consider that this happened ("*this came about*"), and how it could have happened, not as an accident of history but by "*Desolation's mad machine*."

The next image conflates time past with time present, marking a complex shift in scenery and a poignant interweave of texts:

> For each who survived, every numbered
> Arm that tries to hold the wedding guest,— (Ll. 5–6)

The moment echoes and reprises Coleridge's *Ancyent Marinere*,[67] the detainment of the wedding-guest by the wizened stranger who pleads with him to forestall entering that celebration in order to hear his tale of "*woeful agony*," of death and remorse. The allusion is provocative, suggesting that the poet and his readers stand in the same position as the wedding-guest, accosted now by a tattooed survivor, having to forsake the bright pleasantries of the present moment to enter into an abyss of disturbing memory. The transference is acute, for us as for Coleridge's protagonist who "*went, like one that hath been stunn'd . . . A sadder and wiser man.*" The reader of "Summons" is left to draw out the impression the allusion excites, ultimately to consent to what the poem explicitly endorses—to "*Try to see!*" (L. 4)—and through that arresting vision of the living-dead also to grow wise in remembrance.

The image of "figures" as numbers also reappears, acquiring added emphasis because of the dehumanizing circumstances. The poem repeats this motif throughout with expanding proportions: in addition to "*numbered*" arms there are "*endless counts and selections*" (L. 4), "A thou-

---

[67]. An allusion pointed out to me by David Ford. References from the Penguin edition of *Lyrical Ballads*.

sand urgent stories" (L. 7), *"In each testimony a thousand more suppressed"* (L. 8), and finally, *"this infinite nightmare"* (L. 10). "Each" and "every" among the surviving witnesses and testimonies yield to the "thousand urgent stories" of *"The muted dead"* (L. 14) as the poem gradually swells towards an "infinite" horizon. The word play with numbers serves to signify the disproportion between the scant surviving evidence of these lives and the many more whose testimonies are "suppressed," thus underscoring the difficulty of recovering to our remembrance those who remain silenced but who also *"demand their debt of memory."*

The third and fourth images display the paradox of their present-absence or absent-presence:

> A Polish horizon glows with stifled cries:
> Who'll wake us from this infinite nightmare?
> Out of the cone of Vesuvius their lives rise
> To sky-write gaunt silences in the frozen air. (Ll. 9–12)

The paradoxical coalescence of time and space, of the verbal with the visual, of sound and silence, of the visible with the invisible or barely visible, yields an emotional and cognitive density to the experiences of these silent witnesses. With the first image in this quatrain, we are summoned to see and hear simultaneously a Polish horizon *glowing* with their stifled *cries*, though we in fact can neither see nor hear it. The scene conjured here is a scene of writing, but writing that is unwriting itself even as it seeks to enable the reader to somehow see through the paradoxical imagery in order to attain sympathetic awareness. Without the paradox the complexity would evaporate, and naively so. But without the effort to bear witness to the un-witnessed and un-testified, the "debt of memory" would remain unpaid.

The further paradox of attempting to resolve what remains irresolvable accentuates the difficulty the poetry faces. Had the poet chosen to report his own experiences of contemplating the Holocaust he may have settled for paradox. But because the stakes exceed any such *self*-reflection, directing his readers ultimately to remembrance of the other, some form of resolution becomes morally obligatory. Why is this so? To heed Lawrence Langer's commendations from the "literature of atrocity" he upholds as exemplary, one might conclude that our moral obligation to Holocaust remembrance is best fulfilled in literary forms that defy all efforts at resolution. That is, such evidently irresolvable circumstances of nightmarish disorder are better addressed *with integrity* by unresolved, disordered poetic forms. (So when the poem "Never" declares, "*we cannot sing dumb*" (L. 9), Langer might respond, "Why sing at all?"). On the one hand, Langer's view has considerable merit when a literature of atrocity aims to evoke the perverse and acutely disorienting character of Holocaust experiences. On the other hand, remembrance as memorial, if it is to have any substance, must include in its aim to honor the memory of victims *the meaningfulness of their lives*. How else can we refer to their destruction as an "atrocity" and a violation of their humanity at all?

The poem "Summons" enacts this distinction in response to this evocation of the human: the moral resolve to remember *them*—these *others*—finding expression in the formal, aesthetic resolve of the poetry. The deep patterning of the poem's verbal-musical texture provides a form of resolution without sentimentality or presumption, as rhythm and rhyme interact with images to elicit emotional proximity to the irrepressibly human experiences of the camps. We see, and hear, this in the third quatrain as "*stifled cries*" re-emerge in the phrase "*their lives rise*," and in the buoyantly alliterated end couplet,

> A summons to *try to look, to try to see.*
> A muted dead demand their debt of memory. (Ll. 13–14)

The unnamed, and not their murderous un-naming, are given their song, the poet's song of remembrance. The "living-dead" introduced at the beginning of "Summons" are now the "dead living," memorialized in the imagination. That debt of memory abides, however, as living memory requires—here paid not as if it were an economic transaction or a form of absolution, but paid through the musical economy of poetry as a revitalizing witness to the enduring humanity of Holocaust victims. As one of the final poems in the suite proclaims ("Faces," 122), quoting the hopeful strain of the prophet Jeremiah in whose "*darkest scroll*" we find "*a jazz of hope*" ("Stretching," 116):

> I'll change their shame to praise and renown in all
> The earth . . . Always each face and shoeless footfall
>
> A breathing memory behind the gossamer wall. ("Faces," Ll. 11–13)

Conclusion: The Strains of Hope and/in "a moment when testimony and story meet"

"*A breathing memory behind the gossamer wall.*" The line captures the ambition of this poetic suite as well as the poet's own stance in respect of his material. Together with the preceding couplet, it is also, notably, an eloquent line—in this instance an act of lyric *retrieval* that once more brings the "*mute presence*" (L. 2) of "millions" within emotional proximity to the poem's readers. The poet repeats the phrase, slightly modified, and the sense of hope it brings in the final lines of the suite:

> To love the range and fullness yet to recall.
> *Your golden hair, Margarete, your ashen hair* . . .
>
> Next year in Jerusalem! Parting toast and prayer.
> And still they breathe behind a gossamer wall. ("Reprise," 124)

The injection of a line from Paul Celan's disturbing Holocaust poem "Fugue of Death" in Line 10, alluded to earlier in the phrase "*Fugues of detours*" (L. 5), provides the necessary counterpoint to the risk of sentimentality and naïve hopefulness that might otherwise attend such lyric expressiveness. References to the Passover *Seder* also serve to temper any facile or merely felicitous appropriation of the strains of hope, as we recall the circumstances in which that memorial was inaugurated. Sobriety as well as celebration attends this act of remembrance, as it also does O'Siadhail's "reprisal."

In addition to reiterating the aspirations of the poet in this suite, these passages return us to a topic raised in my introduction to this chapter: how to bear witness to hope in a broken world. As we have observed, O'Siadhail situates that challenge within a journey of scrupulous inspection and interrogation, pressing the strains of hope's prospects against the formidable demands of human experiences (in time) that resist it. In order to situate *The Gossamer Wall* more definitively within the interests and priorities of Christian theology, we also ask: How does this poem demonstrate a model for doing "good" theology, and if it does, what kind of theology would it be? As noted, O'Siadhail has not produced a "Christian" poem in the sense outlined above. At the same time, in addition to the frequent evocation of Judaeo-Christian motifs, there is a persistent undercurrent of problematics that register issues of great concern to theology.[68]

Discussion of any of these issues as they appear in *The Gossamer Wall* would prove fruitful in its appropriation for theological reflection.[69] My abiding interest in matters of form, however, directs us to approach our theological reading of this poem from a different vantage point. Through our close readings I have emphasized the formal features of intensity, musicality and angularity, presented in an invitational and interrogative mood (and mode), as qualities of the poetic imagination that facilitate fresh proximity to these experiences and foster recognition of the human. In this regard, we see how poetic form inspires a new way of reading historical content, bringing to the primary witness of testimony a method of commemorating the lived experiences of the past in such a way that we can enter into them without presumption. The poetry represents an embodiment of this attitude, recreating the scene of remembering as a scene of reading and of writing; in its poetic cast assuming the shape of a verbal-musical invocation out of which issues the ultimate summons of the poem—directed towards *us*. As a distinctively Christian model of theological expression, then, I highlight three additional features of O'Siadhail's poem, all of which convene around acts of remembrance and the notion of bearing "true" witness. Broadly, these are what I have called an "ethics of form," the status of testimonies and their recovery as a means of historical and theological redress, and the issuing of a "summons"—to hope as well as to remembrance. In order to refine further our theological focus, and in response to these features, I will also introduce ideas from the thought of Paul Ricoeur, whose own interests parallel those I have highlighted and whose influence on O'Siadhail will become evident.

To begin, we might first ask further: Is it imperative that Christians seek to remember at all—not their own story but the stories of others—

---

68. To name only a few of the most outstanding examples, the poem raises questions related to the problem of evil, Christian-Jewish relations, and the implications of Christian views of salvation and salvation history. Perhaps most disturbing of all, difficulties related to the presence or absence of God also appear in a number of poems, as in the provocative passage from "Haunted" that speaks of *"a god in hiding"* and *"A lover's/ Invitation rumouring through the dark./ Rustles of absence in a silent ark"* (88–90).

69. For excerpted essays that range across this spectrum of issues, see the recent *Holocaust Theology*.

in the strong sense of remembrance we find in *The Gossamer Wall*? To elaborate, in what sense does a summons to remember in witness to the other constitute a priority for the Church in regard to her witnessing task? On the one hand, Christians clearly cannot ignore the Holocaust if their witness to hope is to have any substance; that is, if it is to be effective as an engagement with the world in which the Church now lives. Not only has the Shoah pronounced the "death" of "*Our long and trusted dream of progress*," but it fractures the foundation of trust on which hope is based—making hope "fragile,"[70] and leading the poet to ask, "*Out of this eruption, can we prepare another climate?*"[71] Can trust, in other words, be restored, and in such manner that would allow a witness to hope to regain credibility? Because Christianity, or at least "Christendom," is also implicated in the Holocaust, this breakdown in trust not only challenges the plausibility of a gospel of hope in general, but the authority of a *Christian* witness to hope in particular. Overcoming both communicative challenges raises one priority for the witnessing Church in her "gentle defense" of hope—the "preparing of another climate" in which broken trust transfigures into "healing trust."

On the other hand, to approach the matter of Christian priorities in our reading of *The Gossamer Wall* in terms of effective engagement *only*—even as a means of regaining trust—risks violating the integrity O'Siadhail has sought so assiduously to maintain. There is no necessary conflict in this regard, but the poet's ethical priority towards the other demands that we qualify further the Church's expressive interests. Indeed, his witness to the Holocaust reprises the very notion of witness, as it calls upon readers to look and to listen *before* speaking, as a crucial element for the restoration of trust. In this light, the lesson for theologians (as well as the Church as a whole) is to adopt the view that theology is also a listening discipline, encouraging us to look for models of attentiveness that instruct us in this endeavor. We return, then, to the matter of form, both in regard to interpretation—as a means of gaining sympathetic insight—and in regard to articulation: the shape we give our response to the other being a feature integral to the notion of "true" witness. Hence, we ask: How does *The Gossamer Wall* bring such

---

70. "Cataclysm," 10, L. 14.
71. "Dust-veil," 9.11, p. 112.

a discipline of listening well in order to remember well and, implicitly, to witness well within a distinctively Christian purview?

One of the most poignant effects of this poetry is that its summons in response to the summons of the other asks first that we be *co-rememberers*, even as it confronts us with the possibility that we too may be co-conspirators—that is, of forgetfulness. By this effect, a range of responsibilities accrues to our account, among which is the responsibility to take seriously the question enjoined by the Huguenot citizens of Le Chambon: *"who is my neighbor?"*[72] The injunctions to "meditate that this came about," "to try to look, try to see," "to imagine," all reinforced by the poetry's capacity to evoke acute attention to the particular, have that primary summons to heed our neighbor as their motive force. Significantly, it is in this same poem "Risk" that we find the provocative appeal of *"an interrogative mood."* Conjoined as it is to this poem's first reference to the Good Samaritan parable—delivered by Jesus in his own "interrogative mood" (Ll. 10–12)—we feel immediately the pressure to assess our distant observation of the human face of suffering in terms of this same self-interrogation, and to align our own response with a similar impulse. By staging this confrontation directly in his final section "The Prisoners of Hope," O'Siadhail weds the prospect that *"The desert through which we pass will bloom again"* announced in his overture poem to our *present* response to the face of our suffering neighbor. It is this recognition of a universal summons in the *faces* of the particular that gives his act of remembrance its distinctive ethical-theological urgency: on behalf of "neighbors" who have died, but also for the sake of present as well as future generations of neighbors. To tell the story of others with and through their own testimonies enacts this exchange—*as a condition for our speaking.*

Is O'Siadhail, then, telling a *Christian* story within his poetic witness to the stories of others, and in what sense would we comprehend his project as such, and thus as a model of Christian discourse? Generically, as an act of remembrance familiar under the rubric of memorial or anamnesis, and ethically as a summons to care for our neighbor, the theological promise of his *Gossamer* suite seems at least partially assured. Moreover, its capacity to provoke our attention and engage our response to its subject-matter—generating a dialectic between the

---

72. See "Risk," 98.

particular and the universal—demonstrates a model of effective communication of great general value to the task of public witness. But to refer to this long poem as a public theological *discourse* and to consider its status as a distinctively Christian mode of presentation raises further expectations of its form.

As our first pass at these questions, in the final sections of the suite O'Siadhail pursues a strategy whose aim is not immediately apparent. Turning again to the poem "Risk," for example, by invoking the second commandment reprised by Jesus in his parable—still in the "interrogative mood" and as the testimony of the people of Le Chambon which the poem holds forth as *their* motive—O'Siadhail injects a new narrative into his poetic account. In addition, through his invocations of the Prophets, the Passover and its enduring rehearsal by Jews, and various other allusions to "sacred" history, he opens up an even broader narrative field of reference within his *"narrative struggling to understand."* Having cautiously avoided imposing or overlaying his witness to the Holocaust with his own explanatory framework, the poet nonetheless subtly introduces a context for the meaningful affirmation of hope—not in order to resolve the many complexities of these events or to falsely attenuate our recognition of evil and suffering, but to advance a possibility.

To be clear, that possibility emerges only from the shadows cast by the history:

> A story squeezes at the edge clamours of music;
> Out of darkest histories, profoundest gaiety.
>
> . . .
>
> Dream and reality feeding circuitries of hope.[73]

The poem's own "clamours of music," made manifest through its chiastic structure and prosody especially, offers traces of a second narrative that activate these "circuitries." The moment the poetry stages "when testimony and story meet" in witness to the Holocaust thus invites reflection on a similarly patterned witness: the biblical narrative of redemption celebrated at Passover and in the Eucharist. We find this imparted beautifully in an image evocative of both: "*A feast of rich food and well-aged wine*" ("Stretching," "Glimpses," "Reprise"). The poem's redress includes this poignant redirection, without compromising the priority of the one witness for the sake of introducing the other. Indeed, its primary wit-

---

73. "Glimpses," 117.

ness to the Holocaust prompts us to read these experiences back into a biblical narrative of redemption, not in order to revise the latter but to re-inscribe it as a site of tension as well as promise. Conversely, we are called upon to read the biblical witness itself differently, as an account that is accountable to the lived experiences of others, and whose readers are also made accountable to those experiences. As a result, Scripture becomes more, not less, vital. The Bible's own "complex yes" of hope becomes a living language inscribed into our ongoing struggle to arrive at a complex yes in the face of human suffering. This reciprocal economy allows the emergent movement "*out of*" one dominant testimonial landscape towards the faintly traced but arresting features of a new testimonial horizon, accumulating enormous suggestive power as an authentic witness to hope in the process. The moment when testimony and story meet re-enacted by *The Gossamer Wall* thus emerges as a fusion of narratives of witness. And it is through reflection on this pattern that we gain further methodological footing for our appropriation of this poetry within Christian discourse, both reflective and public.

Among those who have charted a connection of this kind, Paul Ricoeur stands out as one of its chief expositors. His reflections on testimony and witness, and on narrative and poetic "discourse"—folded within a biblical as well as a philosophical hermeneutic—provide a theological grid to help us situate O'Siadhail's achievement within Christian interpretive and expressive practices. By way of sharpening our focus, we will proceed under the sign of "a moment when testimony and story meet" as a means of directing Ricoeur's thought towards the issues of an ethics of form, the status and recovery of testimonies, and the notion of "summons," as these concerns are involved in remembrance and the bearing of "true" witness. For Ricoeur, as for O'Siadhail, testimony and story (or "narrative"), and their convergence, mark sites of revelatory promise. Ricoeur's "polysemic and polyphonic" idea of revelation, which classifies the Bible as a form of "poetic discourse" whose "poetic function" designates the hermeneutical method by which we approach its texts,[74] makes testimony and narrative prominent vehicles for reality disclosure.

74. His seminal essay on this topic is his "Toward A Hermeneutic of the Idea of Revelation" (*Essays*). In this piece, Ricoeur bases his challenge to propositional, "monolithic' concepts of revelation on the literary variety he find in the Bible's "originary documents of faith," and whose poetic form demand to be read as more than a mere

Ricoeur's principal interest in testimony involves his effort to rebut notions of autonomy based on a "refusal of historical contingency," insisting that testimony in its religious manifestation represents "a moment of history [that] is invested with an absolute character."[75] Sounding a note that resonates with O'Siadhail's stance, he then elaborates that testimonies instantiate a "dialectical moment" between event and meaning that returns us to "an originary affirmation which constitutes me more than I constitute it,"[76] thus authorizing a "letting go" of any pretensions to self-consciousness. It is this "historic density" characteristic of testimony and its power to recall us to "an originary affirmation" that creates what Ricoeur calls in "The Hermeneutics of Testimony" an "irruption of meaning," and leads him to insist that "interpretation cannot be applied to testimony from without as a violence which would be done to it" but "the taking up again, in a different discourse" of this dialectic.[77] Ricoeur's own preferred "different discourse" is that of philosophical hermeneutics; O'Siadhail's is that of poetry. For both, however, they hold in reserve efforts at explanation that would replace the affirmations of "first witnesses" with present interpreting subjects. What emerges in Ricoeur's conception, then, is also a way of reading, a practice that calls for a "generative poetics"[78] which attends to the form(s) of testimony to be "taken up" only as they have come to us. O'Siadhail's contribution to this method of inquiry represents its expansion towards the dramatic re-interpretation of testimony, "envoicing" the humanity of witnesses in the verbal-musical texture of his art.

The effect on us in the form of a summons to be co-rememberers, as well as co-readers, resonates with Ricoeur's commendation of poetic language in general, which he believes stands prior to the ahistorical stance of rational-scientific—or what Ricoeur calls "descriptive"—discourse. He declares,

---

"rhetorical façade" (see esp. 74–75, 90–92, 99–100).

75. *Essays*, 112; cf. 109–10.

76. Ibid., 110.

77. Ibid., 144–45.

78. Ibid., 91, 99. By this intriguing concept, Ricoeur means once more a practical engagement commensurate with the formal character of the texts under inspection, and which promotes a dynamic interplay between texts and interpreters. As he writes in an earlier essay, "Philosophy and Religious Language" (1974), "we need a generative poetics that would correspond at the level of the composition of discourse" (*Figuring the Sacred*, 38).

> My deepest conviction is that poetic language alone restores to us that participation-in or belonging-to an order of things which precedes our capacity to oppose ourselves to things taken as objects opposed to a subject. Hence the function of poetic discourse is to bring about this emergence of a depth-structure of belonging-to amid the ruins of descriptive discourse.[79]

We note how Ricoeur edges towards the ethical in this pronouncement through the ideas of precedence and opposition, as a function of the restorative operation of poetic language.[80] At stake is not only our experience of participation-in and belonging-to, which poetic language fosters, but an implicit summons to heed an "order of things" that such language makes possible. The category of testimony proves crucial to this configuration because testimonies do not signal an abstraction (as "order of things" might connote), but they pronounce the voice of an "other" as its source. The summons to bear witness felt by the witness to events (the "dialectic of testimony and witness") is ultimately understood, says Ricoeur, to "proceed from the *Other*."[81] This also represents an "irruption of meaning" reflected in testimony, forcing a reorientation on our part to assume a similar posture as present interpreters: what Ricoeur signifies as an act of self-divestment ("*se dépouiller*"), and which authorizes his distinction between a hermeneutic philosophy and a "philosophy of absolute knowledge."[82] When he expands the classification of the "other" to include people as well as God, he reiterates the importance of maintaining a similar stance (a point to which we will return presently).

In what sense, however, are we still talking about "poetic language" and poetic discourse? Here Ricoeur makes a further move in "The Hermeneutics of Testimony" to situate testimony within story, once more derivative of his study of the Bible's "'confessional' kernel of testimony."[83] Given that testimonies are not self-validating but beg the

---

79. *Essays*, 101. This conviction marks one of the dominant themes in his classic treatment of metaphoric language and its advantages in *Rule of Metaphor*, as well as in the extension of that project in *Time and Narrative*.

80. That is, poetic language inquires after the status of the "originary," while opposing false oppositions between subjects and objects.

81. Ibid., 146.

82. Ibid., 151, 152.

83. Ibid., 134.

question, "what is a true witness, a faithful witness?" Ricoeur concludes, "the hermeneutic structure of testimony consists in that testimony concerning things seen only reaches judgment through a story, that is, by means of things said."[84] Thus, narratology becomes a crucial element in a generative poetics applied to testimony. It is this economy of the "summoned subject" and self-divestment cast within a larger narrative framework that comprises the trajectory of Ricoeur's theological as well as his philosophical hermeneutics. As he neatly summarizes in a later article titled "The Summoned Subject" (1988), "If salvation is a word-event, the communication of this word-event does not take place without an interpretation of the whole symbolic network that makes up the biblical inheritance, an interpretation in which the self is both interpreter and interpreted."[85] Viewed in this light, O'Siadhail's introduction of Judaeo-Christian narratives of redemption in *The Gossamer Wall* gains its theological cast; the "moment when testimony and story meet" recreated as a fusion of testimonial narratives mirrors the pattern Ricoeur discovers in his study of Scripture.

When Ricoeur then widens his study of biblical narratives to take up issues of time and memory as categories appropriate to a narrative theology, the parallels with O'Siadhail's poetic project become even more pronounced. Contending first in his essay "Toward a Narrative Theology" (1982) that, "theological discourse, however conceptual it can and must be, can only elaborate the horizon of meaning implicit in the narratives and symbols constitutive of the Jewish and Christian traditions," he, like O'Siadhail, challenges the notion of a set chronology in the sense of a "univocally chronological schema of the history of salvation" to be superimposed on the various histories of human beings.[86] The advantage of narrative theology is its recognition of an internal dynamic of complex disclosure in the biblical witness, a method which does not seek to rectify similar complexities in human experience—particularly what Ricoeur calls "the unresolved dialectic of memory and of hope" entailed in human suffering, the alternative to which "amounts to an *in-*

---

84. Ibid., 129, 146.

85. *Figuring the Sacred*, 274. I recognize that the category of 'word-event' is not without its controversy, particularly when issues of how and in what sense God is understood to speak in and through Scripture. For a critique that challenges Ricoeur in this regard, see Wolterstorff, Nicholas, *Divine Discourse*, 130–52.

86. *Figuring the Sacred*, 236, 238.

crease of forgetfulness."[87] Hence, by preserving the dialectic found in the Bible's very texts—its "multiplex network"[88]—we preserve their capacity to be in dialogue with the world of time and "historic density."[89] And it is precisely this form of interplay that we see in the *Gossamer* suite, not only as a work analogous to a scriptural pattern, but in continuity with its inherent method of disclosure—advanced as a "gradual adagio of truth" and a "complex yes." It is for this reason Ricoeur commends "a rebirth of narrative in general" as an integral element in "a specifically Christian task," and encourages "further experimentation in the narrative field" on the basis of the Bible's own "paradigms" of innovation.[90]

Ricoeur's grand statement of poetic discourse's advantage, realized in numerous forms, is its capacity to "redescribe reality," the effects of which are to propose a world beyond the text as its ultimate referent, which we can inhabit and wherein we "can project [our] ownmost possibilities."[91] When he develops this idea in his expansive *Time and Narrative*, he situates the mimetic function of story (what he calls "emplotment") within a matrix of figuration, assigning to it the mediatorial role of "configuration."[92] This sense of bringing together in order to open up new possibilities—made available by a mediating text—designates further the peculiar features of *The Gossamer Wall* I have sought to demonstrate in our close readings. Significantly, Ricoeur includes within this meditation on narrative the aspects of *resonance* and *recognition* that have become familiar to our appraisal of O'Siadhail's poetry and to my thesis *passim*, as well as the importance of testimony to narrative criticism.[93] Of equal significance to our present study, Ricoeur also insists upon the ethical stakes involved in the interpretation of narrative and story. He writes,

87. Ibid., 238; Ricoeur's emphasis.

88. Ibid.

89. Seen from a different vantage point, we hear echoes of Charles Williams' Incarnational theology of images here, as the "taking up" of the temporal into the eternal and the operation of eternity in time.

90. *Figuring the Sacred.*, 238, 240.

91. *Essays*, 102. For some of the earliest statements of these ideas, see his essays "Word, Polysemy, Metaphor" (1975) and "Metaphor and the Main Problem of Hermeneutics" (1974–75), reprinted in *Philosophy of Paul Ricoeur*, 120–48.

92. Op. cit., Vol. 1, 53. Ricoeur's three headings for this mimetic function are "prefiguration," "configuration," and "refiguration" (cf. 53–54).

93. Ibid., see 49, 75, 100.

> We tell stories because in the last analysis human lives need and merit being narrated. This remark takes on its full force when we refer to the necessity to save the history of the defeated and the lost. The whole history of suffering cries out for vengeance and calls for narrative.[94]

One hears in this declaration the "full force" of Micheal O'Siadhail's motive, not for vengeance but the preparation of a "new climate" by which a "healing trust" and the hope that attends it become our possibility—*"Can how we remember shape what we become?"*

As vital as it is for the poet to remember well as the basis for this strain of hope, so too is it for the philosopher. In *Oneself as Another*, for example, where Ricoeur extends further the inherently human character and ethical urgency of story, he takes up Levinas' notion of the summons of the other as a "summons to responsibility" for the other, who- or whatever that other may be. While he approves of both categories—that of summons as well as responsibility—under the rubric of ethics he wants to reinstate a more robust notion of the self who *receives* that summons.[95] For Ricoeur, this is especially critical when the other is a "suffering other" who requires our sympathetic "suffering-with" as well as our duty towards.[96] Hence, in his Shoah memorial homily "The Memory of Suffering" (1989), Ricoeur insists both that "remembering is a *moral* duty. We owe a *debt* to the victims," and that, "To remember, to recount, is a way of becoming such consciousness [of evil], such conscience."[97] When he then elaborates, "the most elementary compensation that we may offer is to give them a voice, the voice that was denied them,"[98] we find ourselves squarely within the ethical impulse as well as the very idiom of *The Gossamer Wall*. What this poetic suite gives us in its redress as remembrance in resistance to time's forgetfulness, and as recognition—including that of our neighbor as well as the narratives of

---

94. Ibid., 75.

95. Ricoeur, Paul, *Oneself as Another*, 190. Ricoeur develops a similar emphasis in "Emmanuel Levinas: Thinker of Testimony," where he says, "Summoned, yes, the self is summoned without having chosen this, but, to this very extent, it is summoned 'as irreplaceable'" (*Figuring the Sacred*, 126).

96. *Oneself as Another*, 190–91.

97. *Figuring the Sacred*, 290.

98. Ibid.

redemption—is a pathway into the particulars of the human as a crucial element in "true" witness. As Rowan Williams has emphasized,

> The resolution of the sheer resistant particularity of suffering, past and present, into comfortable teleological patterns is bound to blunt the edge of particularity, and so to lie; and this lying resolution contains that kind of failure in attention that is itself a moral deficiency, a fearful self-protection ...
> ... the world is such that attention to particularity is demanded of us.[99]

The "us" of this statement includes Christian theologians and the witnessing Church as a whole. When the question is then asked, what makes hope plausible? it is the peculiar ability of poetry such as we find in *The Gossamer Wall* to renew that possibility by virtue of its attentive redescription of a reality we are better equipped to engage with the gentleness and reverence that hope's defense of a larger reality requires.

Our next study takes up these threads of remembrance and attention to the particular in a further exploration of poetry's contribution to Christian theology and witness. Here, we examine the formal elements of Geoffrey Hill's "pitch of attention" and "poetic kenosis" as it develops in his long poem *The Triumph of Love*.

---

99. Rowan Williams, "Trinity and Ontology," in *Christ, Ethics and Tragedy*, 78.

4

Geoffrey Hill's "Pitch of Attention" and "Poetic Kenosis" in *The Triumph of Love*

Love Triumphant?

LIKE CHARLES WILLIAMS' ARTHURIAD AND MICHEAL O'SIADHAIL'S *THE Gossamer Wall*, Geoffrey Hill's *The Triumph of Love* is also a "landscape" poem, albeit in many respects different from our ordinary sense of the term. From its opening, one line section we are presented with an image that introduces a dramatic sense of place: "*Sun-blazed, over Romsley, a livid rain-scarp*" (I, 1).[1] Immediately following, the next section then imbues the lyric geography evoked in the first line with a sense of time and the landscape of personal history. "*Guilts were incurred in that place, now I am convinced*" (II), the poet announces, then in Section III invites the satirist Petronius Arbiter to "*carry us with you to the house of correction*" and the mystic Angelus Silesius to "*guard us while we are there*." In quick succession, the poem thus situates our attention visually and figuratively among tightly compressed layers of place references and allusions. *The Triumph of Love* progresses with increasing density of this kind,[2] interweaving the "landscapes" of European history, philosophical and religious thought, art and literature—all cast as the backdrop or larger context for the poet's confrontation with a contemporary cultural scene in the West. In a similar vein, the poet also pursues the idea of a "*moral landscape*" (LI, LII) as a means of focusing his judgment of this scene, and out of which emerges an acute sense of an historical

---

1. Citations from *The Triumph of Love* will follow the Roman numeral heading of each section, with page numbers added where necessary, as here.

2. As Hill commented in a conversation of 16 July 2004 (Boston University), "It is the density I am looking for," a density that becomes the felt effect of his composition.

moment beckoning a vigorous reassessment of modernity's priorities and perspective.

We may, of course, wonder about the propriety of using the word *landscape* to describe this range of manifestly diverse phenomena. But in addition to the images of place repeated throughout *The Triumph of Love*, Hill's method of presentation lends itself to this nomination. What we discover as we examine the poem is a meditation on place that reverberates with a polyphony, and often a cacophony, of interacting voices and images, presented in such fashion to produce a highly material sensation about the objects of inspection. (We recall in this regard the description of *The Gossamer Wall*'s "verbal-musical texture," though Hill's sequence on the surface bears the appearance more of a mosaic than a suite.) The structure of Hill's poem itself generates this sense of physicality, as it proceeds through its Psalms-like one hundred and fifty sections in the manner of a construction project—as the epigraph from Nehemiah signals, and as, for example, the stage direction to the reader, "*You will have to/ go forward block by block*" (XIX) underscores. In addition, Hill's development of *pitch* and *syntax*, as well as his trenchant images and meticulous diction, likewise accentuate the palpable effects of his style. By such means, his poem gives to the issues of place, of context, of situating oneself in respect to one's history and historical-cultural moment, their corresponding "pitch of attention."[3] In this regard, *The Triumph of Love* as a whole resembles a *textual* landscape, an achievement of the spatial imagination within which the poet negotiates the challenges to and prospects for love's triumph in a world that appears obstinately resistant to that outcome.

Standing at the center of these negotiations, hence dominating the "landscape" of the poem, is the self—more precisely, the figure of the poet himself. Viewed in one way, this placing of the self in the center gives the poem its peculiarly modern temperament. It is this very fixation, however, that Hill masterfully critiques and turns to the purposes of a more penetrating vision. In the end, his exploration of the theme of love from the vantage point of the self subverts familiar expectations of the subjective interest, producing simultaneously disorienting and re-orienting results. As so often happens in Hill's poetry, things are not quite what they seem; and it is from this nexus of intense interaction

---

3. We will treat this concept and its import more fully below.

between the interiority of the poet-persona and the panoply of circumstances and personalities exterior to him that our "apprehension" increases (the word is Hill's, as is the intended ambiguity). "*Talking to oneself,*" the poet says "*half-way*" through "*this maze of my own/ devising,*" "*is in fact/ a colloquy with occasion . . . / or so I tell myself*" (LXXV, 38, 39). To remark, then, that Hill's poem presents a landscape of the self affords a suitable point of departure for our study, although this requires some careful qualification.

At the time of its publication, *The Triumph of Love* represented Hill's most extended development of his own persona in his creative output. From the explicit autobiographical references to his experiences, the prevalence of allusions to his own poetry and critical writings, and a preoccupation with his reputation as a poet we readily enough identify the presence of the poet in the poem. But in whatever measure we read this poem as autobiography (which, Hill himself admits, to a certain extent we can), the development of his persona's character proves far from transparent. In short, the persona of the poet represents a carefully crafted creation of the poetic imagination. It is from this remove that Hill examines the state of the individual in confrontation with his circumstances and his own human condition. As his persona acknowledges about his stance depicted here—a stance also characteristic of a spatial imagination—the poet's re-creation of himself represents "*a formal / self-distancing, but like choreography*" (CXXXIII).[4]

Hence, as we proceed in our analysis we have repeatedly to regard the poem through a bi-focal lens. On the one hand, like the figure of Shakespeare's Cymbeline who, Hill has observed, "is both character and 'climate,'"[5] the poet-persona in *The Triumph of Love* manifests the

---

4. Among the formal influences that have affected his style, Hill includes that of choreography, specifically how "the choreography of Mark Morris . . . has shaped my ideas about how to put words together in new ways" (*Paris Review* interview (*PRI*) with Carl Phillips, 296).

5. "'The True Conduct of Human Judgment': Some Observations on *Cymbeline*" in Hill, *Lords of Limit* (*LL*), 65. In another aspect, however, Hill departs from what he describes as Shakespeare's "association of committed technique with uncommitted observation" (56). Although a feature which Hill insists manifest's "the play's virtuosity" ("Shakespeare stands back not through timidity or unconcern but in order to obtain focus," 57), his own strategy in *Triumph* is to wed technique with *committed* observation, not standing back, finally, but agonizingly *within* his persona "in order to obtain focus."

focused energy of the whole. The poem's own context of "character-as-climate," or the self *in situ*[6] of the poet, governs both presentation and interpretation. In this respect, the poet's self-projection serves as the mediating "text' of the poem, and it is along these lines that we are meant to follow Hill's study in love. It is, however, through an often unstable and complex weave of personal emotions, attitudes, reflections and desires that this self-staging proceeds. In the wake of such complexity, the poet-persona admits in Section CIV, "*Nothing true/ is easy—*"; but then, with evident integrity, adds, "*is that true? Or, how true is it?*" (54). In this poem, Hill attaches great significance to the assertion as well as the troublesome questions it elicits. Through a process of wrestling with both, no pretense is made to speak for all selves, but only *a* self; and no presumption is advanced to hold forth a resolute vision of the self's ultimate destiny. "*I / am an old man, a child,*" the poet confesses in Section CXXI; "*the horizon/ is Traherne's country.*" The Triumph of Love, we may therefore suggest at the outset, is in part a poetic exploration of one individual's toilsome quest for love and salvation.[7]

On the other hand, the principle that "context is everything," for which Hill argues in his essay on John Ransom,[8] demands a wider purview than the individual self. The predicament of the self, of the possibility that one's self-address will amount to little more than a "*lost cause*" (CXL, 76), delivers the poet-persona to an unabated confrontation with his circumstances: those of his age and culture, his personal history and memories, the misperceptions of his critics, even the conditions of his own uneven character and, notably, the intractable nature of his medium. Hill's self-staging as "self-distancing" choreography enables his persona's struggle to stand in dynamic tension with these many contingencies—a situation, his persona avers, of extreme vulnerability and moral conflict:

6. The phrase "self *in situ*" represents Hill's shorthand notation for his extensive preoccupation with, as he puts it in regard to his own poetry, "The self that shows itself in its encounters with ... various forms of contingency and circumstance" (*PRI*, 289).

7. As Hill asserts in his Leeds inaugural lecture "Poetry as 'Menace' and 'Atonement,'" "However much and however rightly we protest against the vanity of supposing [poetry] to be merely the 'spontaneous overflow of powerful feelings,' poetic utterance is nonetheless an utterance of the self, the self demanding to be loved, demanding love in the form of recognition and 'absolution'" (*LL*, 17).

8. "What Devil Has Got Into John Ransom?," *LL*, 123. The complete sentence reads: "in Ransom, as in every writer of significance, context is everything."

> Corner to corner, the careful
> fabric of our lives ripped through
> by the steel claws of contingency. We are made
> to make ourselves instruments
> of violence and cunning. (LXXV, 38)

The insistence that the self be understood to stand here impels a unique approach to issues of self-identity. In effect, the questions of personal identity and destiny, and with it any prospect for a triumphant love, arise not primarily in the form "Who am I?" but "*Where* am I?"; or as Hill's persona later queries, "*where are we, finally?*" (CXLVII).

The poet's redirection in this regard and his method of addressing this question begin to designate the convergence of our theological interests and this poem. The question of an individual's identity and destiny rendered primarily in terms of "where" rather than "who" insists that an adequate account of the self can only be assessed in terms of how one is situated *in relation to* others; in its theological-religious cast, in relation to the "absolute" other as well (see Section VIII). Hence, whatever possibility obtains for love to triumph, this poem argues, it can only arise from this way of seeing our selves in a wider context of relationships, not as self-situating, autonomous beings. Moreover, the struggle for a way of seeing marks one of the dominant strains of the poem, making the formal effort to achieve a heightened "pitch of attention" integral to the journey of the self, portrayed as a process towards increasing attentiveness—not only to one's self but, again, to one's circumstances and to others. It is this pursuit of a renewed, and potentially renewing, perception through acts of attentiveness that commends this poetry as a model for theological speech. Already a quality of poetic speech familiar to us from our studies in Williams and O'Siadhail, Geoffrey Hill's contribution takes us even further in one direction of keen relevance to Christian witness and theological reflection.

Of our three poets and poetic sequences, it is Hill in *The Triumph of Love* (as well as in his critical reflections) who makes most emphatic the primacy of language as a medium of ethical and theological reflection. The endeavor to recover a "moral landscape" and, like O'Siadhail, to remember well—in this case, especially those who were (and many who were not) exemplars of an "Active virtue" (LXX)—is depicted as a fierce struggle with speech as that arena within which such prospects are negotiated. Hill's poem recreates the scene of this conflict, tracing the exertions of the self who stands within his historical and cultural context and, indeed, within himself, wrestling with the medium of his own speaking. Thus, upon contrasting the terrain of a "moral landscape" (LI) with the "*Entertainment overkill*" of his celebrity-obsessed society (LIV), the poet appeals to his "guide" and intercessor the Virgin Mary:

> *Vergine bella* — it is here that I require
> a canzone of some substance. There are sound
> precedents for this, of a plain eloquence
> which would be perfect. But —
> ought one to say, I am required; or, it is
> required of me; or, it is requisite that I should
> make such an offering, bring in such a tribute? (LV)

This pursuit of a "perfect" and "plain eloquence" afflicted with the poet's worrisome self-questioning, later elaborated as "*The struggle/ for a noble vernacular*" (LXX) that seems to have disappeared from the sensibilities of his contemporaries, depicts the emotional, and indeed spiritual, temper of the poet's contest with his medium. Over the course of this quest, the poem's pitch of attention—emerging often as the excrescence of the poet-persona's alternately farcical and outraged, satirical and lachrymose, self-awareness—constantly reflects back upon and exposes the character of its own "devising," even as it seeks to excavate and expose illusion and *in*attention in his culture. What this pattern inspires—rendering the struggle with language as the struggle of the self towards virtue—is reflection on the nature of speech as a phenomenon that stands in direct correlation with the moral and spiritual temperament of both individuals and their age and culture. That the poem sets a question mark against the possibility of virtuous speech, and no less so in regard to the poet's own capacity to produce it, gives added emphasis to the stakes involved when people commit their thoughts to words. As Scripture persistently attests,[9] such concerns are profoundly

---

9. Instruction regarding the inherently moral nature of speech and the principle that the tongue shows the character of a person or an entire society abounds in the Bible. One thinks, e.g., of Jeremiah's condemnation of God's people in precisely these terms—"truth has perished and has been cut off from their mouth" (7:28); "But behold, the lying pen of the scribes" (8:8); "Their tongue is a deadly arrow; it speaks deceit" (9:8); etc.—or of James' exhortation, "If anyone does not stumble in what he says, he is a perfect man, able to bridle the whole body as well" (James 3:2).

theological, though it remains to be shown how Hill's poem raises and elaborates them to distinct advantage.

But what, we ask finally, does all of this have to do with love? Within this pattern of struggle over conflicting forces and attitudes, lingering questions arise that trouble our understanding of the aim and effect of this poem, given the ostensible promise of its title. When, on the one hand, we appropriately ask either, What does the triumph of love amount to or look like when viewed through the prism of this poem? or, more pointedly, Does love in fact triumph in this poem? we are left with some rather unsettling ambiguities. The nature of love and the prospects of its triumph are presented as matters as conflicted as the poet's own stance towards himself, his culture and his medium. So he speaks of "*the hatred that is in the nature of love*" (XCVI), 50), or says in response to the supplicant's lament in The Ordinary of the Holy Mass:

> *Ad te suspiramus,*
> *gementes, flentes:* which, being interpreted,
> commits and commends us to loving
> desperately, yet not with despair, not
> even in desperation. (CIX, 57)[10]

The firmness of "commits and commends" yields to the ambiguity of "loving desperately," while the latter maintains a forcefulness that resists ultimate collapse, giving to the quest for love and the ambition to love a measure of promise, although its fulfillment remains remote.

The same sort of tenuous affirmation can be traced in the poet-persona's attitude towards personal forgiveness, announcing early in the poem "*I cannot/ forgive myself*" (V), then at the end of the poem offering the more moderate assessment, "*I find it hard/ to forgive myself*" (CXLIX). In either mood, as with the commitment to loving desperately but without despair or desperation, the poem sounds no note of ultimate triumph. Indeed, that same attitude of reserve comprises the poet's estimation of his poem and of poetry in general. In a final moment of reflection, the poet-persona, addressing his critics, asks "*what are poems for?*" and replies, "*They are to console us/ with their own gift, which is like perfect pitch*"; he then continues, "*What/ ought a poem to be? Answer,* a sad/ and angry consolation"—a phrase (borrowed from

---

10. The Latin phrase translates "to you do we sigh, mourning and crying."

Leopardi[11]) that he reiterates three times (CXLVIII, 82). We need harbor little doubt about the strength of conviction expressed here.[12] Yet, despite the poet's confidence in making such claims, the mood of these lines seems to offer little consolation, however perfectly pitched is the poem's *gift* of itself in this regard; and "sad and angry" hardly prompts us to contemplate either love or its triumph at the poem's finale. Is there any sense, then, in which we may find some correspondence between the auspicious promise of the title and the decidedly ambiguous presentation of that theme, especially in light of the poet's reluctance to render it thus as a prospect of his own enterprise? Viewed from the standpoint of Christian faith and the intent to witness to a love that believers insist does triumph ultimately, the question bears significantly on the contribution of this poem to theological discourse.

If we concede the poem's ambivalence on this account, and ask, not whether love triumphs but under what *conditions* does love suffer apparent defeat in the world and under what conditions does its triumph emerge as a *possibility*, then, I believe, we begin to get some purchase on the theological import of this poem with respect to the theme of love. Once indicated in the title but then withdrawn as an immediate prospect over the course of the poem, the possibility of triumphant love remains in abeyance until both its defeat and its potential to succeed have been contemplated. Hill's poem, in other words, places love in a state of tension, which has the [perhaps unexpected] effect of giving its possible triumph greater dramatic substance—as that force which is only as real as its capacity to address the actual conditions of the world. As a result, the poet's staging of himself as the central figure of this drama and conflict of conditions admits no easy resolution but only a resolve to "love desperately but without despair or desperation," and to insist towards the end of the poem, "*So what is faith if it is not/ inescapable endurance?*" (CXXI).

At the same time, while the poet seeks to expose those conditions which seem to make love's triumph implausible, he points to an alternative possibility, one born of the very contingencies which he insists authentic love (as well as faith and hope) must comprehend and accept:

11. T. S. Eliot also advanced this view of poetry, writing of the function of poetry in "Shakespeare and the Stoicism of Seneca" (1927) that "it provides 'consolation': strange consolation" (*Essays*, 118).

12. A conviction confirmed as Hill's own in our conversation of 16 July 2004.

the kenosis of God in Christ. In saying that the poet *points to* this act in *The Triumph of Love* I mean to avoid any suggestion of an equivalence between Christ's act of self-emptying and what the poem performs or what the persona of the poet undergoes by way of transformation.[13] There are others who in varying degrees emulate this pattern, and the poet "points to" them as well, but he does not count himself among them in any strong sense of kenosis. Still, what we may call a kenotic element runs throughout, and it is a prominent feature of the poem to make us recognize it. To a significant extent, we see the kenotic element through the poet-persona's effort to unmask himself (the motif of masks occurs repeatedly), and in this way to undergo a process that becomes a form of self-emptying, however incomplete. As we shall observe, this effort in itself sets apart *The Triumph of Love* from other poems of the self. Of more immediate significance to my thesis, it is the manifestation of the kenotic within the texture of the poetry—as, again, that which the poetry enacts, or makes legible, by virtue of its formal composition— which further marks the contribution of this poem to theological reflection and Christian expression. Geoffrey Hill's own classification for this work of poetry or poetic speech is "poetic kenosis,"[14] which comprises a distinct union of form and content at decisive points in *The Triumph of Love*. It is a concept whose meaning we will clarify through our study of the poetry and by reference to Hill's critical works, then subsequently in conversation with the thought of the theologian D. M. MacKinnon in the conclusion to this chapter.

Beginning, therefore, with the poem's portrayal of the "self *in situ*," then examining the poet's pitch of attention and plea for a converted perspective through his self-depiction and protracted meditation on language, our close readings and interaction with the poet's critical thought will seek, finally, to illuminate this christological strain in Hill's strategy. His call to attentiveness in response to the questions "where am I?" and "where are we?" arrives ultimately at the need of the self to yield to an outlook that regards love, and with it, all manifestation of nobility and virtue, within a kenotic framework. In the face of individual and societal depravity, the conditions for love's triumph emerge as a renewed possibility only as a person comprehends his situation

---

13. This word of caution was issued by Hill personally in the same conversation.

14. Hill uses this phrase in his essay "Poetics and the Kenotic Hymn," appended to Richard, *Christ the Self-Emptying of God*, 195–97.

from this vantage point. Hence, the grand paradox of the self so familiar to Christian faith but so difficult to present convincingly becomes the subtle but cogent assertion woven into the "contextures" of the poem (to borrow Hill's idiom). For the poet, the project to tear down and expose in order to build towards this renewal is serious business, "a great worke" (as the epigraph signals) with large stakes weighing in the balance for himself and for his society. How Hill gets us there through his project of poetic re-construction is also a study in effective communication—for our purposes, in how to speak "Christianly" to this present age. To appreciate this quality, however, demands much of our *own* attentiveness as readers, which aligns closely with the poem's designs on us: that is, to see through the eccentricities of Hill's often outlandish self-staging the fuller disclosure of a compelling vision of love.

The Self "in situ"

Geoffrey Hill has said that *The Triumph of Love* contains "a very strong element of autobiographical comedy, or even clownishness."[15] We observe this feature throughout the poem, for example in verbal gags ("*Ur? Yes? Pardon? Miss a throe. Go to gaol*," XC) and allusions to comic figures from Petronius' Trimalchio to Laurel and Hardy. We also find darkly humorous one-off guffaws like, "Boerenverdriet? *You eat it—it's Dutch liverwurst.*" (CXIII[16]), and the frequent use of self-deprecating, but poignant incongruities: "*Ethics at the far edge: give the old/ bugger a shove / gentleman a shout*" (LXXII); "*I may be gone some time. Hallelujah!/ Confession and recantation in fridge*" (LXXIII). Then, tellingly, there is the poet's own identification of himself with the figure of a clown. In a series of vaudeville-like sections (CXXIX-CXXXIII),[17] for instance, each ending in a horn flourish of "*ta-Rah ta-Rah ta-rarara Rah*," he imagines himself in a pie-in-the-face routine "*pedaling,/ grinning inanely*" (CXXXIII), "*The nerve to keep standing*" striking him " (*splat!*)" as something "*more/ than temperamental luck*." The parenthetical " (*splat!*)" verbalizes the physical gesture perfectly, setting up

---

15. *PRI*, 285.

16. *Boerenverdriet* is in fact the iconic term for the depiction of the slaughtering of peasants by soldiers in some seventeenth-century Dutch paintings. The joke, however, is on us if we hear only the word without its historical meaning or moral significance.

17. Hill admits the influence of vaudeville, or "music-hall," on his tone and visual imagination (see *PRI*, 286–87).

the contrast with the more serious matter of personal nerve, but with a refusal to take himself too seriously. The same disjunctive effect is produced in Section CXXXII where he raises the issue of *"whether the hidden part which most engages me/ is closer to nub, crux, crank or orifice."* He answers, *"Crank, probably"* (echoing once more the view of himself that he imagines others hold), and adds, *"Whichever it is, it has my tie."*

This is humorous material, and should be received as such. However, the comedic element has an equally forceful flipside, which Hill incorporates in his summary of the poem's rhetorical tone, referring to it as a "tragic farce."[18] Hill captures this doubleness in the repeated image of a *"glowering carnival, kermesse of wrath/ and resentment"* (CX), which describes the extremes of the poet's society as well as the ambiguities present in his own character. In that societal setting, the tragic as well as the comedic or farcical fills in the context of a modern situation and society characterized as much by imbecility, *"Entertainment overkill"* (LIV), and *"our mutually immature desires"* (CVII) as by palpable loss and deprivation. His description of a desecrated cemetery in Section XIII gives a stark image of the latter, the bodies of the dead

> ditched, divested, clamped, sifted, over-
> laid, raked over, grassed over, spread around,
> rotted down with leafmould, accepted
> as civic concrete, reinforceable
> base cinderblocks:
> tipped into Danube, Rhine, Vistula, dredged up
> with the Baltic and the Pontic sludge: (6)

The clotted series of accented beats, punctuated by the trenchant reverberations of words such as *"ditched," "clamped," "rotted," "dredged"* and *"sludge,"* generates a lurching effect that mimics aurally the process the poem describes: the machine-like procedures of an indifferent industrial polity willing to treat human bodies like so much raw material and superfluous waste. And with those bodies, the section insists in its opening lines, go the memories of the people:

> Whose lives are hidden in God? Whose?
> Who can now tell what was taken, or where,
> Or how, or whether it was received: (6)

18. Ibid., 289.

In these lines and the description that follows, we feel the pitch of indignation and remorse felt by the interrogator.

Furthermore, the loss experienced at the thought of these lives is made as palpable as the substance of their bodies thus abused. In a manner reminiscent of O'Siadhail's *Gossamer* suite, Hill makes both proximate, as in this similarly charged lament for victims of the Holocaust in Section XCVII:

> Devouring our names they possess and destroy
> by numbers: the numbered, the numberless
> as graphs of totality pose annihilation.
> Each sensate corpse, in its fatal
> mass-solitariness, excites
> multiples of infliction. A particular
> dull yard on a dull, smoky day. This, and this,
> the unique face, indistinguishable, this, these,
> choked in a cess-pit of leaking Sheol.

The interaction of the words "*they*," "*this*" and "*these*" which react antiphonally with "*our*," the progression of "*numbers*," "*numbered*," "*numberless*" towards the outcome of "*annihilation*," the dissonance between the impersonal "*graphs of totality*" and "*Each sensate corpse*," and between "*unique face*" and "*indistinguishable*," create a dynamic interplay of the universal and the particular. There is a deep irony at work here, though the mood is far from ironic: "*This, and this, . . . this, these*," effaced and unnamed "by numbers" and numbering, remain a "*mass-solitariness*," an abiding and substantial factuality that cannot be refused though their bodies were cast as refuse "*in a cess-pit of leaking Sheol*." As in the previous section, Hill's language and composition registers a tragic finality about the fate of these victims, one that cannot be mollified by appeal to abstractions ("*Each sensate corpse*" admits of none such). Nor does the poem permit us to stand apart from this reality. The assault on their humanity is an assault against *us*, the "devouring" of "*our names*"—the insertion of the first person plural makes the poem's point emphatic. This, too, is the context in which the poet-persona lives and one he feels compelled to acknowledge and to bring to recognition, comprised as it is of "*the brute mass and detail of the world*" (LXX, 37). Together with the comedic element directed against the clownishness he finds present in himself as well as his culture, through such depictions of destruction the poet infuses *The Triumph of Love* with an energy that intensifies both aspects of "tragic farce." Hill's strategy to conjoin these elements through his depiction of the self *in situ*, however, is precisely where his project is often misperceived.

For one, this combination of the tragic and the farcical is more than descriptive. It also represents an act of resistance, the effort to take a stand through one's art, which challenges the tendencies of a culture towards inattention and dissipation (*"And yes—bugger you, MacSikker et al., —I do/ mourn and resent your desolation of learning,"* the poet decries against his imagined literary critics in Section CXIX). For the poet, moreover, this posture involves keen attention to language and "standing by one's words."[19] Viewed in this light, the refusal of the poet to take himself too seriously does not eviscerate, or falsify, the very serious business of confronting societal as well as individual suffering and destructiveness. Rather, the poet's parody of himself intends to bring into relief those elements and the concerns they elicit, his persona serving both to challenge and to embody in microcosm the larger context of history and society—as a locus of its effects.[20] (His *"wounded pride"* is both *"clownish"* and *"deadly,"* LIX). The necessity of beginning with the self remains—the quest for love and the possibility of its triumph still finally come down to the personal, although not the private. Accordingly, the individual stands within as well as against his physical, historical and cultural setting—circumstances Hill describes as "the world's ineluctable necessity"[21]—and only there must he negotiate anything like a personal quest and carry out acts of resistance. Where else, this "autobiographical comedy" asks, can one begin?

The issue of beginnings or origins, prevalent throughout Hill's poetry, takes on a markedly local as well as personal disposition in *The*

---

19. Hill writes of Ezra Pound's *Homage to Sextus Propertius*, "The status fought for, and accomplished, within the comedy and melodrama of this sequence, is . . . that of standing by one's words in a variety of tricky situations . . ." ("Our Word Is Our Bond," *LL*, 156).

20. As Hill has pointed out, in *The Triumph of Love*, "The author is perfectly aware of the grotesque difference between his own resentments and the plight of millions, between the claims that he makes for himself and the several holocausts of his age. The whole structure of the sequence, particularly the way phrases are shaped, the way certain allusions are made to Laurel and Hardy, and comic papers is an acknowledgement of this monstrous inequality; and to read it in any other way seems to me to reveal humorlessness, and *an inability to listen*" (*PRI*, p.285; my italics).

21. *LL*, 141.

Triumph of Love. Taking the theme of the poem from its title, the question emerges: Where does one begin the elusive quest for love? Here, too, Hill's strategy proves multi-dimensional. The country of his childhood seems an obvious (and in some sense necessary) starting-point. The matter of place, however, as well as time, and of situating or "rooting" one's self with regard to either, is quickly made problematic. Here lie his earliest memories, yet ones disturbed, he says, with guilt ("*now I am convinced,*" he asserts); but then the explanation proffered is unconvincing and satirical: "*self-molestation of the child-soul, would that be it?*" And "*Romsley, of all places!*" he exclaims with apparent sarcasm in Section VII: "*Spraddled ridge-/ village sacred to the boy-martyr,/Kenelm, his mouth full of blood and toffee.*" In point of fact, the poet would honor the memory of his upbringing, and does so elsewhere. Yet, the mood of these passages reinforces the difficulty of making sense of one's place in the world, while poking fun at psychological or sentimental approaches to the endeavor.

No greater prospect emerges when the poet widens his lens to include the larger historical landscape of the Europe and Britain that form the backdrop of his life. These are places also riddled with "guilts incurred" through centuries of self-ruination and barbarism, most prominently evidenced by the devastations of the First and Second World Wars. Hill portrays these periods of destruction with ardent saliency in his persona's first address to "*Vergine bella*" in Section LV: the moment

> when your blast-scarred face
> appeared staring, seemingly in disbelief,
> shocked beyond recollection ... (28)

The startling image of Mary, the unflappable exemplar of faith, "*staring, seemingly in disbelief*" registers a shock of its own on our sensibilities, effecting that acute sense of irretrievable loss which characterizes the poet's attitude towards his age. As we observed from Sections XIII and XCVII, his is a broken and fragmented world, a place littered with abused and dismembered bodies and with the "shards" of a forgotten heritage that provoke his persona to plea for some form of recourse and redress: "*What am I to do/ with these shards of downright majesty?*" he beseeches himself in Section LXXXIII. The question he raises earlier in Section XXIII provides a suitable epitaph for these harrowing images:

Geoffrey Hill's "Pitch of Attention" and "Poetic Kenosis" in *The Triumph of Love*

"*What remains? You may well ask.*" By rendering this familiar turn of phrase in two sentences rather than one, the poem confers new stress on each clause: both the question and the need to find an answer are given fuller amplitude and urgency. Something does remain (as the passage following in XXIII and the remaining portion of LV indicate), and it is the earnest desire of the poet to recognize and, if possible, to recover that remnant and not merely to describe its loss. Yet, by presenting the conditions of the world in such palpable images of deprivation the poem defies facile idealism or sentimentality. Only from the "rubble" of a civilization in ruins, and no less so the detritus of the poet's own moral and spiritual deficiency, can any substantive progress towards restoration proceed.

The questions of "what remains" and of where to begin, therefore, converge as integral but equally problematic elements in the matter of rebuilding. This proves acutely so when the restoration of hope in love's possible triumph in the wake of so much personal and societal evil delimits the blueprint for the project. Again, from what place, or standpoint, can these questions as well as this quest be adequately engaged? When towards the end of the poem Hill's persona asks, "*and where are we, finally?*" his answer decidedly dims the prospect of establishing a place to stand, let alone somewhere from which to launch a quest for love: "*we are nowhere/ finally,*" he opines; and lest his readers object, he adds, "*And nowhere are you— / nowhere are you—any more . . .*" (CXLVII).

As hopeless as these lines make the success of his endeavor seem, there is, this poem insists, a way of proceeding which is both necessity and potentiality. The necessity once more involves beginning with one's self, the self *in situ*. If, however, the effort to rebuild by returning to one's roots (which is not, Hill insists, the same as *recalling* one's roots), like the effort to make sense of one's place in a larger, shattered world—in that world's terms—leads nowhere, what alternatives present themselves? Resignation and escapism are options, but not ones the poet-persona proves willing to endorse (see LXXXII, XXIV). What takes place inside him, as the dominant landscape and climate of the poem, yields whatever potential for love the poem offers. Within his persona the elements of tragic farce collide in a protracted study of the self's modern predicament. That predicament, however, consists of more than events and personalities, whether past or present. The poet's earnest meditations on these conditions unfold within the context—that is, the *text*—he creates, thus returning us again and again to one set of conditions in particular: that of language. In what way(s) is the predicament of the self *in situ* and the endeavor to address it substantively also a predicament of language, specifically a dilemma that poetry can or cannot resolve?

As in our study of Williams and his theology of images, to appreciate the many valences of Hill's views on the subject of language—of its potential as well as its predicament—some attention to his critical thought is in order. Such elaboration helps us to refine our understanding of Hill's method; that is, how the vehicle of the self *in situ* and his method of "character-as-climate" function as effective modes for the contemplation of love as a *poetic* enterprise. Because in many respects *The Triumph of Love* represents the poet's dialogue with himself, it is not surprising that we find in his critical thought numerous resonances with his poetic project, and vice-versa. The reciprocity between the one and the other therefore illuminates the principal urgencies of the poet in the staging of himself, a way of proceeding to which the poet also gives demonstrative "pitch."

The Self's Pitch of Attention

Hill appropriates the phrase "pitch of attention" from John Crowe Ransom's *The New Criticism*, applying it in his discussion of that poet's verse. He writes, "It is certainly open to suggestion that Ransom's particular technical achievement has been the conversion of 'strain' into 'pitch.' To be 'contemplative' is to achieve 'pitch of attention.'"[22] By *pitch*, Hill means, with I. A. Richards, the "density" of poetic language as well as its "richness," qualities that give fresh charge and energy to words and which explore (and expose) the depths of their "connotativeness."[23] Moreover, in Hill's view, as with all manner of speech pitch is a trait that designates quality of thought and character. Reflecting upon Ransom's assertion that poets have to "consider technique as a charge upon their conscience," for example, he then adds,

---

22. *LL*, 128.

23. Ibid., 129. In his assessment of T. S. Eliot's poetry and criticism, Hill distinguishes pitch from *tone*, asserting that Eliot's later work was characterized more by tone, and as a result, lost much of its vitality. See "Dividing Legacies" in Hill, *Style and Faith* (*SF*), 153ff.

> To write at Ransom's pitch of attention is to be in ontological and semantic "straits." Acute sensitivity to the richness of "denotative content" is also vulnerability to acoustical din, a situation in which the very finesse of the poet's perception becomes a source of bafflement and panic and, at worst, of self-destruction.[24]

In this light, the sense of "apprehension" as it appears in Section XIV—when his persona opines, "*As to bad faith, Malebranche might argue/ it rests with inattention,*" then adds, "*However, the status/ of apprehension remains at issue*"—acquires a double sense: as anxiety, even fear ("*What choice do you have?. . . / Fear is your absolute,*" LXIX), as well as perception. These "straits" felt by the poet are also the "strain" against which he must press and which he must convert in order to achieve attentive contemplation. For Hill, as for Ransom, this activity of poetic technique involves the poet in an ethical undertaking, his verse tuned by the pitch of poetic composition, with the latter having as its aim a vigilance of attention that returns as both moral and rhetorical action. As he asserts in his essay "Our Word Is Our Bond," "'rhetoric' is a part of the ontology of moral action."[25] Here we find ourselves at the *crux* of one of Hill's most persistent arguments, which he recreates in the dynamics of the poem. The image of the author standing vigil over his medium in sustained acts of attention becomes synonymous with diligence about his moral vocation and responsibility.[26]

Diligence and attention also represent the poet's criteria for the assessment of his intellectual culture, especially its literary pundits,

---

24. Ibid., 129.

25. Ibid., 158. Or, as Hill observes of George Eliot's "achieved style" with its "detailed accuracies" in her novel *Middlemarch*:

> in its demands upon both author's and reader's powers of attention, [it] shows itself the moral equivalent of those very qualities it describes. . . . [F]or the author of *Middlemarch*, intrinsic value is not so much in things, or even in qualities, as in a faculty: the faculty of sustained attention; attention conceived of, moreover, as a redemptive power. ("Rhetorics of Value" [*RV*], 263).

26. As this merging of craft with calling pertains to pitch specifically, Hill has commented (in a discussion of Yeats' poetry) that pitch involves the combination of syntax and intelligence, an intelligence "activated by the pitch of words" ("'The Conscious Mind's Intelligible Structure,'" *Agenda*, 21). He continues, "A poet who possesses such near-perfect pitch is able to sound out his own conceptual, discursive intelligence . . . The poet is hearing words in depth and is therefore hearing, or sounding, history and morality in depth" (ibid.).

to which he gives commensurate rhetorical pitch. In Section CXIX, for example, having censored his fictional critics "*MacSikker et al.*" for "*your desolation of learning,*" he turns to commend the *Scientia* of the Scholastics,

> that enabled, if it did not secure,
> forms of understanding, far from despicable,
> and furthest now, as they are most despised.

The syntactical arrangement and wordplay of "*despicable*": "*despised,*" each accentuated within the metrical and structural pattern, gives added pitch to the idea of indictment evoked. That idea, however, takes a significant turn, also achieved by syntax. The poet's own resentment gives way to an appraisal of Scholastic "*forms of understanding,*" affirming them as "*far from despicable*"; but the following line—"*and furthest now, as they are most despised*"—interjects a subtle, but for that reason more poignant evaluation of those who hold Scholastic *Scientia* in contempt. To wit, the greater the contempt shown by those who gainsay these "forms of understanding," the more these forms show themselves to be "far from despicable," their increase in value inversely proportionate to the decrease in estimation of critics such as "MacSikker et al." In effect, these critics' indictment of *Scientia* returns as an indictment of their own judgment, as that which stands at such a remove from understanding that it fails to recognize any longer its appearance. "Despicable" and "despised" are thus given fuller connotative range and applicability by virtue of Hill's own "syntactical intelligence."

His persona has not finished, however, but elaborates the issues of understanding and of attention and attentiveness already introduced. He continues,

> By understanding I understand diligence
> and attention, appropriately understood
> as actuated self-knowledge, a daily acknowledgement
> of what is owed the dead.

The arc of "*understanding*"—"*understand*"—"*understood,*" coupled with the alliterated progression of "*attention*"—"*appropriately*"—"*actuated*"—"*acknowledgement*" and the relationship created by aural as well as semantic resonance between "*self-knowledge*" and "*acknowledgement,*" generates a field of energy for this set of markedly dense, even cumbersome words and concepts. Any one of these words in a more prosaic setting is susceptible of either an overabundance of energy or of inertia—so familiar and yet so loaded are such concepts as "understanding," "diligence," "attention," and "self-knowledge."[27] Hill's poetics, however, enable us through rhythm and syntax to sound out the words in succession while simultaneously considering the collective meaning of his assertion about the "true" nature of understanding.

Hence, even as his persona argues for the recovery of these now despised but enabling "forms of understanding," the poetry engineers a process by which the virtues they display are given renewed vitality. Hill's method and its effect recall his assessment of Wordsworth's "Immortality" ode in the essay "Redeeming the Time." He writes, "If language is more than a vehicle for the transmission of axioms and concepts, rhythm is correspondingly more than a physiological motor. It is capable of registering, mimetically, deep shocks of recognition."[28] "Shock of recognition" we may take as a product of pitch of attention, and it proves an apt description of his achievement in this section, especially in its final line. As in the sections portraying the ravages of war, he produces his own shock of recognition, here through a further shift in rhythm and diction. In this manner, he punctuates one of the primary concerns of *The Triumph of Love*. Echoing the earlier statement from Section CIV where Hill's persona declares, "*I/ write for the dead*" (54), he here commends "*a daily acknowledgement/ of what is owed the dead.*" From the iambic pentameter of the previous lines to the compacted iambic trimeter of this last, and from the use of three-, four- and five-syllable words to the crisp succession of heavily accented one-syllable words in "of-what-is-owed-the-dead," Hill's rhythmic "disjuncture" heightens the pitch of this statement. The line sounds out an act of recognition even as it sounds *like* an act of recognition by virtue of the emphasis he achieves.

In this manner, Hill presses to the fore the poem's preoccupation with remembrance. In short, with a focus and urgency recalling that of O'Siadhail, we are meant to attend to the testimonies of those who have

27. Hill makes a similar claim for the poetry of Ransom and other "writers of significance," stating that such a poet "takes care not only to purge and enrich clichés by exactness and resonance but also to abrogate the pathos which certain words and phrases might excite in isolation" (*LL*, 123).

28. Ibid., 87.

gone before us. The enigmatic meaning of an inquiry pursued early on by the poet in Section XVIII now becomes clearer. There he asks, "*is this a dead/ march or a death march?*" His reply that "*It is a dead march*" hints at the perspective we find clarified in the phrase "a daily acknowledgement of what is owed the dead": both in the sense of determined and diligent observance and in the sense of awakening our attention to the character and witness of our predecessors. In Hill's view, it is a testimony and a debt too easily dismissed and discarded in this age of inattentiveness—of indifference and forgetfulness.[29]

That neglect comprises the failed attention that this poem seeks to challenge, delivering as an outcome two aspects of indictment. On the one hand, what judges us is the witness of those who have both sought and shown understanding, and who, though dead, endure in the testimony of their integrity. On the other hand, what may also indict us is our failure to acknowledge *daily* "what is owed" them. As the poet conveys his attitude towards his own native England,

> Ingratitude
> still gets to me, the unfairness
> and waste of survival; a nation
> with so many memorials but no memory. (LXXVI, 40)

Hence, he ("*mourning's autodidact*") delivers this charge to himself:

> proud,
> not willing to drop the increasingly
> evident burden of shamed
> gratitude: to his own dead,
> and to those not his own — (LVIII, 30)

Here again, rhythm and syntax enable heightened pitch, as "*proud*" is made to collide aurally as well as semantically with "*shamed*" because of their line placement, but then merge into one singularly enriched combination of aspects to describe "*gratitude*"—by virtue of *its* setting. The poet-persona is both too proud and too shamed not to acknowledge his debt of gratitude. In effect, Hill turns ambiguity to advantage, giving added intensity and texture to the individual's relationship to the larger context of his life and provoking a reassessment of the same across a range of attitudes. Shame and pride, gratitude and ingratitude,

---

29. Hill states in "Diligence and Jeopardy": "Indifference and forgetfulness are lamentable characteristics of our time" (*SF*, 27).

egotism and "self-mockery," all figure as elements in his protracted call to attention, and in turn reciprocate a heightened form of engagement for the reader.

Not surprisingly, the poet's direct appeal for a conversion of perspective also involves the issue of attention. In a further address to *Vergine bella*, he implores her: "*mend our attention/ if it is not too late*" (LXXXVII). The request for healing, and for healing of this feature of our humanity in particular, makes clear the nature of the "conversion" that Hill's poem seeks to effect. The necessary pre-condition for the restoration of love and of hope in its triumph, this plea supposes, rests with the struggle to hear and to see anew. In "Redeeming the Time," Hill makes this need explicit, relating it to the role of art and of artists as practitioners of what Coleridge called the "secondary imagination." Hill writes: "the secondary imagination, the formal creative faculty, must awaken the minds of men to their lost heritage, not of possession but of *perception.*"[30] This, again, represents the thrust of his aim, and the very conflict his persona engages. If the heritage that holds this deposit of perceptive power is indeed lost, the question arises: by what means and with what attitude might it be recoverable? "*What am I to do/ with these shards of downright majesty?*"

What, however, are we to make of the persona who issues this plea, weighing his admiration for the majesty of some against his estimation of others and the conditions of his age—its unconscionable amnesia and "'*savage torpor*'" (LIV)? The poetry captures the needed proportion of a response in the locution "*Laus et vituperatio*" ("praise and invective"), "*the worst/ remembered, least understood of the modes*" (XXIII); "*lost, rediscovered,/ renewed on few occasions this century*" (XXVI, 15). The poet-persona's endeavor to rebuild includes his own effort to reinstate this mode, though not in the form of a resolution:

> I have introduced,
> it is true, *Laus et vituperatio*
> as a formality; still this formal thing
> is less clear *in situ*. That —
> possibly — is why I appeal to it. (CXLII, 78)

Within the admixture of context, in other words, the dynamics of this approach provide the range of notes to be sounded, the necessary pitch of

---

30. *LL*, 97; my italics.

polarities which Hill's persona pursues with vehemence as he alternately praises those worthy of memory and excoriates those guilty of inattention, ingratitude and pride (both past and present—the poet-persona neither valorizes nor deplores any age *per se*). And nowhere does he show such vehemence, such *pitch*, more than in his own self-appraisal, including that which he imagines others hold of him. But how, we also need to ask, does the poet-persona's protracted attentiveness to himself constitute a means of recovering and restoring "shards of majesty" and of reawakening recognition of a *"moral landscape" "in which particular grace,/ individual love, decency, endurance,/ are traceable across the faults"* (LI)? These are the elements of the vision he commends, but his own self-preoccupation would seem to vitiate the integrity of his appeal. The poem presses such questions upon us with force. The answer we derive, however, represents the most misunderstood element in the poet's plea for attention—not for himself, but for something more that these qualities comprise.

The much-criticized presence of the poet in the poem, with all the portrayals of his disgruntled attitudes, feelings and anxieties, as being so incompatible with the great calamities he laments, misses this point about the pitch of Hill's self-staging entirely. The poet may be the clown or fool his critics (both fictional and real) and even he himself portray. But the sneering depictions of his character—"*Obnoxious chthonic old fart*" (XXXIV), "*Rancorous, narcissistic old sod*" (XXXIX), "*Shameless old man, bent on committing/ more public nuisance*" (XXXVII)—are so vehement, so "over the top," that one wonders why Hill's critics have not thought past its obviousness to consider the subtler purpose for the hyperbole.[31] The vehemence of these characterizations is integral to the poet's strategy, but it also creates a minefield of potential misreadings; and this, too, is the point. Hill has set a trap for the inattentive reader (or

---

31. Peter McDonald, showing himself to be one of Hill's most sensitive, and sensible, critics comments on this tendency to read the poem only on its surface without understanding why the surface is presented as it is. He writes, "the reception of *The Triumph of Love* has been marked by a number of more or less disgusted reactions to what the poet has chosen to bring up. Few, on the whole, have paused to consider how immediately they were able to come up with these reactions" (*Serious Poetry*, 208). With regard to "the sheer extravagance of Hill's 'vehemence' " in particular, he adds, "Not irony, then, but transparency is involved ... To complain that Hill's codes in *The Triumph of Love* are easy to see through is both to get the point and to fail to get the point" (211).

critic). But for the alert reader who hears *through* these vituperations the more demanding call to attention Hill's poem seeks to elicit, provocation registers an invocation. Similarly, Hill's critics have also apparently forgotten what Hill himself has said about the importance of "the heckler" to the "drama of reason" towards which, he believes, literature ought to aim.[32] In *The Triumph of Love* he has included the heckler in numerous guises as an integral element in the "climate-as-character" method of the poem in order to intensify the dramatic urgency of his persona's situation.

We observe this strategy to generate attentiveness through heckling and clamorous self-portrayal from the outset of the poem where we are introduced to an old man recalling his childhood. Here we find not a person with wisdom to dispense ("senex/ sapiens *it is not*,"[33] V), but an apparently angry, misunderstood, and yet sympathetic figure:

> What is he saying;
> why is he still so angry? He says, I cannot
> forgive myself. We are immortal.
> Where was I? Prick him. (2)

The self appears here in three voices—that of the old man's *un*sympathetic observer(s), what he is saying or is reported to have said about himself, and the poet who interrupts the exchange with "*Where was I?*" (sounding himself like an old man who has lost his train of thought). The rapid shifts in point of view and verb-mode, aggravated further by the absence of inverted commas, creates a complex syntax that disrupts our ability to distinguish who in fact is speaking and who listening. Is the old man also the poet-persona talking to and listening to himself? Are there others looking at him, even as he regards himself? The effect of this derangement of syntax and point of view generates an impression of muttering: of trying to give voice to something crucial (in the sense

---

32. It is on this basis that he criticizes George Eliot's 1868 pamphlet *Address to Working Men by Felix Holt*: "Eliot has denied us the cross-rhythms and counterpointings which ought, for the sake of proper strategy and of good faith, to be part of the structure of such writing. In short, she has excluded the antiphonal voice of the heckler;" and as a result, he adds, she "has denied us 'the drama of reason'" (*LL*, 90).

33. The allusion here comes from The Rule of St. Benedict, chapter LXVI, which describes the role of a porter for an abbey who was to be alert enough to answer questions but too feeble to wander off. The allusion thus doubles as a description both fitting and not fitting the image of the poet as he is portrayed.

of *crux*) that cannot be heard. It presages the passage from CXXXII in its meditation on "*the hidden part which most engages me,*" and with equal abruptness simultaneously holds forth then withdraws a matter of supreme importance.[34] Initially, then, the pitch of attention is cast as the pitch of *in*attention. The pathos of "*I cannot forgive myself*" (a statement itself broken by enjambment) and the profundity of "*We are immortal*" succumb to the force of the interjection "*Where was I?*" and the curt "*Prick him.*" Both phrases are thus reduced to verbal palimpsests, barely traceable in the aural environment of the section.

Hill's technique in these passages, indeed throughout the poem as a whole with its repeated verbal interruptions and disruptions of syntax and trains of thought, signals the poem's preoccupation with matters of context and attentiveness. The lighter side of "Where was I?" is the image of an old man who forgets what he is saying. A more serious aspect of this image, also present, is that of an individual trying to hear himself think and of a poet trying to write a poem, but who finds it difficult to progress because of the noise of disparate and distracting voices. Indeed, this is, by design, a poem that finds it difficult to begin, let alone progress.[35] At the same time, the struggle to proceed in the midst of constant disruption, which the poem both replicates and reflects, demonstrates the demands placed *upon* the poet. All that Hill has said about "words, contexture, and other circumstances of language" and the poet's struggle to find his own voice by mastering "the acoustical din that surrounds us all,"[36] he transposes into the portrayal of his persona and his situation.

This situation does not remain the poet's or his persona's only, however. Hill's manner of holding forth then withholding imposes a

---

34. The device in part reverses but also resembles the achievement Hill observes in Ovid, that poet's "realization of the manner in which 'holding forth' can be a way of withholding" (*LL*, 150).

35. The rapid retreat from the elevated image of a momentary sensation in Section I—"*Sun-blazed, over Romsley, a livid rain-scarp*"—to the flattened, nearly anesthetic first line of Section II—"*Guilts were incurred in that place, now I am convinced*"—immediately casts the entire poem in this similarly disjunctive mode. Moreover, the fact that this image also brackets the entire poem, but remains in suspended animation until it is taken up again (with only one slight modification, from 'a' to 'the') one hundred and forty-nine sections later emphasizes the attitude that the entire poetic enterprise is fraught with disruption.

36. *PRI*, 279.

challenge to the reader, specifically our own ability to hear. By incessantly disorienting focus through shifts in perspective and points of view, *we* are made to experience the effects of an acoustical din, and as a result, feel viscerally the difficulty of paying attention. (Hill adds stress to this predicament throughout by repeating the motif of mishearing as a running gag: "*You can say you are deaf in several languages*" (XXXVI); "*Excuse me — excuse me — I did not/ say the pain is lifting. I said the pain is in/ the lifting. No — please — forget it*" (XLII); "*For definitely the right era, read: deaf in the right ear*" (CV).) Returning to Section V, the answer to "*why is he still so angry*" has been given—it is because he can neither forgive himself nor reconcile himself to his own *im*mortality—but it remains unattended to. Hence, the issue for his readers becomes, Have *we* heard it? Are we listening, or even able to do so? "What is he saying?" becomes the reader's own mantra, a reaction deliberately engineered by the poem. In effect, the reader is required to exert energy resisting the poem's own antiphonal devices; that is, to submit to a process of *reading through* the poem's disruptions in order to attend to the poem's critical concerns. The pitch of inattention, or of disrupted attention, reciprocates a challenge to pursue the opposite. Hence, beyond the "*splenetics*" for which the poet asks *Vergine bella*'s forgiveness in LXXXVII, and of which the poet is often accused, Hill's "choreography" of the self recreates a scene of reading, and of writing, that strains constantly within as well as against its surface. The poet's struggle is to be our struggle to overcome the constraints of language, as he seeks to expose the insipid conditions of his age, culture, and even his own soul, which together have "infected" it.[37]—an aim that requires extraordinary vigilance.

The Self within "Words, Contextures and Other Circumstances of Language"[38]

In this vein, we need to distinguish further between Hill's method and the approach of other poets who likewise focus their theme through

---

37. Hill uses the image of 'infection' to designate the poet's struggle with language. Borrowing Auden's metaphor, he writes, "'Infections' are 'ordinary circumstances' and the dyer's hand, steeped in etymology if nothing else, is by that commonplace craftsmanlike immersion, an infected hand" (*LL*, 153).

38. Taken from Hobbes' *Leviathan*, the locution provides the subtitle for his tellingly titled book, *The Enemy's Country: Words, Contexture, and Other Circumstances*

the lens of the self. One such distinction, already indicated, involves the recognition that Hill does not permit his persona to extricate himself from his circumstances or "contexture"—for example, as a form of self-transcendence or escape, in the company of other *"artists of escape"* (XXIV, 13) or *"others well-tried in the practical/ worlds of illusion, builders of fabled masks"* (XXV, 13). Most significantly, he insists that the circumstances which bind his persona (in the sense of obligation as well as contingency) include language, words. Thus, the poet's address *"a se stesso"* ("to himself")[39] proceeds:

> *A se stesso.*
> Not unworded. Enworded.
> But in the extremity
> of coherence. You will be taken up.
> *A se stesso.* (LXI)

"Not unworded. Enworded."—that is, the self folded within speech, or con*text*ualized—as the section itself is enfolded and given its own context by being bracketed with *"A se stesso."* "Enworded" and enfolded do not mean self-enclosed, however, *"But in the extremity/ of coherence."* At first glance, the statement strikes us as odd. In what sense is one *in* (as opposed to "at") an extremity, and does the phrase mean "extremely coherent" or coherence that is discovered only in an extremity of circumstances (a *"colloquy with occasion"*)? References to the Catholic martyr Thomas More elsewhere in the poem suggest all of these meanings: More (*"Morus"*) who *"enacted extreme measures"* by his willingness to sacrifice his life for his convictions, which the poem sets against appeals for *"moderation"* (CXVI). Hill's notion of extremity, then, bears connotations of both the measure of limits and of that which is extrinsic to, and/or out of, the self.

The next sentence, *"You will be taken up"* communicates the range of this dual possibility. On the one hand, there is in this statement the idea of being "taken up into"—in this context, into one's words as, in a sense, their captive, and as the site wherein things come together or

of Language (EC). In this series of essays, Hill explores the poet's struggle "to resist the pressure of circumstances" (5)—political, cultural, linguistic (cf. the epigraph from Ezra Pound).

39. This phrase comes from Giacomo Leopardi's (1798–1837) poem of that title in which the poet implores his *"tired heart"* to *"Rest now"* in the face of life's vanity and his own despair.

"cohere." Whatever coherence is achieved, it must be sought and rendered in speech—that is, "enworded." On the other hand, the allusion to resurrection opens a further possibility for the self, one which directs the self towards a greater "extremity" (the "*reach of resurrection*," XCI) that situates the self in a larger frame of reference: that of one's imminent mortality and the possibility of transcending it. In either sense, the self remains, but exists—actually and potentially—in a context; as, again, the bracketing with "*A se stesso*" reiterates. The implication we draw from this section—remarkable for the range of meaning achieved through such economy of words—signals the inclination of the whole. Hill's self-depiction does not aim merely to relate or excite a series of private emotions, but, as we have said, to disturb and to re-orient our very notion of the subjective interest. (This is not a poem in the "confessional mode" that Hill disparages.[40]) Indeed, his ambition to effect a change in perception, and with this a *conversion* of perspective, along these lines places a question mark against the private ruminations and foibles of any one individual. The poet is a public figure, however received by his public, and his medium of speech is, in regard to common practice, the most public of all the arts. As Hill's persona avers in his commentary on the poet Eugenio Montale, "*publicities, public life,/ [are] the anteroom to the presence-chamber/ of self-containment./ ... one man's privacy is another's/ crowded at home — we are that circumscribed*" (CXXXIV, 72–3). To be "circumscribed," "enworded," is to stand within one's medium but as the site of *public* negotiations (that is, "*negotium*,"[41] reprised in the poem as "*unending* negotium," CXXV, 68), and so, as the bearer of a public responsibility.[42]

In a similar vein, in addition to insisting that the self remain inextricable from one's circumstances, including the contexture of words, Hill's pursuit of a converted perspective helps to reconcile two strains in his thought that on the surface may appear contradictory. One is his

40. In "Poetry as 'Menace' and 'Atonement'" Hill admits: "I ... disdain the 'confessional mode' as currently practiced" (*LL*, 1).

41. Hill borrows this word [from Dryden] to describe the poet's laborious confrontation with the "unhappy circumstances" of his own language. He writes, "the poet is necessarily engaged in a competitive *negotium*; he is competing with the strengths and resistances and enticements of the English language" ("Unhappy Circumstances," *EC*, 9).

42. Hill states in the Phillips interview, "I think men and women who write poetry or write music or paint are finally responsible for what they do" (*PRI*, 279).

"disdain for the confessional mode" noted above, which he reiterates as the "naïve trust in the unchallengeable authority of the authentic self" so prevalent in recent poetry.[43] A second strain, enunciated in the same interview, involves the poet's (and by implication, our own) struggle "to hear and to elicit the voice of the authentic self from the many voices of the not-self and, indeed, from the many voices of our time, which are themselves drastically inauthentic."[44] The difference between these statements that overcomes the apparent contradiction hinges on the phrase "unchallengeable authority," which in this same context Hill equates with "inadequate knowledge and self-knowledge."[45] At issue, in other words, is the matter of intelligence, not sincerity—an intelligence that aligns authenticity with moral authority.[46]

The matter of authority is one Hill raises frequently in *The Triumph of Love*, and it has significant bearing on the poem's central aim to elicit a change in perspective as one necessary pre-condition for love's triumph. We may put the matter in the form of two interrelated lines of inquiry: First, by what or whose authority are society and its more prominent representatives subjected to the often blistering critique displayed in this poem, and by virtue of what means, if that critique is valid, are we enabled in some sense to transcend those conditions? Second, if a change in perspective is warranted, *is* there an "authentic self" present in this poem who successfully negotiates that transformation without succumbing to a "naïve trust" in his own authenticity? As we see, the poet-persona emerges as an acutely conflicted individual, one burdened as much by his own depravity as by his earnest desire for rectitude.

Mea culpa,
I am too much moved by hate —
pardon, ma'am? — add greed, self-pity, sick

43. Ibid., 282–83.
44. Ibid., 279.
45. Ibid., 282.

46. Hill comments: "it would be naïve to contend that sincerity confers absolution" (*LL*, 106), meaning that sincerity does not "absolve" us from either the "unconditional"constraint of the moral law or of language. Both require extraordinary alertness, which leads him to take up Allen Tate's question of "how the *moral intelligence* gets into poetry" (ibid., 115; my italics). This does not dissolve the pertinence of sincerity for the poet, but recognizes its complexity (its lack of transparency) within the ambit of moral law. "Sincerity," Hill writes in "Dryden's Prize-Song," "is a complex, not a simple state" (*EC*, 77).

> scrupulosity, frequent fetal regressions, *and*
> a twisted libido? Oh yes -- much
> better out than in. (LXXV, 39)

The self-deprecating humor of these lines relieves one intensity—that of self-preoccupation—only to encourage another, taken up in the next section's lament over ingratitude. Still, we are left to wonder: to what extent and in what sense are we to trust him and his own self-presentation as a vehicle of witness and conversion?

It is my conviction that Hill has created a figure who is *not* to be trusted in respect of his sincerity or intensity of feeling. The trajectory of the poem leads constantly away from such presumptions, its "self-distancing choreography" pointing us in another direction entirely. Accordingly, having admitted his own cowardice in Section CXXXVIII, he concludes, "*I am saying (simply)/ what is to become of memory?*" (75). At the same time, I hold with equal conviction that Hill means for his *poem* to be trusted, or at least taken seriously—*where* the poet takes his stand remains within the contexture of his verse, "enworded." In the very acts of pointing up his deficiencies, Hill's persona repeatedly clears away any appeals to his own character in order to stand us within the poem as the site of a more significant appeal to that which exceeds the self.[47] This does not remove the difficulties of his persona's quest for love, nor does it resolve all issues of authority for the poem (as we shall see presently); but it radically reorients the focus of attention to that space a poem uniquely inhabits, and by implication, where its redemptive potential is brought to the test.

To stand within, as well as by, one's words is, this poem insists, a difficult and hazardous place to stand. To be "cunning" of speech[48] in the craft of words is not a hazardous "hook" from which the poet excuses himself, but proves all-inclusive: "*We are made/ to make ourselves*

---

47. Hill has confirmed such a strategy elsewhere, saying, "I have come to see that the closest approximation of truth requires that the shortcomings of the self be admitted into the most intimate textures of the work. You can at one and the same time firmly believe that your position on certain issues is right, and acknowledge that one's feelings are far from pure..." (*PRI*, 284).

48. As with Williams' senses of the word "cunning" in "Taliessin's Song of the Unicorn," Hill sees in its various nuances the value of its use, particularly in "the practical eloquence of controversy" (*SF*, 89). Or as he says in "'The Conscious Mind's Intelligible Structure,'" "sincerity is not enough,... creativity means cunning and artifice and ... 'spontaneity' is an illusion'" (op. cit., 21).

instruments/ of violence and cunning. There seems no/ hook on which we are not caught . . ." (LXXV, 38). The "hook" includes that of language especially, and manifestly so. If, as Hill avers in his commentary on Henry Vaughan's poem "The Night," "Sensuous experience is what is evoked; the sensory material I take to be language itself,"[49] what kind of sensory material is language, and how does its use return an estimation of the one who works with, or in, it? That the latter proves to be the case we may take as axiomatic for Hill. He commends the observation advanced by Robert Burton, "It is true, . . . our stile bewraies [betrays] us," a principle Hill extends to include issues of character: "One can see how a question of rhetoric might well be construed as a matter of spiritual fidelity and how 'stile' might indeed 'bewraie' the author."[50] (Hill echoes this conclusion in Section CXVI where the poet-persona asks, *"how could it fail, that lineage?"* to which he replies, *"As before, the question stands as one/ of rhetoric."*)

His elaboration of the theme of style and rhetoric as organs of character and the very "contextures" wherein the ethical and spiritual fidelity of individuals as well as communities and societies find their measure runs throughout his works. This interest can be approached variously as a plea for clarity of both perception and perspective, as well as for integrity of speech, from numerous points in *The Triumph of Love*. So, for example, he petitions the *Vergine bella*:

> Overburdened with levity, the spirit found
> in carnal disarray — so what do you know,
> *Amarilli, mia bella*? Say it is not
> true that mockery is self-debasement;
> though already I have your answer: We
> are to keep faith, even with self-pity,
> with faith's ingenuity, . . . (CXV)

"Overburdened with levity" returns us to the poet-persona's commentary on his own character (as well as, perhaps, that of the poem itself), and

---

49. In "A Pharisee to Pharisees" (*SF*, 79). Later, in this same essay he adds, "Language is a vital factor of experience, and, as 'sensory material,' may be *religiously apprehended*" (86; my italics.).

50. "Keeping to the Middle Way" (ibid., 53). In his Preface to this collection of essays, Hill makes the connection even more emphatic. Commenting on John Donne's view of authorship, he elaborates: "With Donne, style *is* faith: a measure of delivery that confesses his own inordinacy while remaining in all things ordinate" (ibid., xiv).

on a society typified by a lack of seriousness or wise judgment. Both the individual and the society in which he finds himself risk remaining in "*carnal disarray.*" A further risk is that the use of mockery as a mode of [self-]correction will only further debase the self. Hence, his appeal to "*mia bella*" solicits the poise that the poem once more seeks to achieve between the pitch of the tragic and the farcical, as a point of juncture and of potential disjuncture. At that point what proves determinative is the prospect of an altered perspective (rendered graphically by the enjambed "*We*" in Line 5). The answer to his question (which is also not a direct answer) lifts attention away from the self towards resources that lie beyond it: "*We/ are to keep faith, even with self-pity,/ with faith's ingenuity.*" By bracketing "*self-pity*" between "*keep faith*" and "*faith's ingenuity,*" the poem reinforces this shift in focus

The meaning of this last phrase signifies something else crucial to the argument of the poem. As an attempt to generate a new perspective on the predicament of the modern self in its contemporary context, it too reflects a departure by Hill from the "confessional mode." "*[F]aith's ingenuity,*" as a mode of keeping faith, marks a shift in this section's thematic trajectory made manifest through its self-reflective compound words, as the poem moves from "self-debasement" and "self-pity" to,

> self-rectifying cadence,
> perfectly imperfected: e.g., the lyric
> art of Spanish baroque, seventeenth-
> eighteenth-century Italian song . . .

The answer the poet "already has" from the Virgin releases him (ironically) to a new constraint; and, significantly, the image for such rectitude is poetry. More than emblematic, the example of poetic styles from the past registers the poet's aspiration to marshal the resources of his own medium as an act of resistance to "overburdened levity" and a "spirit in carnal disarray," whether his own or the spirit of his age. This poem is also to be "*self-rectifying cadence,/ perfectly imperfected,*" as if Hill's persona needs to jar himself (and any who care to listen) into an awareness of what stakes are involved and what stands in need of recovery. The principal goal, he insists, is not self-realization but self-*correction*, indexed to the transformation that a faith perspective uniquely affords ("*And if not faith,*" he adds to the list of "what remains," "*then something through which it is made possible/ to give credence—,"* XXIII), and which poetry, at least of the kind invoked here, in some sense embodies.

Here also the substance of one of Geoffrey Hill's arguments about the power and limitations of poetic speech resurfaces, that power being the capacity of poetry to effect moral and spiritual rectitude—an assertion Hill advances here by his own poetic technique. The poet's parenthetical note to himself (*"End with that reference, in the Ludlow masque,/ to* haemony, *plant of exilic virtue."*) marks a definitive break in the poem, a "disjuncture" common throughout *The Triumph of Love* in a variety of forms. Here, as elsewhere, such disjunctures amplify an attitude towards self-inspection, which is simultaneously aggressive and resigned, both self-assertive and self-questioning. It is a variation on the achievement Hill commends in Ben Jonson, who, as with Hill's perception of his own challenge, struggled to subdue a world reflective of "a barren age," and whose "qualifications worry the verse into dogs-teeth of virtuous self-mistrust."[51] As we have observed, Hill's own procedure similarly involves endless qualifications, as a means of tearing down and shaking up—in this case, the conventions of his own medium—in order to build anew.

In these lines, as one instance of this strategy, we note that the poet's departure from his own poem proper creates a duplicitous effect. The line is both part and not part of the poem, thus not diminishing but strengthening and reiterating the notion of "exilic virtue": as a voice that speaks from beyond conventional boundaries and which preserves its own integrity by doing so. The poem *enacts* that same ethos, not lyrically—like the *"lyric art"* of Spanish and Italian poetry—but structurally. In effect, the parenthetical device generates a shift in attention that disrupts our expectations of poetic flow by interjecting a voice "from beyond" the poem, but still in keeping with the poem's own theme of faith and self-correction. The disjuncture in the poem proper with its reference to *"haemony"* (which, notably, sounds like *harmony*) thus folds back into the sense of the whole as another form of "perfectly imperfected," "self-rectifying cadence." The result, a product of poetic *style* and not literal statement, serves to make manifest the contention that poetry can run parallel with and can further instantiate faith's "self-rectifying cadence."

51. *LL*, 52, 53, 54.

Hill's move here recalls his interpretation of Pisanio's line "*Where I am false, I am honest, not true, to be true*": he comments, "This is the taming of 'false relation' to a new constructive purpose. *Dissonance is the servant preparing the return of harmony.*"[52] The statement, and others like it,[53] could stand as another epigraph to Hill's style as well as his aim in *The Triumph of Love*. As we find this pattern reproduced in the poetics of Section CXV, Hill's own poetic "ingenuity" demonstrates another instance of "keeping faith," as a prolonged endeavor to stand vigil over his medium even as he in the persona of himself stands vigil over his soul (recalling also that this entire section is a *prayer* to the Virgin). The self-rectifying cadence of Hill's poem advances the moral aspirations of his persona as a single movement towards self-correcting faith. As Hill has asserted, "The instrument of expression and the instrument of self-knowledge and self-correction is the same,"[54] or as he says of Dryden's "constant vigilant negotiation" within his art, "it is one of the virtues of his style to transform a driven condition into a cadenced vehemence."[55] Poetry, in other words, does not merely elaborate themes of faith and rectitude, but as Hill's technique through his parenthesis demonstrates, it is capable of *performing* an act of integrity for the poet who is likewise "overburdened with levity" and whose spirit is "found in carnal disarray."

This may appear a large claim for poetry, but one Hill carefully elaborates in his critical works. We meet it early in his celebrated inaugural lecture at Leeds University, "Poetry as 'Menace' and 'Atonement'" (1977), in which he asserts that "the technical perfecting of a poem is an act of atonement, in the radical etymological sense—an act of at-one-ment, a setting at one, a bringing into concord, a reconciling, a uniting in

---

52. Ibid., 66; my italics.

53. In his essay "Redeeming the Time," e.g., Hill argues that the pattern of "stress-pitch-juncture" familiar to linguistics needs modification when giving an account of the kind of effect Wordsworth achieves in his "Immortality" ode. The rhythmic break at one point in that poem, he contends, requires a new term—'stress-pitch-*dis*juncture'—as a means of describing the sometimes startling effect of rhythmic patterning distinct to poetry (*LL*, 88).

54. *PRI*, 283. In this same context Hill also uses the phrase "self-rectifying," applying it in this case to the power of seventeenth-century metaphysical poetry "in which the language seems able to hover above itself in a kind of brooding, self-rectifying way" (ibid.).

55. *EC*, 69.

harmony."⁵⁶ Together with this potentiality of effecting "the atonement of aesthetics with rectitude of judgment," and as a strain against it, Hill also insists that, "The arts which use language are the most impure of arts," a condition due to both the fallenness of language *and* the poet.⁵⁷ Thus, he concludes, Karl Barth's definition of sin as the "specific gravity of human nature as such" leads to the conviction "that it is at the heart of this 'heaviness' that poetry must do its atoning work, this heaviness which is simultaneously the 'density' of language and the 'specific gravity of human nature.'"⁵⁸

It is within the "force-field" of these dynamics that the phrases "*self-rectifying cadence*" and "*perfectly imperfected*" not only attest to the ambiguous promise of poetry but also acquire the moral and spiritual resonances that Hill believes underlie all manner of language use. And it is the peculiar task of poetry to disclose language's condition of imperfection even as it aims towards its own perfection and "at-one-ment" as a means of self-correction.⁵⁹ Hill develops this combination of both aspects in his more recent Tanner Lectures (2000). On the one hand, he insists, "For the poem to engage justly with our imperfection, so much the more must the poem approach the nature of its perfection," while on the other hand arguing that, "the great poem moves us to assent as much by the integrity of its final imperfection as by the amazing grace of its detailed perfection."⁶⁰ The tension remains as the abiding situation of the poet's own endeavors, and it is not one that Hill ameliorates in *The Triumph of Love*. Rather, his scene of writing reprises this situation as the poem struggles to progress and as his persona wrestles *in situ* within the contextures of his medium and the cacophony of distractions and even more disturbing malignancies of his age and personal character. At the same time, the poem strains to direct us towards a different horizon that is in fact born of these same contingencies. Hill's effort to

---

56. *LL*, 2.

57. Ibid., 10, 2. The fallenness of language, as constitutive of human fallenness, also represents a common strain in Hill's thought. As he writes elsewhere, "There *is* something 'mysterious,' some 'dark and disputed matter' [Hopkins] implicated in the nature of language itself" (ibid., 151).

58. Ibid., 15.

59. We note the affinity of this view with Charles Williams' delineation of the "ostentation of verse."

60. *RV*, 269.

accomplish poetic "at-one-ment" leads ultimately to, and indeed enacts, the very properties and features of the doctrines that address our imperfect condition. As an outcome, poetic technique converges with theological insight to produce a style of faith that is recognizably christological.

Style and Faith: From "Kinesis" to "Kenosis"

Hill's diagnosis of the "cross-thwartings" of Gerard Manley Hopkins' poetry[61] is apposite to his own method and "style of faith" in *The Triumph of Love*. He writes, "Hopkins's theological crux is necessarily a linguistic crux."[62] The statement expresses further the idea of poetry's "atoning work"; a pitch Hill finds in Hopkins that carries overtures of dogma "arduously and perilously" set forth within the constraints of language. Although Hill's persona questions the truism that "nothing true is easy" (as, by its own logic, he must), it suggests this reciprocal economy of "crux," connoting the strain experienced in the pursuit of something central or pivotal. Pitched within the contextures of language as the site of *negotium* with "the world's ineluctable necessity," the difficulty of speaking truth involves a general state of affairs for those who would discover and hold forth a "word of truth" to their contemporaries. The poet's punning in Section CXXXII ("*whether the hidden part which most engages me/ is closer to nub, crux, crank or orifice* . . . ," etc.) elicits this same dynamic tension: the poet who is thought to be a "crank" and an "eccentric" is the self whose pursuit of the truth *turns* on matters of speech.[63] If, however, as Hill asserts, language is a party to human fallenness, infecting the "dyer's hand" of the poet and any human speaker with the danger of corrupt speaking, how can a theological crux be converted to a linguistic crux with "spiritual fidelity"? What manner of speaking proves both instructive with regard to our infected condition and promising in terms of redeeming it? Of what quality is a language of faith?

61. I.e., between "freedom of pitch" and "freedom of field"—regarding the former, in a reversal of our common construal, as "the right-keeping of will" and the latter as that which language manifests.

62. *LL*, 157.

63. Hill's observations of Ransom's play on the word 'eccentric' leads him to make a similar association with speech: like the mechanical device, it too "can convert rotary into rectilinear motion" (ibid., 123–24).

Particularly in light of the testimony of Scripture about speech, but also with respect to various currents within theology as well as academia and the culture at large, there is perhaps no more significant fusion of concerns for the Church's thinkers to explore. Hill's poem advances the prospect for poetry to formulate a trenchant redress in this regard on two fronts: by drawing our attention to conditions of "false" speaking (as well as defective *hearing*) while holding up models of "right" speaking, and, in the process of doing so, performing his own acts of at-one-ment. The pitch of his style when tuned to matters of theological import especially inculcates the conviction that human speech can achieve a measure of virtue, and return insight into our condition and need—supremely our need for grace and love.

When, in Section LXX, Hill's persona announces "*The struggle/ for a noble vernacular*" as an effort towards "*Active virtue*," and adds, "*Still, I'm convinced that shaping,/ voicing, are types of civic action*" (LXX, 36), the poem raises this possibility explicitly. At the same time, his persona asks in this section, "*But where is it?*" (that is, this "struggle for a noble vernacular"), and "*Where has it got us?*" The issue does not progress along the lines of an essentialist debate: not "what," we note, but "where" he twice asks. Thus, when he admits, "*I cannot/ say how, precisely*" active virtue has "*Intrinsic value*," this is *precisely* the point—he affirms the value of active virtue because he knows what something of value *looks like*:

> Partaking of both
> fact and recognition, it must be, therefore,
> in effect, at once agent and predicate:
> imponderables brought home
> to the brute mass and detail of the world; (37)

To make an abstraction of active virtue would be to deny its evident nature, as "*that which shall contain/ its own passion in the public weal*" (36)—that is, "*in effect*." By teasing out the semantics of "where" and "how" in this manner the passage deposes a commentary on the very issue of semantics, confirming by his own "*shaping, voicing*" that the presence, or absence, of active virtue is not reducible to semantic games. Rather, active virtue entails a quality of speech characterized as a "noble vernacular" that materializes "fact and recognition," but which is disappearing from the landscape: "*the cherished stock/ hacked into ransom* and ruin; the voices/ of distinction, far back, indistinct" (36)—hence also among the list "*of things betrayed*" (37).

To recover from "ransom and ruin" the "voices of distinction," then, marks the aim of the poet-persona's endeavor to revive this struggle. For him, this is not the pursuit of an ideal but of recognizable values both constituted and disclosed in "noble" speech, values that stand among other "*imponderables brought home/ to the brute mass and detail of the world;/ there, by some, to be pondered.*" Once again, the image of construction appears, but the labor of the poem towards that possibility, its dominant mode of "shaping, voicing," involves *excavation*—a digging down and laying bare in order to expose. It is an image that also receives commensurate pitch in the composition of the poetry, and depicts as well an attribute of poetic form by which Hill divulges the "theological crux" of his poem.

In Sections LXVI and LXVII, Hill gives this work of excavation a particularly theological temper. In Section LXVII his persona appeals to Justice, "*Instruct me further in your travail,/ blind interpreter,*" then continues,

> Suppose I cannot
> unearth what it was they buried: research
> is not anamnesis. Nor is this a primer
> of innocence exactly. Did the centurion
> see nothing irregular before the abnormal
> light seared his eyeballs? Why do I
> take as my gift a wounded and wounding
> introspection?

The "they" of this section refers to the previous one, in which the poet levels his complaint against an Anglican church whose "*strange guild/ . . . practices daily/ synchronized genuflection and takes pride/ in hazing my Jewish wife,*"[64] but who nonetheless benefit from Christ's resurrection: "*But since he is/ risen, he is risen even for these/ high-handed underlings of self-/ worship*" (LXVI). The word "*buried*" in LXVII intensifies the irony at work in these sections, cooperating with, as well as reacting against "*he is risen*" and "*risen indeed.*" On the one hand, we hear the words of Paul's summation of the Gospel, that "Christ died, was *buried*, and rose again." On the other hand, the poem's qualification on the heels

---

64. Hill refers here to an actual situation involving his wife Alice Goodman.

of the word—that "*research/ is not anamnesis*"—offers a tacit rejoinder to those who fail to "see" the import of that proclamation (who do not "unearth" Christ in that confessional sense, and so, ironically, leave him buried). The satire of "*Did the centurion/ see nothing irregular before the abnormal/ light seared his eyeballs?*" and of the final comedic lines reinforces this point. In sum, the task of research may certainly involve attentiveness, but it seeks to unearth in order to gain one kind of knowledge; anamnesis constitutes a form of attentiveness that seeks to translate knowledge into memorial and reflective wisdom (and in this case, ultimately, worship).

The marking of such a distinction can, in fact, be taken as paradigmatic for one of the poem's principal objections to the current state of the intellect—including the theological or religious mind. Issues of authentic knowledge and knowing obtain especially for a Church that does not "see," that does not hold in remembrance the "searing" implications of its own confession and, as a result, becomes a "*blind interpreter*" of a different kind whose

> rule is clear enough: last
> alleluias *forte*, followed by indifferent
> coffee and fellowship. (35)

The choice of "*rule*" has teeth, evoking the "rule" followed by various monastic orders known for their extensive discipline and diligence. The mocking satire reiterates the poet-persona's lament for what the church has lost, or, more precisely, has "buried," and to such degree that he earlier comments, "*It seems weird/ that the comedy never self-destructs*" (LXVI). And once more, the arena of *negotium* is language and the meaning of words. Repeatedly in Section LXVI the poem refers to "Christ risen"—"*Christ has risen yet again*," "*If Christ/ be not risen*," "*But since he is/ risen*," "*proclaim him risen indeed*"—following the progression of the Easter liturgy, but within a context created by the poem that simultaneously diffuses and concentrates sense. What the statements become when made the appendages of "ritual supplication" and "synchronized genuflection" or merely the precursor to "indifferent coffee and fellowship," and what they nonetheless entail "since he is risen," scrutinizes a further crucial distinction: the difference between making or keeping words vital and rendering them "inert."

In Hill's estimation, the latter is the product of inattentiveness as well as a form of accommodation whereby words become merely expressions of, or are subjected to, the vagaries of "general taste."[65] So, his persona instructs in Section XL:

> For wordly, read worldly; for in equity, inequity;
> for religious read religiose; for distinction
> detestation. Take accessible to mean
> acceptable, accommodating, openly servile. (20–21)

The play on "typographical mishaps" solicits a serious point,[66] and illuminates the concerns of LXVI–VII. For the words "he is risen," the poet exposes the anemia of their "worldly" and "religiose" expression while, by repeating them, he gives fresh charge to their appearance. The implications we draw for the witnessing as well as the confessing church are pointed, and should provoke believers to engage in some rather worrisome—perhaps "wounded"—"introspection" of their own. In light of these sections, particularly troubling is the often-evoked category of relevance—whether it is a virtue to be sought in witness or a guise that masks the church's anxiety to be "acceptable," thereby offering little more than a "servile" accommodation to "general taste." The issue of rhetoric as Hill expounds it in his verse leaves little room for equivocation in this regard. A noble faith, we may say, requires a "noble vernacular," characterized by "fact and recognition" rather than "acceptability." Again, it is a matter, and a measure, of spiritual fidelity, which makes all manner of diligence, not relevance, the virtue this poem commends.

At the same time, the poet-persona admits his own difficulty in heeding properly the gravity of faith's confession. When he turns to his need for instruction and to his own condition in Section LXVII, he makes the import of "he is risen" personal—what these words mean, and what believers mean when they say them, brings us once more to

---

65. "The difference," Hill clarifies in "Redeeming the Time," is "essentially, between vital and inert structures" of speech, the latter being such that can lead even to a "malign activity . . . made possible by the inertia of general taste" (*LL*, 95). Hill raises a similar concern in his review of Yale's 'modern-spelling' translation of Tyndale's New Testament—"Of Diligence and Jeopardy"—where he contrasts "the newer spirit of accommodation" (on the part of "merchants of 'relevance,'" 35) with "an old humility" characterized by diligence of attention to words (*SF*, 23; cf. especially 31, 35, 39).

66. The phrase appears in "The Weight of the Word," *SF*, 138. Here as elsewhere in this collection of essays, Hill illuminates the import of the line "research is not anamnesis."

the question of what the poet means, and whether he or his poem are exceptions to the "rule." Hill's persona confesses, "*Nor is this a primer/ of innocence exactly*"—a colloquialism that hangs on the end of the line a further implicit appeal for precision ("exactly"), also a virtue classified under diligence of attention. But the poet-persona's innocence remains questionable and inexact. Hence, although his own excavation project would incline away from "attenuation" (cf. LXVI, L. 5) and towards anamnesis, here again the barrier to doing so, he insists, belongs as much to himself as to those whom he criticizes. He is a man whose "gift" is that of a "*wounded and wounding/ introspection*" (an ironic allusion to the Eucharist), and who pleads in the following section: "*Remove my heart of stone. Replace/ my heart of stone.*" *Self*-excavation, therefore, is the "rule" he would follow and the "cross" he would bear, as well as a feature of the theological-linguistic "crux" the poem manifests.

The choice of cruciform words here is appropriate. The "*lost cause*" of the self (CXL) is, again, the cause of the lost self—a condition, the poet insists in the previously cited Section LXXV, applies to us all: "*Corner to corner, the careful/ fabric of our lives ripped through/ by the steel claws of contingency*" (LXXV, 38). The words "*Corner to corner*" and "*ripped through*" evoke the Crucifixion, associating the situation of both poet and reader with that of the "*hook . . . of the thorns and nails.*" We, like Christ, are also in one sense "*caught*" and torn; although, in a different sense, we perhaps are not, paradoxically, set free "*by lot*" as a result of his sacrificial act. In either sense, to be bound by contingencies specifies the condition of both the poet and the poem (which the statement "*Talking to oneself is in fact/ a colloquy with occasion*" (39) reiterates), as it also designates the very condition to which Christ subjected himself. The outcome does not seem promising for the poet-persona, however, who confesses (with Dantean overtones), "*Vergine bella, now I am half-way/ and lost — need I say — in this maze of my own/ devising*"; then, having admitted his own deficiencies, concludes this section on a note of passive lament: "*Forget my own name next* in hac/ lacrimarum valle" (39).

In effect, the theological "cross-thwartings" between crucifixion and contingency in this passage do not relieve but intensify the felt condition of the persona. And significantly, that condition is both constituted and conveyed by language (the phrase "maze of my own devising" recalling Ransom's "ontological and semantic straits"). The effort to recover "what remains" and the "shards of downright majesty," like the endeavor to set "at one" or, indeed, to reinstate the possibility of love's triumph, all lie within the common province of the contingent, and all return the poet-persona to his own lostness and the apparently dubious prospects of his art. Still, despite the challenges that also accrue for Hill's persona in light of his cultural context and the vehement opposition of his detractors,[67] he refers to his poem as his "*self-giving*" (VIII), which he subsequently offers to *Vergine bella* as a "tribute," pleading:

> I ask that you acknowledge the work
> as being contributive to your high praise,
> even if no-one else shall be reconciled
> to a final understanding of it in that light. (LV, 29)

Is the poet-persona, then, both a sinner and in some sense a suffering servant, as the allusion to Job in Section XXXI indicates: "*Scabpicking old scab: why should we be salted/ with the scurf of his sores?*" The identification with Job implies an appraisal of his own situation, not only as he stands before men but before God. Does he, then, also imagine being put to the test in order to disclose his own frailties and return glory to God? The poet as servant does appear as a motif in *The Triumph of Love*, and the constant harangue of heckling and invective he is made to endure, including his own self-inflicted variety, certainly comprises suffering of a sort. But to identify the poet-persona with the figure of a "suffering servant" once again risks a form of self-aggrandizement smacking of a contradiction, given the aim of the poem to return praise to others. Yet, the allusion is here, and references to other "suffering servants" abound in the poem.[68] Is the poet-persona of such ilk as these?

The question remains in tension, and Hill himself eschews the identification of his persona with a martyr.[69] Indeed, his clownishness only further accentuates the distance he feels from the suffering of

---

67. "*A noble vernacular?*" he imagines his detractors asking, "*We could screw him,/ finish him for all that . . .*" (CXVII).

68. In addition to Job, Hill refers to numerous biblical figures, most prominently the Virgin Mary and Christ (*Isaiah's prophetically/ suffering servant*," XXIII), as well as saints and martyrs from Church history. To this pantheon of servant-witnesses he also adds artists (Rouault, Bach), and poets (Herbert, Donne, Milton, Wordsworth, Péguy).

69. "The autobiographical element here," he has stated, "would be totally undeserving of the word *martyr*. I think that martyrdom can come in many forms, but I can't think of a clownish martyr" (*PRI*, 284).

others and the virtuous self-sacrifice of those he lauds. Hill has also insisted, however, that he is a *witness*. By and large, as noted, his witness through this poem aims to retrieve the testimonies of others. Hill is also a poet, and he understands both aspects of his vocation in these terms. Accordingly, when he asks himself, "Why should a poet bother to write poems?" he replies, "Everybody has to find his or her own way of witnessing, and the only way I can effectively witness is by writing and by trying to write as well as I can."[70] He continues, "There are things one has to witness to. I return constantly to what I think is one of the major outrages of modern life: the neglect of the dead, and a refusal to what we owe to them, and a refusal to submit ourselves to the wisdom of the dead and, indeed, to the folly of the dead...."[71] Accordingly, his persona declares, "*I write for the dead*" (CIV).

In witnessing to Christ, however, does he also not witness to (and for) the living? His answer, as we have seen in Sections LXVI–II, is yes; or as he earlier affirms, "*If the gospel is heard, all else follows./ We shall rise again, clutching our wounds*" (XVII, 9). True to the habit of mind of Hill's persona, the lines from these sections are as much analyses of the meaning of confession as they are forms of confession itself, and in this respect create space for even the uncommitted to contemplate their significance. In that space, however, the wealth of testimony included in the poem combines to form an assertion: the witness of others represents the deposit of that lost heritage of perception (a "moral landscape") in need of recovery, as much for the poet as, by implication, for ourselves. The "field of assent" that Hill engineers consists of our response to that witness—of our attentiveness to it through the aperture of a converted perspective. His persona's "*shamed gratitude*" represents one form of response. How does the poem also [re-]direct our attention to Christ, and how does Hill's self-staging of a beleaguered poet constitute the potential recovery of a "noble vernacular" suitable for this witness, which, like Sydney's "*Augustinian grace-notes*" and "*Italianate-/Hebraic Milton*" offers a voice "*pitched exactly — / somewhere — between* Laus Deo *and defiance*" (CXVIII, 63)? The poet could not be more explicit in his testimony to Christ when he reprises the "*modalities*" in nature that "*stoop to re-enter the subtrane of faith*" and clarifies, "*faith, that*

---

70. Ibid., 298.
71. Ibid.

is, in real Being;/ the real being God or, more comprehensively, Christ—" (XXXVIII, 20). In such "*harsh times/ with hag Faith going the rounds*" (LXXXVI), however, it seems a greater subtlety is required, which the poem provides through its meditation on and, ultimately, its enactment of that feature of a Christian vision that (strange as it may be to say) encompasses all: *kenosis*.

As the poet-persona continually empties himself of [self-]presumption through repeated acts of "virtuous self-mistrust" that we feel in the very texture of the verse, the energetic pitch of *vituperatio* directed against himself and others follows an arc towards its alternate emphasis. *Kinesis* yields finally to *kenosis*; and it is the kenotic that constitutes the grounds for *Laus*. (The poet-persona's joking about the theme of "*Kinesis* to *Kenosis*" as the title of an imagined literary conference in Section LXXXVI signals this movement. Like other instances of the poem's subtlety, do we catch it?) What this poem ultimately points to through its own series of self-divesting acts is the self-emptying of Christ ("*Isaiah's prophetically/ suffering servant*," XXIII) as the pattern, or model, by which love's triumph emerges, albeit paradoxically. As a result, between the termini of *laus et vituperatio* the poem also carves out a space for the gracious work of God, a need the poet-persona feels keenly. His pride, his anger, his "*Savage indignations/ plighted with self-disgust*" (CIV, 53), collectively paint the portrait of a guilty man. Yet, he is one who knows an experience of grace: "*No matter that the grace is so belated;/ . . . no matter how/ grace is confused, repeatedly, with chill/ euphoria.*" (CIX, 57). His is a plight familiar to many, underscored by the conviction that faith is "*inescapable endurance*" (CXXI), and the confession at the poem's end, "*I find it hard/ to forgive myself*" (CXLIX). Whether or not he numbers himself among "the elect," chosen "*by lot*" to be set free by the "hook" of Christ's "thorns and nails," remains in suspense, as does any final pronouncement regarding the nature or extent of God's grace (see CXXXIX). What is portrayed, and what forms a prism through which this modern poem of the self enables us to glimpse facets of hope in love's triumph, are the acts of self-sacrifice and self-denial he sees in Christ and finds in others (in *imitatio Christi*).

Hill discusses the kenosis of Christ directly in his rarely cited appendix to Lucien Richard's book on this subject.[72] In this short essay

---

72. Op. cit. (n. 14).

"Poetics and the Kenotic Hymn," Hill contends for "a rectified Christian poetics . . . that would compromise itself as little as possible with Christian aesthetics . . . [which are] scarcely to be distinguished from a 'surrogate post-Christian religion of artistic gratification.'"[73] Hill takes his first cue for this argument from the "*negative* ground" established by Barth in his comments on the limits (or "points") of human power in the Epistle to the Corinthians. The human assertion of freedom as an expression of power over things, so Barth contends, tends to decay into a slavery *to* the power of things. Thus, concludes Hill, "if there is to be such a creature as the individual voice, or style, it can exist only as an expression of sustained vigilance along a line that may be understood as a continuum of Barthean [sic] 'points.'"[74] The failure to recognize this, he adds, amounts to "Corinthian self-delusion."

The *positive* ground for "a rectified Christian poetics," Hill then argues, may develop generically out of Rahner's notion of "symbolic reality," but is captured ultimately in the *kenotic* as Fr. Richard describes it: "'An authentic Christology must affirm that Jesus' life is simultaneously characterized by power . . . and by powerlessness.'"[75] This combination, Hill adds, made manifest in space and time and the contingencies of human existence, cannot be accounted for in terms of an "equivalent" expression rendered through "occult" gestures (his summary of "post-Christian" aesthetics). Rather, it requires a "real" expression of that reality, captured most forcefully in the words of the Kenotic Hymn in Philippians 2:5–11. Accordingly, a "poetic kenosis," when true to this pattern, drives towards this original form. Hill writes,

---

73. Ibid., 196. By "Christian aesthetics," Hill means a naïve valorization of artistic effect that draws equally facile identifications between Christian doctrines and their supposed appearance in the thematic strains of literature (e.g., "redemptive themes in 'X'"). As he asserts in "Poetry as 'Menace' and 'Atonement,'" "The major caveat which I would enter against a theological view of literature is that, too often, it is not theology at all, but merely a restatement of the neo-Symbolist mystique celebrating verbal mastery . . . If an argument for the theological interpretation of literature is to be sustained, it needs other sustenance than this" (*LL*, 17).

74. "Kenotic Hymn," 196.

75. Ibid., 197.

> If, as it must be, character is something other than personality, each true act of expression is the making of a character, kenotically conceived: an affirmation of selfhood which, even in the instant of expression, is self-forgetting.[76]

In this light, Hill advances the category of "pure kenotic poetry," found in the Kenotic Hymn as its original statement (as well as a "statement about origin"),[77] replicated in Tyndale's "Englishing of Philippians 2:5–11," and further expressed in, for example, George Herbert's "magisterial . . . yet recurrently and finally self-humbling" verse.[78] It is my contention that *The Triumph of Love* offers a "kenotically conceived" presentation of the self, or at least inclines insistently in this direction—a presentation which is at once self-affirming and "self-forgetting," and through this conception holds forth a peculiarly Christian understanding of love. Nowhere do we see this vision of the kenotic more in evidence than in the section that contemplates the Kenotic Hymn directly.

When Hill's persona introduces the Kenotic Hymn in Section CXLVI, he does not first cite the passage or offer any exegesis of it, but, tellingly, directs attention to Tyndale's faithful *translation* of it:

> A hundred
> words — or fewer — engrafted by Tyndale's
> unshowy diligence:

It is the worker in words acting as the servant of *another* who manifests the qualities that the poem seeks to emphasize. The parenthetical "*— or fewer —*" and the colloquial "*unshowy*" plainly capture this attitude, and render the poem's own rhetorical tribute to the character esteemed in the theologian-scholar.[79] In effect, the passage conveys the view that the truly diligent, and so faithful, laborer does not set out to parade his own gifts, but when a servant of another, employs those gifts to display the other's glory. (We are reminded here of John the Baptist's declaration, "He must increase, but I must decrease," John 3:30.) Thus, the section

76. Ibid.

77. Richard's conclusion, ibid.

78. Ibid. Hill would include Hopkins as well in this category of "kenotic" poets. In Section IX, his narrator states that Hopkins "*had things so nearly right, as did Herbert,/ though neither would have flown solo. . . .*"

79. On Tyndale's diligence and humility, in contrast to the "accommodating" promotional tendencies of contemporary publishers, see once more his essay "Of Diligence and Jeopardy," *SF*, 21ff.

brings two servants to mind: the first being "Isaiah's prophetically suffering servant," the Christ of the "Kenotic Hymn" who, though God,

> ... *made himself of no reputation* ... *took*
> the shape of a servant —

The poet's own reinscription of this passage gives due emphasis to the astounding character of this act: his citation reads simply, "*God ... made himself of no reputation*," making more pronounced the implication that it would be sheer arrogance for human beings to pursue the opposite. (Is this an example of "*a simple text that would strike them/ dumb*" held up in Section LIV as the antidote to the debased and self-promoting manipulations of a celebrity culture?)

At the heart of the account of God-incarnate and of the crucified God is humility, and this, the poet adds with simultaneously disorienting and reorienting effect, "*is our manumission,/ Zion new-centred at the circumference/ of the world's concentration.*" The paradox of kenosis and its outcome could not be stated more cogently. God's self-emptying and "shaping" of himself as a servant subverts the world's proportions, announcing freedom from bondage won at a remove from "*the world's concentration*" (connoting power as well as focus of attention), while establishing a new center of reality, and with this, a new foundation for love. "*Zion new-centered*" conveys a stability that counteracts the "carnal disarray" of the human condition, bringing to the fitful drama of love so trenchantly displayed in this poem the shape of its potential to triumph.

The second servant, or kind of servant, is the human who situates himself or herself within this pattern and seeks to emulate it; who is, in this respect, "Christ-like." Tyndale, with his "*unshowy diligence*," provides one such example; Augustine, Paul and, interestingly, John Ruskin provide three others. On the one hand, what these individuals share in common, according to the emphasis here, is that each labored in language to render and to summon a vision of reality greater than them. Tyndale was a translator and martyr, Augustine a theologian of comprehensive reach and enormous literary output, Paul a martyr-witness, portrayed here as a "reinscriber," and Ruskin the "*Fellow-labouring master-/ servant of* Fors Clavigera" (his letters of exhortation on behalf of British workers). Unlike his literary predecessors, however, Ruskin's style showed "*wedded/ incapacity, for which he has been scourged/ many* times with derision."⁸⁰ But the allusion to Christ subverts that assessment; and so, the poet adds, their derision "*does not/ render his vision blind or his suffering/ impotent.*" As with the charges leveled against Scholastic *Scientia* in Section CXIX or the hypocrisies portrayed in LXVI–VII, judgment returns as an indictment, in this case of the critics for their own lack of vision.

At the same time, all of these "fellow-laborers" (also an allusion to Philippians) are "masters" of their craft. There is no necessary contradiction here. As Hill contends in his discussion of the phrase "our word is our bond," "'Mastery' is as much as is not servitude."⁸¹ Still, the doubled aspect of "*master-servant*" inscribes a further paradox, made explicit here but present in various forms throughout the poem. We hear the same complex of attributes in the phrase "*the Law's/ majesty of surrender*" and in a statement Hill appropriates from Ransom's notion of "the Hebraic *ruah*" present in verse, whose "perfected" result is "'majesty combined with contingency.'"⁸² We needn't press the metaphor of *ruah* towards a vatic claim for poetic inspiration in order to see how this effect nonetheless fits Hill's notion of kenosis and of the master-servant poet who seeks to render it. The poet's "unending *negotium*" with language, his endeavor to "atone" for the fallenness of speech with speech that shows the nature of imperfection while striving towards its own perfection, aims at this same combination of majesty and contingency through the mastery of his craft. In so doing, the master-servant poet mirrors in his work (albeit imperfectly) the economy of kenosis made manifest supremely in Christ. In bearing witness to this example or pattern, however, Hill's persona refuses to lay claim to any finality in this regard, identifying his poem more with the "wedded incapacity" of Ruskin than the "perfections" of Augustine, Tyndale or Paul. His own "kenotically conceived character" once again confirms this estimation, *kinetically* charged as it is with vehement but ambiguous confessions of weakness and sin ("*In whatever direction/* kinesis *takes me, it is no distance*," he confesses in CII).

Still, even here in the poet's complex self-staging we find positive strains of the kenotic at one terminus of its paradox. The poet-persona's

---

80. There is also a double entendre in these lines, as Ruskin was rumored to be sexually impotent.

81. *LL*, 151.

82. Ibid., 133.

description of his "proud-shamed gratitude," for example, or his charge, "*Is it so unjust/ to say to the State Church you lack pride/ and are not ashamed?*" (LXXXIII), strike an antiphonal chord similar in tone to the ones we hear in "master-servant" or "majesty-contingency." More to the point, the place of self-assertiveness made manifest as pride and anger and of *laus et vituperatio* in the economies of virtuous character and virtuous speech reflect their own subtle form of humility. Although the poet-persona fittingly suspects his own innocence as he rails against inattention, forgetfulness and the idols of self-promotion, a passionate regard for truth, this poem asserts, nonetheless calls for aggressive defiance of these aberrations. No claim to be a servant of truth, in other words, can be sustained by one who refuses to defend it. But again, to take such a stance is perilous, fraught with the dangers of self-presumption and a triumphalism that defeats the very thing one would promote ("*But vulnerable, proud/ anger is . . . Pride is our crux: be angry, but not proud/ where that means vainglorious*," CXLVIII, 81). For a poem that ends by insisting that "*we are nowhere/ finally*" and that its own achievement is "*a sad and angry consolation*" the tension of "nothing true is easy" remains unresolved—as unresolved as the piercing ambiguity of its title-theme.

But the paradox of kenosis has another terminus—that of yielding, finally, to the "claws of contingency," and more profoundly, to "the hooks and nails"—not in desperation or despair but in service to a higher calling that promises an eventual alternative outcome. With a restraint in keeping with the poet-persona's tentative "self-giving," his work of excavation approaches this aspect of kenosis indirectly—that is, as something he forcefully indicates but does not claim as his own achievement. Turning again to Section CXLVI, Hill's persona offers this estimation of Tyndale's diligent, "unshowy" translation of the Kenotic Hymn: "*it is all there/ but we are not all there*," adding "*read that how you will.*" (Once more, the matter of place, of "where" we are, resurfaces, only here it is cast within the kenotic.) This last rejoinder, familiar in its ambiguity and eliciting the semantic range which the statement itself connotes, recalls attention to one of the poem's principal concerns: How are we to read? The invitation to read the poem's two-fold reflection from Tyndale's "*hundred words*"—"*it is all there/ but we are not all there*"—issues a challenge both to decide to read and to recognize through reading where one stands with respect to the poem's claims.

What is "all there" is not elaborated directly, though the implication seems clear. The words Tyndale translated and his *manner* of doing so share a common deportment: that of a servant who relinquishes all aspects of personal entitlement and self-promotion. "All there" and the invitation to read thus solicit a distinctively Christian form of self-examination, in response to the question: Where and, significantly, *how* do we find ourselves? The poem pries open that possibility, which becomes the reader's own dilemma and prospect; one that redirects us towards a "new center."

The image of prying, or prising, appears in the final lines, the portrait of Ruskin depicted here concluding:

> to us he appears
> some half-fabulous field-ditcher who prised
> up from a stone-wedged hedge-root, the lost
> amazing crown.

The allusion to Jesus' parable of the Kingdom of God is poignant.[83] The irony that we may dismiss a man as "*some half-fabulous field-ditcher*" when the prize of his labor is "*the lost amazing crown*" reiterates the challenge leveled above, "*it is all there/ but we are not all there.*" The failure to perceive what lies beneath appearances recalls as well Jesus' injunction to the hearers of his parables: "He who has ears to hear, let him hear." It is to what lies at the roots that the poet-persona ultimately presses his reflections, and which he would extract for our own contemplation. The succession of compound words with hard consonants, reminiscent of Hopkins' "sprung rhythm," replicates aurally this act of digging. Thus, when we hear the phrase "*the lost amazing crown*" it appears as if it has been "dug out" of or "prised up" from the language that precedes it. In fact, the inclination of the entire section is designed to culminate in this image, as it progresses through a series of blocked reflections in telescoping fashion. Beginning from the wide scope of "*The whole-keeping of Augustine's City of God*" and "*the Law's/ majesty of surrender*," it narrows through reference to Tyndale's "*hundred words — or fewer*," then contracts further in the citation of two statements from "*Paul's reinscription of the Kenotic Hymn*," arriving finally at "*the lost amazing crown*" that Ruskin has "*prised/ up*" from a "*stone-wedged*

---

83. "The Kingdom of God is like a man who finds a treasure buried in a field, and for joy over it sells all that he has and buys that field" (Matthew 13:44).

hedge-root." Commensurate with this movement, we find increasing density of composition, as the use of bracketed phrases in each of the first three "blocks" compresses into the compact series of accented compound words in the final block.

By such means, Hill creates a vehicle for an intensifying semantic impression: the sense of digging down in order to unearth, conveyed through the pitch of his composition. As a result, the "amazing crown" emerges as the "crux" of attention, capturing in an image a sensate focal point for the "centering" pronouncement that also falls in the central lines of this section: "*God . . . made himself of no reputation . . . took/ the shape of a servant — .*" Where the section leaves us provides as well a point of *departure* for the entire poem: an act of self-forgetting that displaces the persona's preoccupation with his own reputation—managed, finally, but paradoxically, by the mastery of the poet's craft—which prompts the reader (if one is willing to heed the implicit invitation) to seek out the same. As the poem slides from the pronouncement "*it is all there*" to the lament in the following section "*we are nowhere/ finally*" and the pitched cry "*to be healed . . . to be/ healed, and die!*" (81), "the lost amazing crown" receives its contrapuntal accent, returning us once more to that condition which makes the poem's witness to its appearance cognizant of our deepest spiritual need.

Conclusion: Contingency, Intensity, and Indirection

Thus, the poem concludes by registering the same complex of emotions which Hill has cultivated throughout—a poignant sense of deprivation coupled with urgent longing for restoration and for a place to stand. In effect, the temper of Hill's tragic farce of the self inclines more towards the former mood. At the same time, the kenotic strain of the poem and its meditations on Christ and other emulators of self-forgetting service poses a question we are left to contemplate: Whether the tragic marks a finality about our existence or an element susceptible of a new possibility? That Hill does not present the latter as an *inevitability* but only permits its prospect to emerge from the disfigured landscape of the self *in situ* he depicts intensifies the tragic stress in his persona's (and our own) condition. We feel the pitch of lostness as well as longing in the "brute mass and detail" of the broken world and in the "acoustical din" he re-creates; and much of his poetic power consists of his ability to imbue his verse with the reality of these imperfections—even, as we have seen, as the conditions of his own medium.

Yet, in his witness to the kenotic he weaves into these very contextures the remnant of a different order of perception, however neglected or forgotten even by those who confess adherence to its claims. Here also we find undertones of the tragic, but it is a tragedy that bears the promise of transformation: "*our manumission,/ Zion new-centred at the circumference/ of the world's concentration.*" Tragedy, in other words, is both the condition of our own *un*making and the seedbed of our remaking, and it is a tribute to Geoffrey Hill's poetic skill and his insight as a Christian thinker that both aspects are held in creative tension throughout *The Triumph of Love* as the pressure points of a personal drama. Hence, although his persona insists, "*We have already been sent to the dark/ wood, by misdirection . . ./ and are there still, in a manner of speaking*" (CXXXV), the poet's own method involves redirecting our attention through mostly *indirect* appeals to a Christian economy of redemption, one which unfolds *within* the contingencies of existence.

To say, then, that Geoffrey Hill demonstrates a "style of faith" in *The Triumph of Love* requires us to situate this poem within a distinct mode of theological thought as well as a distinctive method of theological expression (Hill's style we will return to presently). Central to both, and the focus of our regard for this poem's contribution to Christian theology and witness, is an understanding of the Incarnation as the meeting point of majesty and contingency and of mastery and servitude made manifest in the self-giving of God. To inquire after a language of faith from this poem, therefore, is to ask: What does the language of *kenotic* faith look like, and what is its significance to Christian witness in this age?

The theological reflections of moral philosopher D. M. MacKinnon offer cogent insight in response to these questions. Three themes from MacKinnon's thought, which form a nexus concentrated on the meaning of God-incarnate, serve to illuminate and confirm the merits of Hill's "kenotically conceived" presentation of the self. The first involves MacKinnon's Incarnational epistemology, derived through his own protracted *negotium* between the abstractions of metaphysical idealism and the narrowness of the Positivist critique of knowledge. MacKinnon found in the Incarnation a mode of theology that permits both streams, or "styles," of thought. On the one hand, he admitted that "no religion easily survives without a theology and theology is almost inevitably drawn to the style of metaphysics,"[84] while on the other hand he emphatically insisted that the Incarnation demands adherence to the facts, or as he often put it, a commitment to recognizing the "way things are." MacKinnon gives this realist position its distinctively Christian theological and historical emphasis in his use of the phrase "*in concreto*" to describe the "manifestation of omnipotence" we see in John's presentation of Christ.[85] Elsewhere, he declares succinctly, "Jesus is sheerly concrete, sheerly particular," the one who consequently makes the love of God "concrete in the depth of human history."[86] For this reason, MacKinnon—sounding a theme that proves crucial to Hill's poetic vision—delineates the relationship between philosophy and christology (and, significantly, the relationship of the latter to "Christian theology") as "the problem of *contingency*."[87] He writes, "To acknowledge the supremacy of the Christology [sic] is to confess that finality belongs somehow to that which is particular and contingent . . ."[88]

In this last statement, and as we have seen from our study of *The Triumph of Love*, the question of "where" emerges as a central concern in the pursuit of meaning: Where do we look for truth and where has truth been disclosed? Where does the self look in order to find itself? And, as MacKinnon elaborates directly and Hill intimates, where do we find love? For both, the answers lie not in concepts or abstractions, but in the "stuff" (as MacKinnon, echoing Charles Williams, calls it) of existence, *in concreto*—that is, that place where we find ourselves and can only find ourselves, both in the sense of our condition and any prospect for redeeming it. For MacKinnon, as again more implicitly for Hill, such a prospect emerges within the contingent because that is where we find God in Christ, or more precisely, the "*deed*" of God performed by Christ. He writes, "the deeper we penetrate the ultimate conditions of human existence—the sheerly intractable that seems to defy the imposition of rational order—the nearer we approach that with which

---

84. MacKinnon, *Borderlands of Theology*, 217.
85. MacKinnon, *Problem of Metaphysics*, 119; cf. 7, 120, 121.
86. *Borderlands*, 67, 68.
87. Ibid., 75; my italics.
88. Ibid., 58.

the deed of Christ seems to engage."[89] In this respect, Hill's presentation of the human condition (with its "*steel claws*" and the "*thorns and nails*") and the arc from kinesis to kenosis track a similar approach—and destination. As we find in Hill's poem, MacKinnon's mediations on Christian perception compel a relentless return to "the rich and dark complexity of human reality" that Christ engaged, to which he delivered himself, and which his interpreters must not alleviate or diminish in the name of acquiring a false "intellectual security."[90] Thus he speaks repeatedly of "the tragedy of Jesus" and of a "Christian faith [that] is ultimately to be found . . . in the stuff of human tragedy."[91] MacKinnon's sensibility here explains his prolonged attention to literary works, particularly tragedies. In that they too explore and expose the complexities, ambiguities, and "the genuinely tragic texture of the human condition," they are incomparable resources for Christian self-reflection that weigh against a tendency to "belittle" that aspect of our condition—that is, he contends, if we are to understand aright the import of the Incarnation and not "hide" from others "the features of . . . Christ."[92]

The evident affinity between MacKinnon's Christian realism and Hill's "tragic farce" in their determined regard for the contingent as the context of meaning and of meaning-making grows only more profound when we turn to the closely related second theme of the kenosis of Christ. Not surprisingly, MacKinnon's meditations on this theme show the same motifs as we find in his treatment of Incarnational epistemology. What he calls (echoing Hill's vernacular) the "theological crux" of the Incarnation[93] he expands to include kenosis, which, he contends, is "always to be understood in close connection with a *theologia cruces*."[94] Furthermore, says MacKinnon, although God's self-giving is finally an "ontological mystery," it manifests "the manner of the presence of God

---

89. "Absolute and Relative in History," in MacKinnon, *Explorations in Theology 5*, 68. In this vein, he clarifies that the mystery of God is "a mystery of action" (67), and "that mystery is of a God engaged to give sense to history by receiving from human existence the very depths of its problems" (68).

90. Ibid., 69. Accordingly, he chastens a "tendermindedness which would diminish actuality to the level of human concept, which would evacuate human life of its deeply tragic element in the name of an intellectual security" (ibid., 67–68).

91. MacKinnon, *Stripping of the Altars*, 50, 93.

92. *Explorations*, 10; cf. 6.

93. "Scott Holland and Contemporary Needs," *Borderlands*, 108.

94. *Explorations*, 67.

... to his creatures."[95] In Christ's consummate act of self-emptying on the cross we see once more not the expression of an idea or a concept, but "a raw piece of human history"—"that human deed in which the abysses of existence are sounded."[96] The kenosis of the Son, in other words, takes us further into the fabric of the familiar; though in the depths it "sounds" we are confronted with the ultimately unfathomable (a "*fathomless pool*," as the Arthuriad images it). As MacKinnon says of our response to the phenomenon of God-incarnate in general, "We must perceive the thing in its strangeness, in order to school ourselves to grasp its ultimate reality in the desperately familiar..."[97]

In addition, he insists, there is in the kenosis of Christ made consummate in his "obedience unto death" "an unmistakably tragic quality" seen especially in John's perception of Christ's sufferings.[98] His view here militates against a simplistic triumphalism,[99] and calls upon interpreters to see once more how thoroughly Christ has entered into and accepted the conditions of our humanity. "[I]n Christ," he writes in "Kenosis and Self-Limitation," "the invulnerable made itself vulnerable, and this vulnerability is not something episodic, but belonging to heaven itself."[100] That there is triumph in the Resurrection MacKinnon harbors no doubt, declaring its certainty as "the way it is" (and with a great deal less ambiguity than we find in *The Triumph of Love*).[101] At issue for him, rather, is what "posture" we adopt with respect to Christ's means of achieving it. Hence, he affirms that the suffering of Christ

---

95. *Borderlands*, 80, 79.

96. "Atonement and Tragedy," ibid., 102, 104.

97. "Miracle, Irony, Tragedy," *Metaphysics*, 121. MacKinnon strikes a similar note in his appraisal of Christ's parables, writing, "they have the unquestioned advantage of focusing in completely concrete terms the central metaphysical concern – that of reaching through the familiar to its alleged transcendent ground, without evacuating that familiar of its own proper dignity" ("Parable, Ethics, Metaphysics I," ibid., 82).

98. "The Transcendence of the Tragic," ibid., 125.

99. As MacKinnon argues in his "Conclusion" to *Metaphysics*, "Inevitably tragic perception rejects any method of dealing with the reality of evil by appeal to a facile teleology" (ibid., 169).

100. "Epilogue" to *Themes in Theology*, 232.

101. See *Resurrection: A Dialogue*. Although MacKinnon elsewhere will in a qualified sense speak of "the *finally* tragic failure of Christ's passion" (*Stripping of the Altars*, 93), in "Parable and Sacrament" he admonishes his readers of our need to be "schooled to perceive tragedy without loss of hope" (*Explorations*, 179).

presents "the only key we have to the inner ways of God, and the only sure guide to the posture befitting us in the world he has fashioned."[102] It is a posture that admits "life's roughest edges," and takes its measure from the deed of Christ—"its rough, untidy, always concrete actuality"—as that very "shape" or "restored patterning" which God has given to our existence.[103] And here there appears the ground for our third theme from MacKinnon, which regards the matter of theological *styles*.

In *The Stripping of the Altars*, MacKinnon sets before the Church and her teachers the task "to seek the forms of post-Constantinian existence *both in respect of inter-Church relations and in respect of presence to the world*."[104] Central to this quest, he contends in "Kenosis and Establishment," is "the way of kenosis," "one of the key ideas required for the renewal of the Church's understanding of its mission."[105] In this trenchant critique of the Church's institutional posture, MacKinnon pleads for "a radical reformation of ecclesiastical styles" vis à vis "the radical application of the law of *kenosis*," which, he believes, will help to "reconstruct" how Christians commend their faith to others.[106] Thus, MacKinnon envisions a Church whose "witness to the truth ... no more relies on the compulsive power of superior propaganda than it does on that of physical force," but is "receptive, expectant, always seeking to fulfil [sic] the law of self-emptying," a form of receptivity that, from Christ's own example, we find "belongs to God as he is in himself."[107] Christian witness in its multiple forms, therefore, assumes an open posture, in keeping with the radically vulnerable character of "the Incarnate."[108] In sum, taken together with his commitment to the contingent as the ground of meaning, MacKinnon's appeal for a *christocentric*, kenotic

102. *Borderlands*, 111.
103. *Explorations*, 68.
104. Op. cit., 10; MacKinnon's italics.
105. Ibid., 14, 15.
106. Ibid., 25, 28, 19 respectively.
107. Ibid., 21–22, 24. It is this same kenotic temperament that he commends in the style of Scott Holland who, MacKinnon comments, recognized through an emphasis upon the *Christus-patiens* of Jesus that "persuasion is superior to force in being" (*Borderlands*, 114; cf. 118).
108. Here again, MacKinnon includes the element of the tragic as an integral feature in this witness—a feature constitutive of Christ's as well as our own experience from which, for this reason, we needn't seek deliverance "but the presence of the ground that alone makes possible the endurance of its burden" (*Stripping of the Altars*, 40).

theological style and witness commends that which takes us deeply and receptively into the fabric of human existence as we find it and as Christ engaged it. It is in his sustained attention to the "actuality" of God-incarnate that both his analysis and appeal prove most convincing in respect of the Church's comprehension of its public tasks.

We may, of course, imagine multiple forms of a kenotic style, including those which wed boldness with receptivity in the endeavor to persuade, and which return others to a contemplation of the central revelation of God in Christ.[109] We have observed also in *The Triumph of Love* a further strain of the kenotic as MacKinnon understands and applies it, one which we have named Hill's *implicit* approach to the theme of kenotic love that "signals" its potentiality (however muted), and which we may also designate as a style of *indirection*.[110] MacKinnon provides this appraisal of Hill's poetry with a theological context for its merits as a method comprising the Church's public tasks, finding in indirection an approach that bears the stamp of his kenotic christology—which insists upon the supreme importance of the "proximate object of faith" while admitting our own inadequacy to grasp and articulate it fully. He observes this dynamic in the "peculiar indirection" of the parables, whose genius it is "to hint, or more than hint, at ways in which things are" and at "that which transcends."[111] In their "openness of texture" and "interrogative quality" MacKinnon finds a pattern for theological speaking that is commensurate with Christ's own stance in the world.[112] In Hill's vernacular, a "theological crux" inhabits a "linguistic crux," whereby words *enact* sense in a convergence of form and substance. MacKinnon's sympathy with Wittgenstein's "*thrusting against the limits of language*" as an epigraph for what it means to be "metaphysically minded" is apposite to this same pattern or style, as is his belief (paral-

---

109. MacKinnon's respect for Holland's sermons notes this blend of elements, which includes the preacher's "bold, almost extravagant language" as well as his patient receptivity (*Borderlands*, 109).

110. In his essay "Some aspects of the 'grammar' of 'incarnation' and 'kenosis': reflections prompted by the writings of Donald MacKinnon," Kenneth Surin appraises the philosopher's style similarly, writing: "MacKinnon's is very much a method of 'indirection'" (*Christ, Ethics and Tragedy*, 93).

111. *Metaphysics*, 79, 80.

112. "Parable and Sacrament," *Explorations*, 168, 179. In this vein, he speaks of the "desperately human speech of the Incarnate" (173).

leling those of Janet Soskice and Paul Ricoeur) that theology inevitably involves "a metaphorical groping" for the ultimate.[113]

What Geoffrey Hill brings to this method or style and to the distinctively christological overtures we find in *The Triumph of Love* is pitch of attention—a dramatic intensity conveyed through its densely textured, spatial imagination. The poem's manner of holding forth then withdrawing, of disorienting in order to reorient, and of generating intense moods that ricochet between the farcical and the tragic while insisting that a force as stable as "active virtue" and a rich deposit of grace, dignity and individual love have been evident—all combine to create a pitch of inattention that reciprocates acute attentiveness. In so doing, Hill's poem produces a textual environment, a "contexture," for his self-excavating choreography that refracts through the shadows and din of stark contingency the traces of a kenotic vision. Viewed in this light, his persona's confession that "nothing true is easy" defines both the urgent aim and the expressive challenge of the poet's "struggle for a noble vernacular," as, I would argue, it does for the witnessing Church.

At the same time, in regarding *The Triumph of Love* as a form of Christian theology it is crucial to affirm that indirectness does not mean vagueness. As we have seen from our study in Hill, and as MacKinnon confirms, a method of indirection grounded in a kenotic form of humility does not require passivity on the part of those who bear witness to the self-giving of Christ, and who seek to do so in the very manner of that self-giving. On the contrary, the persuasive power of suggestiveness bears with it (if I may appropriate for a different context a phrase from MacKinnon) "capacities of recognition" that enlarge perception and our ability to apprehend.[114] In that much of this recognition in *The Triumph of Love* directs our attention to and enacts the strains of the tragic does not displace but, as MacKinnon asserts, deepens our awareness of God's profound participation in our condition in the shape of a suffering servant. The persistent return to one's self *in situ* that Hill engineers—a self who confronts the depredations of his world and of his own fallen character, and a self who would, nonetheless, remember love—is the portrayal of a self who stands in this place of the tragic and

---

113. *Metaphysics*, 17 (my italics); "Metaphor in Theology," *Themes*, 72.

114. MacKinnon uses this phrase to describe the nature of Kant's concepts, *Metaphysics*, 8.

finds there not only the things that are "irrevocable"[115] but the potential for things to be redeemed.

Finally, and in conclusion, it may be that, as Donald MacKinnon says regarding the response of Christ to his executioners, "silence is the most eloquent witness of all."[116] We find a similar appeal, but with a paradoxical twist, made by Hill's poet-persona when he pleads:

> Even now, I tell myself, there is a language
> to which I might speak and which
> would rightly hear me;
> responding with eloquence; in its turn,
> negotiating sense without insult
> given or taken.
> Familiar to those who already know it
> elsewhere as justice,
> it is met also in the form of silence. (XXXV, 18–19)[117]

To speak eloquently to the eloquence of justice and of silence, to articulate the *mot juste* that rightly responds to justice's often-silent refrain—however we attempt to anatomize the ligatures of this appeal, in the end the poet-witness remains the servant of his own medium. And there, finally, we find him: still troubled by his own immortality, but having pronounced the possibility of love, "*still writing.*"

---

115. The word is MacKinnon's, when he warns against a view "which leaves out of account the presence in human life of the sheerly irrevocable, of that which has been done, and it is now too late to undo, of the damage inflicted on others that cannot be put right and that no interpretation can possible [sic] render edifying" ("Good Friday and Easter: An Interpretation," *Resurrection*, 83).

116. "The Controversial Bishop Bell," *Stripping of the Altars*, 92.

117. Hill addresses the 'eloquence' of silence in his provocative essay "Language, Suffering, and Silence."

5

Conclusion

Capacities of Recognition (and Resonance) and the Public Tasks of Christian Theology

W<small>E MIGHT APPLY</small> M<small>AC</small>K<small>INNON'S SALIENT PHRASE TO ALL MANNER OF</small> discourse, insofar as it captures a common ambition (if not always a result) to make recognizable the object(s) being contemplated or the subject being conveyed. In the discourses of Christian theology the endeavors to clarify, to confirm, to compel attention and to persuade, may all be said to involve the pursuit of such capacities. Because theologies of the Christian faith inherently look towards a public horizon—comprising a *holding forth* as well as a *holding together*—the aim to make Christ and Christian beliefs recognizable seems specially urgent as the Church stands within as well as in dialogue with the cultures in which it finds itself. To reiterate the familiar contention made at the outset of this thesis, the very substance of Christian faith's deepest conviction—that God assumed our humanity in order to 'explain' himself to us (John 1:18) on the way to redeeming us—forcefully suggests one conclusion on the part of Christ's followers. Their task as thinkers and witnesses seeks commensurate patterns of disclosure—an active embodiment of their faith in deeds, including the deeds of speech. Put otherwise, God's *accommodation* to us in Christ (in a more robust sense of the word than Geoffrey Hill intends in a different context) inaugurated an interminable work of translation of the Christian message into idioms that can be comprehended by the Church's audiences—an unending 'colloquy with occasion', to borrow Hill's apt phrase.

In this light, we may argue further that an unrecogniz*able* Christianity is a contradiction in terms. The gospel itself makes recognition paramount as a feature of theology's formal presentations—not only to the Church but to the uncommitted as well, wherever Christians seek to bear witness effectively. We hear pronouncements of this sensibility in Paul's aim "to become all things to all men" as the proper burden of the witness who "has made himself a slave to all that he may indeed win some" (1 Cor. 9) or, from our own study, in Charles Williams' "Way of the Affirmation of Images." As again Rowan Williams insists in his description of a responsive theology's "communicative task," the effort to persuade calls for "a theology experimenting with the rhetoric of its uncommitted environment," making its message communicable "across the boundaries." Christian faith's own gospelled convictions confirm this ambition.

Accordingly, my argument for the contribution of poetry to Christian theology's public tasks may also be construed as a study in the capacities of recognition that these poems afford. My answer to the question "Can poetry matter to Christian theology?" has proceeded to demonstrate a method of reading poetry theologically (a "demonstration in pursuit of a method") with a view to discovering how these poems present a distinctively Christian form of engagement and a significant resource for Christian persuasion. This has required us repeatedly to situate the poetry within a theological context (without abrogating its own integrity), even as we endeavor to situate theology within its late-modern cultural context; and to do both in regard to the missionary task of the Church. It is along these lines especially that the matters of recognition, and with it, resonance, acquire their urgency. That the poems of Charles Williams, Micheal O'Siadhail, and Geoffrey Hill manifest a scrupulous intelligence commensurate with the rigors of academic theology is evident from our analyses of their art (as well as their critical thought). But more to the point of my larger theme of poetry as a form of theological discourse and witness, we have said that through their verse these poets "make legible," and so recognizable, facets of a Christian vision that finds its center in God-incarnate. In the following summary, this common thread will help to synthesize the results of our study and to refine our analysis of its import for the challenges now facing the Church in its public witness.

Although I did not intend it when selecting these particular poems, they each in turn take up as a prominent theme a central feature of the Christian confession and experience: those of faith, hope, and love. In each of these poems we do find reflection on all three of these themes; but without over-determining the theological thrust we discover in each, we may in broad strokes align them accordingly. In Williams' Arthuriad we observed how his presentation of a world proceeds "under the sign," and signs, of Incarnational faith. In the battle of perspectives he stages between his king's poet Taliessin and the king, the images derivative of an Incarnational vision of immanent glory, and a *"capacity of faith"* (*RSS*, 122) in keeping with that vision, emerge as decisive with respect to human flourishing. The "complex yes" of Micheal O'Siadhail's redress of history in *The Gossamer Wall* then issues in a meditation on hope—on its difficulty as well as its eventual demands in the face of undeniable evil, and in the *faces* of those who have been evil's victims. And Geoffrey Hill's troubled engagement with the prospects for love to triumph in the wake of irrepressible human suffering, frailty and fallenness leads to intimations that such a possibility resides ultimately in a kenotic love. When we consider that faith, hope and love are all closely tied to witness in Scripture (See, e.g., Heb 11:1–12:3; 1 Pet 3:15; and John 13:35; 17:21 respectively), their presentation in these poems more firmly establishes the potential contribution of these works to the Church's public witness.

Still, in drawing attention to the development of Christian thematics we have only begun to appraise the results of our demonstration. More than critical readings imbued with a theological gloss, I have sought to show how these poems manifest works of theological engagement in the substance of their formal composition. Our studies in images, diction, rhythm and rhyme patterns, structure and syntax have pointed to one common emphasis: that Christian theological sense is conveyed through the form of these poems. That is, the formal elements serve to *enact* the strains of a Christian vision of life and of an Incarnational theology rather than merely embellishing Christian ideas, and do so to advantage in regard to Christian witness. That a poem's *peculiar advantages* include embellishment or enhancement is readily apparent, although the nature and import of that phenomenon and its *affective* results are rarely explored within christological categories such as I have emphasized in this study. So, for example, what Charles Williams contemplates under the rubric of a "feeling intellect," or the wedding of emotional intensity and intellectual insight characteristic of images and of poetic speech in general, he transposes into a pursuit of "more vivid forms of glory and grace," which finds its impulse and ultimate grounding in the acts of Christ the "arch-natural image." In his Arthuriad, the result is a "conversion of Christian thought into images"; and by the development of his christological figures and Incarnational pageantry he offers a *dramatization* of immanent glory instantiated by the "in-Godding of man." His presentation of Christian faith re-imagined within the contextures of history and myth yields an enlargement of the deeply human implications of God-incarnate, such that by the visionary power of his art, we—like his poet-protagonist Taliessin—might also be "*caught by a pulse of truth in the image*."[1] In this regard, Williams' "Christian habit of mind" made evident in his imagistic verse confirms what Janet Soskice contends is the capacity of figurative discourse to generate "new possibilities of vision"—possibilities that extend the proper task of theology understood, in Williams' formula, as "the measurement of eternity in operation."

Micheal O'Siadhail's "poetics of testimony" and "poetry of remembrance" in *The Gossamer Wall* effect a similar convergence of form and theological substance, and of careful reflection and emotive force. Through the architecture of his poetic suite and the verbal-musical texture of his images and rhythm and rhyme patterns, he invigorates traditional poetic forms with the capacity to recognize and to heed the human face of suffering and evil. His achievement as a "witness of witnesses" to "clear away and lay bare" in order to distil and disclose brings to the anxious plight of hope the power of the poetic imagination to exact a recovery of the past that "brokers" a present redemptive possibility—the prospect of a "*healing trust.*" And by recasting history in the shape of commemoration or of "remembering well," he displaces the imposition of overarching interpretive schemes in favor of impelling our attention to the *particulars* of the "other." As a result, he creates proximity to their lived experiences as a means of issuing a summons to readers to be "co-rememberers." It is here, in this transfiguration of "living-dead" victims into the "dead-living" faces, and voices, of *neighbors* that O'Siadhail's *Gossamer* suite discharges its distinctively Christian impulse. Under the pressure he induces to take seriously the demands of loving our neighbor, his poetics of testimony and remembrance manifest what we referred to as an "ethics of form," the very urgency of which derives from

---

1. *RSS*, 127.

the keen acts of attention which his poetry *performs*.[2] This "recognition of a universal summons in the *faces* of the particular," also re-inscribed through the poet's subtle fusion of testimony and story (including biblical narratives), manifests in turn what Paul Ricoeur emphasizes as the distinct advantage of poetic discourse. Ricoeur's contention that such language bears a unique ability to "redescribe reality," and in such capacity that it "restores to us that participation-in or belonging-to an order of things," O'Siadhail reifies in the "complex yes" of his poem and its gentle but insistent invitation "*to try to look, to try to see.*"

Also in a pattern of the spatial imagination and with a similar mandate to remember and to *see* rightly, Geoffrey Hill's "tragic farce" and "choreography of the self" in *The Triumph of Love* interfuses density of expression and moral as well as spiritual intelligence. His persona's struggle to recover, to hear and to see anew a 'lost heritage of perception' within and against an "acoustical din" makes the conditions of the self *in situ* he portrays and the urgency of the questions "Where am I?"/"Where are we?" palpably available. And with equal intensity, through the kinetic *pitch* of his "self-rectifying cadence" and his work of excavation he "*prises*" from "the ontological and semantic straits" of language the strains of a kenotic vision born of the tragic, fallen fabric of the human condition (its "claws of contingency"). This "kenotically conceived" presentation, we noted, both reflects and enacts what Donald MacKinnon referred to as "the way of kenosis," which for him—as with Hill's notion of "poetic kenosis"—calls for distinctively christological *styles* of thought and expression. It is within the very "contextures" of his medium that Hill focuses our attention in this direction, conveying through the composition of his verse a "theological crux," which is also a "linguistic crux"—a style of kenotic faith that provokes us to

---

2. In this vein, from O'Siadhail and especially Hill, I take issue with Oliver Davies's contention in *A Theology of Compassion* that poetry has no *performative* value for Christian ethics: that it is a powerful but ultimately self-referential "*aesthetic*" phenomenon, for which theology—because it is a "*critical*" discipline responsive to the word(s) of God—has little use when it seeks to convey Christianity's ethical stance in the world. Davies bases his distinction entirely upon an amalgam of structuralist and post-structuralist theories of poetry, and not at all on a reading of *poems* such as I have offered here, in order to see what they in fact *do*—thus demonstrating the *opposite* of his position. I have critiqued Davies' views along these lines and contrasted them with Hill in particular in a paper titled "Poetry and the Ethics of Speech," delivered at Oxford to the Society for the Study of Christian Ethics (September 2002).

contemplate our own stance and place in the world ("*it is all there, but we are not all there*") under the tutelage of a kenotic love. Furthermore, his scene of writing that reciprocates in our experience of the poem the scene of reading *attentively*—of reading through in order to regain lost or dulled *capacities* of perception and apprehension—comprises the suggestive power of his poetic vision. His persona's prayer, "*mend our attention/ if it is not too late*," both captures the poet's aim and indicates the donation we receive from his achievement.

In significant ways, Geoffrey Hill's poem and critical reflections articulate much of what I have sought to demonstrate regarding the contribution of poetry to Christian theology and witness—a poetry that itself, in the verse of these poets, manifests its own form *of* theological expression. Still within the category of capacities of recognition but under the aspect of Hill's emphasis on pitch of attention, we are led to consider a range of formal advantages that accrue around the 'patterning of particulars' that these poems perform. Charles Williams' insistent plea for "accuracy, accuracy, and again accuracy! accuracy of mind and accuracy of emotion" is apposite in this regard. (As we have observed, to his Christian habit of mind accuracy reflects both a virtue of successful poetic statement *and* the "exact" nature of glory made manifest in the "acts of Messias.") The achievement of pitch and the attention it engenders depend upon such precision, and we have seen how each of these poets proves a master of this quality through his own variety of poetic composition and deployment of formal devices. Accordingly, poets both attend (and cause us to attend) to the particular and also vivify the "brute mass and detail" of human experience and the human condition, accomplishing both as a function of their ordered speaking. We think again in this regard of T. S. Eliot's insistence upon the interfusion of "precise emotion" and "precise thought," and his estimation of "the poet who thinks" as one "who can express the emotional equivalent of thought."[3] The combination of these intellectual and affective qualities of precision facilitated by attention to particulars indicates two further distinct benefits of poetry's pitch of attention to the tasks of Christian witness.

---

3. "Shakespeare and the Stoicism of Seneca," in *Essays*, 115. Eliot elaborates, "We talk as if thought was precise and emotion was vague. In reality there is precise emotion and there is vague emotion. To express precise emotion requires as great intellectual power as to express precise thought" (ibid.).

First, as it pertains to the Church's engagement with its various publics, against the tendencies to generalize noted in my Introduction there is an urgent need for accuracy in any assessment and critique of culture. Viewed in this light, we may add to Ricoeur's appraisal of poetic speech's ability to redescribe reality (by way of enlarging and refining our capacity to apprehend an order of things) the commendation of poets as able *describers* of reality;[4] or as Charles Williams puts it, as ones who help us to apprehend "things as they are."[5] There arises in this regard an ethical concern as well as an issue of effective persuasion. Hill solicits our alertness to it under the category of an "*Active virtue*" made evident in "*the struggle for a noble vernacular*" and the "*shaping, voicing*" that "*are types of civic action*," which he advances in his own verse through his respect for the contingent. Similarly, underlying Micheal O'Siadhail's "*summons* to try to look, to try to see" is an obligation to virtue required of witness-bearers; a "gentleness and reverence" made possible only by sustained attentiveness to the other, to one's *neighbor*. The pitch of attention he achieves in *The Gossamer Wall* bears that responsibility directly, demonstrating evident restraint in the very textures of his composition even as he elicits provocative reprisals of human experiences of the Holocaust.

The lesson for the witnessing Church seems plain, and can be plainly stated. Attention to the particular and accuracy of description comprise a first order task, indeed duty, of Christian persuasion—of a Church that would listen and seek to see clearly as a prerequisite for speaking. In the "school of the poets," Williams' Arthuriad reminds us, we find the "study of precision";[6] and it is this attribute they return to a Church in need of "education in attentiveness or reverence, and in alertness to the languages we use," as Nicholas Lash admonishes; and who, adds Lash, must therefore engage "the unending *discipline* in learning how to speak." Or as David Ford contends, making explicit the

---

4. In "The Language of Faith" (1973), an essay to which we will return in our next section, it is in fact Paul Ricoeur who calls for "*a philosophic anthropology*" because it offers "a description of human existence, of the human condition, [which] has value as *prediscourse* with respect to preaching . . ." (*Philosophy*, 227; his italics).

5. Commenting on Dante's *De Monarchia*, Williams writes in *Figure*: "The chief business of man is at any moment to be realizing his powers of intellectual apprehension—to understand, to the utmost of his capacity, things as they are" (91).

6. *TLL*, 48.

connection I want to establish, "To be just in our seeing requires a long apprenticeship, learning from those with practised eyes ... Artists can draw us into the complexities of this apprenticeship."[7] In light of our study, we would say also that it is poets who excel in this apprenticeship in speech.

A second benefit to Christian theology and witness derivative of the poet's pitch of attention regards *resonance* as well as recognition. Although I stated in my Introduction that resonance is a "vehicle" for recognition, we observe from our studies in these poems that both qualities interact simultaneously within a common dynamic, and produce a united effect. At issue is the capacity to foster identification and with it participation (though, as we shall observe, not without provocation) as crucial elements in efforts to persuade.[8] In that a supreme challenge confronting gospel witnesses in late-modern societies involves gaining the attention of the unbelieving and uncommitted *at all*—that is, persuading them even to listen attentively—then the need to "realize the contact," as Charles Taylor puts it, becomes as much an imperative as the need for accuracy of description (the latter, of course, is also a condition for the former). Here again, these poets school us in methods of doing so in speech, in an ordering of words that express a particular—that is, a "particularistic"—quality. Donald MacKinnon puts the matter cogently within its theological purview when, speaking of the Incarnation, he admonishes that we must "school ourselves to grasp its ultimate reality in the desperately familiar."

It is the word "desperately" that conveys the sense of pitch, which our poets evoke with such force that their readers' capacity to identify with their vision increases in proportion not only to the familiar, but to what may be wholly unfamiliar to them as well. So, Charles Williams' dramatization in images of kingdoms in conflict and the machinations of power, of ambition, of human bodies, romance and sexuality, indeed of the poetic imagination itself and the "passionate reason" that attends

---

7. *Self and Salvation*, 22.

8. David Cunningham offers a helpful survey of the elements of persuasion and a convincing case for the revival of rhetoric in the discourses of theology in his book *Faithful Persuasion*. See especially his section on *pathos* (42ff.) in which he advance and elaborates the profile of a "rhetorically sophisticated theologian" (51) who seeks to reverse "the general neglect of rhetoric [that] has allowed the audience to disappear from most theological discourse" (43–44).

its pursuits, all provide touchstones of the desperately familiar. By speaking "the language of our common blood," his poetry offers pathways to a supervening vision of immanent glory. His development of images—like those of O'Siadhail and Hill in their more manifestly lyric moments—displays a passionate intelligence that not only retraces the very ligaments of our familiar desires and gives them body, but simultaneously retrieves them within an Incarnational vision that holds forth the promise of their fulfillment. So too, Micheal O'Siadhail's recovery and re-presentation of "*spoors of memory*" by and through which he engraves the hallows of history and the "*gaunt silences*" of millions of "*muted dead*" with the 'fondled faces' of real people, endows his appeals to hope with substance. Because he enables us to feel the import of their humanity, his endeavor to "convey the possibility that memory can deepen then re-emerge in a new vitality" advances with the full force of conviction towards the prospect of a "healing trust"—proportionate to the value and dignity he so assiduously asserts and restores. We assent to such possibilities, in other words, because they *emerge from* his acts of attention. Hence, when O'Siadhail introduces the traces of Judeo-Christian narratives of redemption, their hopeful strains also acquire new vitality for readers because, through the "reciprocal economy" he generates as "*a moment when testimony and story meet*," he "re-inscribes" these narratives with the lived experiences of others with whom we are enabled to identify.

In *The Triumph of Love*, then, resonance with Hill's vision of love—or more precisely, of its *plight* and the conditions necessary for its renewed possibility—largely depends upon our capacity to identify with the figure of the poet himself. As a self-conscious "other" who becomes the fulcrum for Hill's acts of attention, we have noted the difficulty (prompted by the poet) that arises with respect to the integrity of his voice. Less difficult is our identification with an individual who feels harried and distracted, who struggles to comprehend his place in the world, who also finds it 'hard to forgive himself' and so feels an earnest desire for grace. We also may readily align ourselves with his remorse and indignation at the travesties of his age, the "desolation of learning," and the "Entertainment overkill" that comprise the tragic farce of a broken and forgetful world as he sees it (and as he enables *us* to see it); and we may even share his sense of "clownishness" as a fitting portrait of our own character in the midst of it. In advancing the poem's work of atonement "from kinesis to kenosis," however, the demands upon the reader to accept self-excavation, self-correction and self-forgetting as the self's own requisites for virtue and love increase precipitously. On the one hand, of course, a poet who assumes an ambiguous stance towards his ostensible theme and who insists that his poem is "its own gift" and "a sad and angry consolation" doesn't worry over the measure of assent his art engenders—or fails to incur. Indeed, the assertion "*I write for the dead*" itself conveys a rebuff of such anxiety (as well as a subtle rebuke to his present audience). On the other hand, by insisting that a poet bears a public responsibility Hill refutes any tendency to sanctify a private vision. In witnessing to the exemplars of "active virtue" whose traceable attributes create the furrows of a moral landscape—a witness that subverts the subjective interest and directs us eventually to contemplate the kenosis of Christ and "the lost amazing crown"—Hill's poem does issue a summons to attention that calls for a form of assent and for our identification with his persona's concerns. In his manner of doing so he highlights a feature characteristic of all three poems, which significantly qualifies our appraisal of capacities of recognition and resonance as appropriate categories for Christian witness.

We have observed that through Hill's self-staging, provocation registers an invocation, and that by this dual effect he challenges us to *read through* the disorienting pitch of his self-presentation in order to attend to his project of recovering right perception. The form of assent this strategy inspires involves our willingness to take up his challenge, which he prompts by creating such pitch of inattention and distraction, and with it *lostness*, that the need for clarity and conversion becomes our own felt urgency. In this respect, his pronouncements that "it is all there, but we are not all there" and "nowhere are you" throw down a gauntlet of sorts that is familiar to a Christian rhetoric—made manifest supremely, I would argue, in the evangelism of *Jesus*. Although Jesus' use of creative devices in parables and figures of speech in particular do commend the imagination to the discourses of Christian faith (as many have emphasized), his strategy cannot be construed merely as an aesthetic performance. As he clarifies in Matthew 13, for example, in telling parables he did not aim ultimately to attract but to distinguish—between those who could or could not, and who would or would not listen and perceive (Matthew 13:13ff.; cf. Mark 4:11–13). In the imaginative rhetoric of the Gospels resonance is meant to bring about a challenge to *our* capacities of recognition, creating new possibilities for identification through the familiar, but in that very place transforming it into a site of confrontation.

We see this dynamic at work in all three of our poems. Through his development of Incarnational images in the Arthuriad, Williams transfuses the modern pursuit of satisfaction through a "recognition of the inner in the outer" with a *Christian* imagination of the universe. By indexing the "sensuous apprehension of our satisfied capacities" to the coordinates of an Incarnational vision, like Geoffrey Hill he impresses a larger framework for personal as well as societal meaning than any private vision can discharge.[9] In *The Gossamer Wall*, Micheal O'Siadhail's invitation to the reader reciprocates a challenge to recognize not only the other but ourselves. His poetics of remembrance exposes our possible complicity in bigotry and violence and also prompts us to heed his summons to look and to see the face of a neighbor through the vanishing testimonies of their suffering, the very form of whose memory dictates the shape of our own future ("Can *how we* remember shape what *we* become?"). As in *The Triumph of Love*, capacities of recognition in these poems include the opportunity for discovery that the poetry distinctively affords, while simultaneously requiring readers to increase their own capacity in proportion to the vision these poets elaborate and enlarge. Not only, then, do they make legible and enact the strains of a Christian sense of existence in the world—in the expressive shapes of faith, hope, and love—but in so doing they elicit our participation in the very process of self-examination they advance; a feature we again find in Jesus' public uses of imaginative speech. In short (to once more appropriate Hill's vocabulary), resonance has "teeth" and recognition involves "shocks"; both of which we experience as a product of the poetic textures these poets weave, and which give substance or density to their witness. We recall in this regard Hill's appeal to a "rectified Christian poetics," which opposes and corrects a Christian aesthetics amounting to little more than "a surrogate post-Christian religion of aesthetic gratification." In that Christian witnesses seek a "faithful

---

9. In this respect, Williams' Arthuriad (like, in their own ways, O'Siadhail's and Hill's poems) fulfills Charles Taylor's call for "new languages of personal resonance," bringing to "the exploration of order," which Taylor believes such languages facilitate, an expansive Incarnational sensibility that simultaneously affirms and reorients the very notion of a "personal vision" as an "index" for "seeing good" (cf. Introduction, 13ff).

persuasion" (David Cunningham's helpful moniker) and not merely to gratify popular sensibilities, their deployment of imaginative speech aims to hold forth "*voices of distinction*" that *prepare for* the conversion of their audiences.

I am being scrupulous in my choice of words in this last phrase. The language of conversion is of course appropriate to any discussion of gospel witness. However, not only does such an outcome involve a mysterious work that ultimately lies beyond the capacity of Christian witnesses to effect,[10] it conveys what many late-moderns would regard with suspicion if not outright offense. Despite that sensitivity, however, the aim to "persuade men" towards gospel faith, as Paul described his task, ought not incur embarrassment on the part of witnesses ("*I am not ashamed of the gospel*," the Apostle declared). On the other hand, the recognition that attitudes of suspicion and postures of resistance prevail among many contemporary late-modern people calls upon North Atlantic Christians to respect that sensitivity (however warranted and in whatever forms it takes) even as, by their witness, they seek to move people to consider afresh the vision of Christ.

For both aspects, then—the ultimate mystery of conversion and the sensibilities of contemporary uncommitted people—the language of "preparation," or *preparatio evangelica*, seems to suit best a description of the witnessing task in light of its present challenges. With regard to contemporary sensibilities, we have asked in various ways: How can the witnessing church make available the features of a gospel vision that have grown remote to the sensibilities of late-modern individuals? And in this same vein: How can the Church revitalize its speech in such manner that its own language regains a foothold in the discourses of the public square and, indeed, in the *imagination* of late-modern audiences, such that the gospel once more becomes intelligible as well as compelling to them? I have insisted that such questions appropriately reflect the burden of gospel witness as an outflow of the very nature of the Gospel of God-Incarnate.[11]

---

10. So Jesus tells Peter at his confession, "Flesh and blood did not reveal this to you, but My Father who is in heaven" (Matthew 16:17).

11. Hence, although there is significant truth in Karl Barth's insistence that "the gospel does not require our assistance," the theologian misses one of the most salient features of that very gospel, and ignores the fact that the Church has always owned the responsibility to "translate" it in accordance with the needs of its endlessly varying

It is a burden that Paul Ricoeur recognized and, indeed, one he assumed, and which designated for him one of the principal aims of his entire hermeneutical project. In his early essay "The Language of Faith" (1973), Ricoeur poses a problem similar to that which we have just outlined. He asks, "How can one communicate to another and to oneself the meaning of the kerygma in such a way as to develop something approaching a comprehensible discourse?" The question obtains, he elaborates, particularly in the face of a 'secularization' that has led to "an estrangement from the kerygmatic situation itself" within which the very questions the kerygma addresses have lost their meaning.[12] Significantly, he assigns this concern to "the tasks of Christian preaching" which "not only has to continue the language of Scripture, but to restore a signifying language . . . in order to find a cultural expression."[13] Hence, prior to the question of preaching but a constitutive element in it, Christian preachers must make it their aim to restore this lost ground, "this kind of humus of meaning," without which the kerygma cannot be heard intelligibly.[14] Ricoeur's category for this endeavor is *"prediscourse,"* which, he contends, it is the responsibility of Christian preachers to reconstruct. Relevant to our own interests, that ambition, he says, must proceed to formulate "a language which awakens possibilities," a form of speech that is most effective when imbued with "the grace of imagination."[15] When, therefore, we speak of preparation and of

---

audiences. It was in fact Barth's "positivist doctrine of revelation" that prompted vigorous criticism from Dietrich Bonhoeffer, who objected to Barth's "'Like it or lump it'" attitude towards Christianity's encounter with the world, calling it an *unbiblical* position. Against a "positivism of revelation [that] makes it too easy for itself," he wanted to contend for a this-worldly understanding of the gospel: "What is above this world is, in the gospel, intended to exist *for* this world" (*Letters and Papers from Prison* [*Letters*], 286; cf. 328).

12. *Philosophy*, 223, 227. He clarifies, "Cultural distance is not only the altering of the vehicle, but also the forgetting of the radical question conveyed by the language of another time. It is necessary to undertake, therefore, a struggle against the *forgetting* of the question, that is, a struggle against our own alienation in relation to what operates in the question" (224). That forgotten question, he adds, regards "the origin and meaning of our life," which, in its Christian context, includes "the question of 'to be lost' or 'to be saved,'" and which stands in need of being "rediscovered" (226).

13. Ibid., 227

14. Ibid.

15. Ibid., 231, 237. Also with respect to such a goal he writes, "We are in quest of a language which would be appropriate to the kind of *imagination* which expresses

a language of *preparatio*, we may employ this category of "prediscourse" and the directions Ricoeur takes it as a way of designating the kind of language a publicly viable theology is compelled to construct for its disaffected late-modern audiences. It is also an appropriate category to describe the achievements of our poems, which, distinctively, "continue the language of Scripture" *as* a signifying language by virtue of their creative "re-inscriptions" of biblical themes, thus awakening new possibilities for Scripture to speak today.

Furthermore, as forms of prediscourse they add one other feature to a language of preparation. In addition to pitch of attention, but akin to it, these poems accomplish the interfusion of resonance and recognition with such persuasive effect by virtue of their *calculated restraint*.[16] By this phrase I mean in broad strokes that these poets engineer through their formal technique a *process* of discovery whereby meaning—for our interests, theological or christological meaning as we have highlighted it—emerges gradually but forcefully as a *possibility* (with Ricoeur, a word we also have used throughout our study to describe the effects of the poetry). It is here that the peculiar advantages of poetic performance—of what these poets do in their verse as forms of effectual witness-bearing—show their potency in the face of growing indifference, ignorance and inertia. To the extent that, in at least significant quarters of North Atlantic societies especially, this is an age with "*hag faith going the rounds*," calculated restraint represents a style of Christian expression befitting the Church's persuasive tasks among those who can no longer hear more direct forms of proclamation, and so, require fresh, compelling translations of the gospel.

It is Charles Williams and Geoffrey Hill who put their finger on this need as well as its potential redress when, for example, the one speaks of "turning the formulae of belief into an operation of faith," or the other speaks of a poetry "which intersects with direct meanings obliquely, yet cogently," and of a "doctrinal poetry" that "is finally made meaningful, is finally made to be understood, by something other than the doctrine."[17]

---

most characteristic existential possibilities," a quality he finds in literature especially by which, he adds, "I can participate imaginatively in the meaning deployed . . ." (231).

16. "Restraint," again, is a word Charles Williams used in praise of poetry's peculiar quality (cf. 52, n. 95).

17. "Language, Suffering, and Silence," 243. In a similar vein, Williams attested, "Doctrine, of course, may be an intense part of poetry; but in that case it must arise for us out of the poetry" (*RB*, 56).

(We think once more of C. S. Lewis's appraisal of the Arthuriad in this light, when he said that it "restated to my imagination the very questions to which the doctrines are answers.") As Hill adds in this same essay, "that 'something other' is a gift of *technē*," a skill of speech that involves "the imagination's kneading process, the theme identifying itself with and in the language; the language identifying itself with and in the theme."[18] It is this intersection with direct meanings "obliquely, yet cogently" that through their "gift of *technē*" these poems demonstrate an able *preparatio evangelica*. Indeed, the various "conversions" that these poems effect themselves comprise robust forms of preparatory persuasion: what we have called a "conversion of our sensibilities" and a "conversion of perspective" characteristic of the aims as well as the results of this poetry.

Each of our poems demonstrates its own form of calculated restraint, which is also a strategy of holding forth doctrinal meaning. We have observed in Williams' Arthuriad "an atmosphere of disclosure rather than an attitude of closure" advanced by the "mediat[ing] capacities" of his images (indeed, by the "sacramental symmetry" of the whole). Similarly, in O'Siadhail's *Gossamer* suite we noted its "angularity," "interrogative mood," and "gradual adagio of truth"—creating "*a conversation so rich it knows it never arrives/ or forecloses.*" In our study of Hill, then, we referred to his style or "method of indirection," a "holding forth then withdrawing" that comprises "the persuasive power of suggestiveness." ("Nothing true is easy" or, we may add, *easily conveyed*.) In each of these manifestations of calculated restraint we observe the imagination's kneading process at work, allowing theological meanings to emerge gradually,[19] though punctuated at various points within these texts at moments of keen Christian self-consciousness: Williams' cruciform images and direct references to Christian ideas and practices; O'Siadhail's allusions to sacred narratives and the Eucharist; Hill's references to the Crucifixion and Resurrection and to historical figures of the faith, his addresses to the Church, and his more direct witness to Christ and his kenosis. Even here, however, the poets load these moments with ambiguity (in the sense of multi-valence) that still

18. Ibid., 244.

19. It is, in fact, one of the further advantages of poetic sequences or long poems, which "realize meanings" (Alter) by the swell of an overarching impression towards which the poem builds over the course of the whole.

preserves an open-textured quality to their presentation. In this manner their poems allow readers to explore their implications as, again, a *possibility*, even as they are confronted with a challenge to make that possibility their own—"*accipe*," "take, read," heed this "*summons*," seek "*the lost amazing crown*."

In all, these poems create fresh contexts for meaning by which the features of a Christian vision *become* visible as well as viable—in this respect also a form of prediscourse that prepares new ground for receptivity. Yet they do so without loss to the intrinsic challenge (the "teeth" of resonance) which that same vision invokes against the deficiencies, the fallenness, the idols of self-promotion they expose, and which the poets represent as a condition of limitation intrinsic to their own medium of words. In this way also these poems demonstrate extraordinary poise, not in the form of stasis but with earnestness and intensity of focus that is an enlargement as well. They provide not only the images, the vocabulary, even the grammar and syntax for the theological possibilities they elicit, but by such formal means they imbue these possibilities with a precision of thought and emotion that translates their appearance into a language that is vital and not inert.

Together with the poetry's pitch of attention, this achievement of reorientation or redirection through indirect means comprise those capacities of recognition that these poems exude. There is, of course, a great deal more they achieve as "works of the productive imagination" (Ricoeur). But in that we have inquired after their contribution to Christian theology and witness specifically, we have highlighted those features which demonstrate their resourcefulness to a thinking and expressive Church in its contemporary late-modern environment.

In having put forward a case for poetry's advantages in this regard, however, as well as, implicitly, for a method of confirming the same by reading *poems* closely, there remains a fundamental question we have asked throughout this study for which some final clarification seems in order. We have asked both whether this poetry demonstrates a model of "good" theology and of *doing* good theology, and, if so, what kind of theology would this be? We may apply the same question to my method of reading poems theologically. In both aspects, by situating these poems and our study of them within the public, missionary tasks of Christian theology and by demonstrating their merits as resources distinctively fitted to these tasks, we have made significant strides towards establishing that works of poetry can be works of theology. When we say that something offers a *model*, however, we strongly suggest that it ought to be studied and in some sense emulated. Accordingly, in our final section we will consider further how, and *where*, we might appropriate the results of our study within the discourses and practices of Christian theology.

Modeling Theological Styles: Christian Discursive Practices in the School of the Poets

By referring to discourses and practices I have implied a distinction that I would like quickly to reformulate as an integrated whole. Christian discourse, in whatever form it takes, *is* a practice. For this reason, when Christians speak—whether as scholars within an academic setting or as witnesses to their neighbors—they seek to do so *Christianly*: their very manner of speaking itself exhibiting the content they believe and which they hope to convey to others. Following Miroslav Volf's emphasis on the "intimate link between beliefs and practices" within a Christian vision such that we can conceive "belief-shaped practices" and "practice-shaping beliefs,"[20] we may adopt the phrase *Christian discursive practices* as a descriptive heading under which to consider our appropriation of poetry as a model for theological speaking. Because practices embody Christian beliefs and those beliefs are embedded in our practices, Christian discourse is not only *about* faith but involves "speaking faith" in ways that the Christian gospel distinctively informs. Hence, when we solicit "theological virtues of speech," for example, or appeal to "a noble vernacular for a noble faith," we place ourselves firmly within a set of values that asks not only what this poetry does, but what *theology* does, or is meant to do, in its speaking. And in this regard, we return once more to the 'issue of rhetoric' and of theological styles.

In the projects of Janet Soskice, Paul Ricoeur and D. M. MacKinnon, among others (e.g., Robert Alter, Rowan Williams, David Ford, Frank Burch Brown), we have found convincing exceptions to a tendency to treat matters of form and style as [perhaps] interesting

---

20. Volf and Bass, eds., *Practicing Theology*, 250–51ff. In response to this formulation, he later adds that practices "are Christian insofar as they are 'resonances' of God's engagement with the world" (260), and concludes, "we should resolutely place theology at the service of practices..." (263).

but superfluous concerns. Instead, they bring to the table a vigorous assessment of Christianity's formal practices as constitutive elements of theology's interpretive and expressive tasks. In so doing, they also provide a theological and scriptural conceptual framework (as well as a vocabulary) by which to assess the contributions of poets and poetic speech to theology.[21] By creating a conversation between these thinkers and the poets at work in their poetry, my own project has attempted to confirm, first, that a formal or stylistic interest is not an idiosyncratic brand of theological reflection hovering about the margins of otherwise serious theological projects. Rather, this interest goes to the *crux* of Christian discursive practices that have as a priority the aim to hold forth an Incarnational, christological or christocentric vision in the public square. Furthermore, as Miroslav Volf also contends, "*at the heart of every good theology lies not simply a plausible intellectual vision but more importantly a compelling account of a way of life . . . .*"[22] In both respects, the poems of Williams, O'Siadhail and Hill offer models of good theology, bringing to their own form of Christian witness the power of the literary imagination to enact aspects of such an account, and by the multifaceted resonances they achieve to make it 'compelling'. Although not theologies in any comprehensive or systematic sense of the word, in their poetic discourse we find exemplary displays of *doing* theology as a work of witness manifested within the textures of language.

Is it towards a "formal theology," then, which studies the conjuncture of effective style(s) with theological substance that my account of poetry's contribution ultimately advances? The label may fit, though to settle there risks reducing the aims of my project to one specialized field of inquiry and neglecting the larger questions I have posed. Another way of refining the question "Can poetry matter to Christian theology?" is to ask, "Does Christian theology have any *stakes* in the literary output of poets, and if so, what do Christian discursive practices gain from the study of poetry?" Space does not permit us to address the larger question implied here, which considers the stakes theology has in culture

---

21. Frank Burch Brown's study of *Four Quartets* in *Transfiguration* offers a remarkable testimony to this emphasis and sensitivity, a work that in many ways mirrors my own study.

22. Ibid., 247 (the author's italics). Volf is careful to qualify this assertion, clarifying, "God is the proper object of theology," and "As the highest good, God matters for God's own sake, not for the sake of a preferred way of life" (260).

and in cultural production generally, and which would require a much wider circle of "conversation partners" in order to fill out my account of poetry's contribution.[23]

My more narrow focus on the works themselves as models of Christian theology and witness, however, returns a number of additional advantages that recognize poems as resources. Specifically, theology's public task concerns itself with the earnest quest for resources that will facilitate and advance the cause of the gospel in society. In this respect, there are significant stakes involved in the appropriation of poetry and poetic studies within the discourses of Christian theology. What this endeavor assumes, of course, is that theology faculties, seminaries, and divinity schools adopt cultural engagement and the witnessing task as integral features of their mission, and do so to such an extent that the quest for such resources finds its proper place in the curriculum. Where this is not the case, very little of what I have to add now regarding the advantages of poetry and its study bears relevance, at least within the professional educational institutions of the Church.

From the kernel of instruction we garner from our close readings of these poems a wider field of application opens up that spans various Christian discursive practices. As "re-inscriptions" of scriptural themes and ideas, for instance, these poems offer a form of biblical commentary, enhancing and expanding the science of exegesis through the *art of exegesis*—a formal sensitivity that, as emphasized already, the Bible itself commends by its own uses of poetic language and figurative discourse. With an eye to this exegetical advantage, for Christianity's various publics within as well as outside of the Church the study of such poetry as we have examined in these pages (and there is a vast corpus of other poetry that we could include!) promises fresh interpretive insights as well as compelling *translations* of the scriptural witness and the doctrines theologians attempt to formulate in response to that witness. We recall in this regard David Ford's appeal for a "long apprenticeship" in learning how to see, here applied to the exegetical task in its public

---

23. In regard to theology's engagement with the ideas of the age and the demands these place on efforts to make Christian discourse intelligible, for example, a more complete treatment would include theology's attempts to grapple with the questions and insights of cultural anthropology, literary criticism, critical theory and hermeneutics, aesthetics (including phenomenologies of art), etc., as they are pursued within theology's own disciplines.

deportment as the refinement of skills in learning how to *read* attentively. To read Scripture as these poets do in light of the human condition and experiences it addresses represents an exercise in interpretation that brings text and audience into new forms of creative dialogue.

In a similar vein, as descriptions and re-descriptions of reality imbued with precise emotion and intelligence, these poems also model forms of effective engagement with late-modern publics that comprise *pedagogies of persuasion* for the witnessing Church. As resources endowed with capacities of recognition and pitch of attention through their "gift of *technē*," they offer a curriculum for the formation of an imaginative intelligence, which brings new vitality and substance to the articulation of gospelled convictions—"*Not unworded. Enworded.*" Moreover, in that the poems of Williams, O'Siadhail and Hill also turn a critical eye towards the Church, summoning Christians to examine and renew their own perception and appreciation of what they confess, this pedagogy not only facilitates the search for effective forms of communication but also compels serious self-reflection on the part of believers. At issue is an integrity of thought that manifests itself in an integrity of speech—an "ethics of form," a "shaping, voicing" that is "a type of civic action" or "active virtue," all of which contribute to an *ethics* of persuasion. To refine the stakes I have in mind here, we may ask: Do Christian witnesses themselves comprehend the depths of their own gospel faith as a faith that intersects vitally with every aspect of humanity, and thus seek to translate the same with a perspicuity of insight and diligence of style equal to that manifested in the work of these poets? Here, the image of a poet standing vigil over his own medium as a "master-servant" returns with force as a model for the witnessing church to show a similar vigilance in their thinking as well as their speaking practices. It is also an image that recalls one of the most provocative suggestions made by a theologian in the last century, and which will direct our concluding comments.

In his *Letters and Papers from Prison*, Dietrich Bonhoeffer advances the notion of a "religionless Christianity,"[24] which he elaborates as "the non-religious interpretation of biblical concepts" or, more positively, a Christianity reinterpreted "in a 'worldly' sense—in the sense

---

24. Bonhoeffer introduces this notion in his letter to Eberhard Bethge ("E.B.") of 30 April 1944 (*Letters*, 278ff). Because he works out this notion entirely in letters to the same, I will henceforth cite page numbers only from this edition.

of the Old Testament and John 1.14."[25] Although Bonhoeffer's idea remained inchoate (thus cautioning us to temper our appropriation of it), his motive for this suggestion and the recommendations he was able to articulate bear striking relevance to the "pedagogy of persuasion" I am advancing for our poems—as models of diligence and integrity in speech. For one, he also recognized "[t]he displacement of God from the world, and from the public part of human life": features, as he described it, of "a world come of age" that brings to completion the movement "towards the autonomy of man."[26] It is at such an historical juncture that he believed 'religious' interpretations no longer prove solvent because they fail to address modern persons in their irreversible "adulthood"— as individuals who do not accept "God as a working hypothesis"[27] and who reject singular appeals to an other-worldly rationale for belief as well as traditional structures of thought that assert humanity's fundamentally religious nature. Bonhoeffer derived his own rationale for this critique from the gospel itself and what he understood as "the profound this-worldliness of Christianity," arguing that "the concepts [of the New Testament] must be interpreted in such a way as not to make religion a precondition for faith."[28] "To be a Christian," he insisted, "does not mean to be religious in a particular way, . . . but to be a man—not a type of man, but the man Christ creates in us"; and again, "The 'religious act' is always something partial; 'faith' is something whole, involving the whole of one's life."[29] Sounding a note that resonates with MacKinnon's sense of the "desperately familiar" and "*in concreto*" character of God-incarnate, Bonhoeffer neatly summarizes, "God is beyond in the midst of our life"; and it is there, in this "secular" environment, that we are meant to "*recognize*" him.[30]

25. Ibid., 344, 286. He also adds the phrase "the secular interpretation of biblical concepts" (346; cf. 361).

26. Ibid., 344, 325–26 respectively. The description of "a world come of age" recalls Paul Ricoeur's similar assessment and the impossibility of "returning to another age" (see, e.g., "Language of Faith," 226).

27. Ibid., 360.

28. Ibid., 369, 329 respectively.

29. Ibid., 361, 362. In his letter to E. B. of 21 July 1944 he adds, "The Christian is not a *homo religiosus*, but simply a man," whose own "this-worldliness" is "characterized by discipline and the constant knowledge of death and resurrection" (369).

30. Ibid., 282. He adds, "I should like to speak of God not on the boundaries but at the centre" (ibid.), then in his letter to E.B. of 29 May 1944 he writes, "We are to find

We have observed in all three of our poems this 'religionless' quality as Bonhoeffer understood and construed it—a "this-worldliness" that situates those Incarnational aspects of faith, hope and love they develop within the contingencies of human existence. They do so, moreover, without loss to the claims upon us which the gospel entails, following Bonhoeffer's further insistence that, "When we speak of God in a 'non-religious' way, we must speak of him in such a way that the godlessness of the world is not in some way concealed, but rather revealed, and thus exposed to an unexpected light."[31] And when Bonhoeffer expresses the hope that Christianity will one day generate "a new language, perhaps quite non-religious, but liberating and redeeming—as was Jesus' language,"[32] we find in our poems manifestations of such a movement through their re-imagined, "oblique, yet cogent" capacities of resonance and recognition with a Christian vision. That is, we see at work in these poems not a departure from the implications of the Christian gospel but, even in their "calculated restraint," a *deepening* of its this-worldly, redemptive import; their own "unexpected light" that serves to disclose the light of the gospel, achieved distinctively as a product of poetic form.

In drawing this distinction we get at the heart of what my entire project has sought to demonstrate. Contrary to the almost instinctive anxiety to make the Christian religion relevant in a "world come of age," and as an antidote to the acute sense of helplessness Christian witnesses often feel in such a context, a robust, publicly viable theology and witness calls for this deeper contemplation of the *gospel*. As Bonhoeffer intimates in his hope for a "new language," or as our theologians have underscored and our poets have both asserted and demonstrated, *the more profound our comprehension of the gospel the more persuaded we become to attend to matters of form*. Moreover, it is the gospel itself by virtue of its constitutive features that supplies the "sustenance" (Hill) for the interminable work of translation and witness it impels. Accordingly, for its witnesses the "Word made flesh" must continually be made flesh,

---

God in what we know, not in what we don't know. . . . God is no stop-gap; he must be recognized at the centre of life, not when we are at the end of our resources; it is his will to be recognized in life, and not only when death comes" (311–12).

31. Ibid., 362.

32. "Thoughts on the Baptism of Dietrich Wilhelm Rüdiger Bethge," May 1944 (ibid., 300).

must be re-embodied and re-enacted in keeping with the gospel's very premises and claims. (As Paul Ricoeur concludes, "Is not the Good News the instigation of the possibility of man by a creative word?"[33]) In their own ways, and as a gift of their speaking, Charles Williams, Micheal O'Siadhail and Geoffrey Hill model this vital connection. Their pedagogies of persuasion that fuse form and substance in the re-formulation of a Christian vision of life offer voices of distinction that Christian theologians and witnesses can ill afford to neglect—at least when the gospel's own premises and priorities are accepted as the decisive elements in their discursive tasks.

If I may advance one final plea for the study of such poetry, it is this: So vast and so demanding are the challenges now facing the witnessing Church in its late-modern contexts that all variety of resources of language and of the imaginative intelligence should be marshaled for this decidedly public enterprise we call theology. Within its many and multifaceted discourses, there may still be a suitable way to designate the nature of my plea. What shall we call it? We could say it is an appeal for a 'theology of the imagination', but that doesn't quite capture the ultimate direction of my study. Perhaps, then, we could say I plea for this: a *missiology of the imagination*.

---

33. "Language of Faith," 238.

Bibliography

Works Cited

Alter, Robert. *The Art of Biblical Poetry*. New York: Basic Books, 1985.

Begbie, Jeremy, editor. *Sounding the Depth: Theology through the Arts*. London: SCM, 2002.

Blake, William. "There is No Natural Religion." In *The Complete Writings*. Edited by G. Keynes. Oxford: Oxford University Press, 1966.

Bonhoeffer, Dietrich. *Letters and Papers from Prison: The Enlarged Edition*. Edited by Eberhard Bethge. New York: Collier, 1972.

Brown, Frank Burch. *Transfiguration: Poetic Metaphor and the Languages of Religious Belief*. Chapel Hill: University of North Carolina Press, 1983.

Brueggemann, Walter. *The Prophetic Imagination*. 2nd ed. Minneapolis: Fortress, 2001.

Cavaliero, Glen. *Charles Williams: Poet of Theology*. Grand Rapids: Eerdmans, 1983.

Cavell, Stanley. *Disowning Knowledge in Six Plays of Shakespeare*. Cambridge: Cambridge University Press, 1987.

Chopp, Rebecca. "Theology and the Poetics of Testimony." In *Converging on Culture: Theologians in Dialogue with Cultural Analysis and Criticism*, edited by Delwin Brown et al., 56–70. Oxford: Oxford University Press, 2001.

Cohn-Sherbok, Dan, editor. *Holocaust Theology: A Reader*. New York: New York University Press, 2002.

Coleridge, Samuel Taylor. *Biographia Literaria*. In *The Portable Coleridge*. Edited by I. A. Richards. Middlesex: Penguin, 1977.

———. "The Rime of the Ancyent Marinere." In *Lyrical Ballads with a Few Other Poems*. Middlesex, UK: Penguin, 1999.

Craig, Kenneth M., Jr. *A Poetics of Jonah: Art in Service of Ideology*. Columbia, SC: University of South Carolina Press, 1993.

Cunningham, David. *Faithful Persuasion: In Aid of a Rhetoric of Christian Theology*. Notre Dame: University of Notre Dame Press, 1991.

Davies, Oliver. *A Theology of Compassion: Metaphysics of Difference and the Renewal of Tradition*. London: SCM, 2001.

Dawson, David. *Literary Theory*. Guides to Theological Inquiry. Minneapolis: Fortress, 1995.

Eliot, T. S. *Selected Essays 1917–1932*. New York: Harcourt, Brace, 1932/1938.

———. *To Criticize the Critic and Other Writings*. New York: Farrar, Strauss & Giroux, 1965.

Farrer, Austin. *The Glass of Vision*. Glasgow: MacLehose, 1948.

Ford, David. *Self and Salvation: Being Transformed*. Cambridge Studies in Christian Doctrine 1. Cambridge: Cambridge University Press, 1999.

Gioia, Dana. *Can Poetry Matter? Essays on Poetry and American Culture*. Tenth anniversary edition. St. Paul, MN: Graywolf, 2002.

Hardy, Daniel W. *Finding the Church: The Dynamic Truth of Anglicanism*. London: SCM, 2001.

Hauerwas, Stanley. *After Christendom: How the Church Is to Behave if Freedom, Justice, and a Christian Nation Are Bad Ideas*. Nashville: Abingdon, 1999.

———. *Resident Aliens: Life in the Christian Colony*. Nashville: Abingdon, 1989.

Heaney, Seamus. *The Redress of Poetry: Oxford Lectures*. London: Faber & Faber, 1995.

Hill, Geoffrey. "'The Conscious Mind's Intelligible Structure': A Debate." *Agenda* 10. 4–11.1 (1972–73) 14–23.

———. *The Enemy's Country: Words, Contextures, and other Circumstances of Language*. Stanford: Stanford University Press, 1991.

———. "Geoffrey Hill: The Art of Poetry LXXX." Interview with Carl Phillips. *The Paris Review* 42/154 (Spring 2000) 270–99.

———. "Language, Suffering, and Silence." *Literary Imagination: The Review of the Association of Literary Scholars and Critics* 1.2 (1999) 240–55.

———. *The Lords of Limit: Essays on Literature and Ideas*. New York: Oxford University Press, 1984.

———. "Poetics and the Kenotic Hymn." Appendix to Lucien Richard, *Christ the Self-Emptying of God*. Mahwah, NJ: Paulist, 1997.

———. "Rhetorics of Value." The Tanner Lectures on Human Values, Oxford, March 6–7, 2000, 255–83. Online: http://www.tannerlectures.utah.edu/lectures.Hill_01.pdf.

———. *Style and Faith*. New York: Counterpoint, 2003.

———. *The Triumph of Love*. Boston: Houghton Mifflin, 1998.

Jones, David. *The Dying Gaul and Other Writings*. London: Faber & Faber, 1978.

———. *Epoch and Artist: Selected Writings*. London: Faber & Faber, 1959. Reprinted, 1973.

King, Roma A., Jr. *The Pattern in the Web; The Mythical Poetry of Charles Williams*. Kent, OH: Kent State University Press, 1990.

Langer, Lawrence L. *The Holocaust and the Literary Imagination*. New Haven: Yale University Press, 1975.

———. *Holocaust Testimonies: The Ruins of Memory*. New Haven: Yale University Press, 1991.

Langer, Susanne K. *Feeling and Form: A Theory of Art Developed from Philosophy in a New Key*. New York: Scribners, 1953.

Lash, Nicholas. *The Beginning and the End of "Religion."* Cambridge: Cambridge University Press, 1996.

Levi, Primo. *Survival in Auschwitz: The Nazi Assault on Humanity*. Translated by Stuart Woolf. New York: Simon & Schuster, 1996.

MacKinnon, Donald M. *Borderlands of Theology and Other Essays*. Edited by George W. Roberts and Donovan E. Smucker. Philadelphia: Lippincott, 1968.

———. *Explorations in Theology 5*. London: SCM, 1979.

———. *The Problem of Metaphysics*. Cambridge: Cambridge University Press, 1974.

———. *The Resurrection: A Dialogue by G. W. H. Lampe and D. M. MacKinnon.* Philadelphia: Westminster, 1966.

———. *The Stripping of the Altars.* Bungay, Suffolk, UK: Fontana Library, 1969.

———. *Themes in Theology, The Three-Fold Cord: Essays in Philosophy, Politics and Theology.* Edinburgh: T. & T. Clark, 1987.

Maritain, Jacques. *Creative Intuition in Art and Poetry.* New York: Meridian, 1955.

McDonald, Peter. *Serious Poetry: Form and Authority from Yeats to Hill.* Oxford: Clarendon, 2002.

McGarry, Patsy. "Making a Plea for Memory." *The Irish Times* (Monday, September 23, 2002) 14–15.

Michaels, Anne, *Fugitive Pieces.* London: Bloomsbury, 1998.

Milosz, Czeslaw. *The Witness of Poetry.* Cambridge: Harvard University Press, 1983.

Moltmann, Jürgen. "The Identity and Relevance of Faith." In *The Crucified God: The Cross of Christ as the Foundation and Criticism of Christian Theology.* Translated by R. A. Wilson and John Bowden. London: SCM, 1974.

Moorman, Charles. *Arthurian Triptych: Mythic Materials in Charles Williams, C. S. Lewis, and T. S. Eliot.* Los Angeles: University of California Press, 1960.

Nussbaum, Martha. *Love's Knowledge: Essays on Philosophy and Literature.* New York: Oxford University Press, 1987.

O'Donovan, Oliver. *Desire of the Nations: Rediscovering the Roots of Political Theology.* Cambridge: Cambridge University Press, 1996.

O'Siadhail, Micheal. "The Art of War." *Insight* (Sept. 28, 2002) 26.

———. *The Gossamer Wall: Poems in Witness to the Holocaust.* Newcastle: Bloodaxe, 2002.

Rahner, Karl. *Theological Investigations Volume IV.* Translated by Kevin Smyth. London: Darton, Longman & Todd, 1966.

Ricoeur, Paul. *Essays on Biblical Interpretation.* Edited by Lewis Mudge. Philadelphia: Fortress, 1980.

———. *Figuring the Sacred: Religion, Narrative, and Imagination.* Translated by David Pellauer. Edited by Mark I. Wallace. Minneapolis: Fortress, 1995.

———. *Oneself as Another.* Translated by Kathleen Blamey. Chicago: University of Chicago Press, 1992/1994.

———. *The Philosophy of Paul Ricoeur: An Anthology of His Work.* Edited by Charles E. Reagan and David Stewart. Boston: Beacon, 1978.

———. *The Rule of Metaphor: Multi-disciplinary Studies of the Creation of Meaning in Language.* Translated by Robert Czerny. Toronto: University of Toronto Press, 1977.

———. *Time and Narrative.* 3 vols. Translated by Kathleen McLaughlin and David Pellauer. Chicago: University of Chicago Press, 1984–88.

Soskice, Janet. *Metaphor and Religious Language.* Oxford: Oxford University Press, 1985.

Taylor, Charles. *Sources of the Self: The Making of the Modern Identity.* Cambridge: Cambridge University Press, 1989.

Thomas, R. S. *R. S. Thomas: Selected Prose.* 3rd ed. Edited by Sandra Anstey. Bridgend: Poetry Wales Press, 1995.

Tracy, David. *The Analogical Imagination: Christian Theology and the Culture of Pluralism.* London: SCM, 1981.

Volf, Miroslav, and Dorothy C. Bass, editors. *Practicing Theology: Beliefs and Practices in Christian Life*. Grand Rapids: Eerdmans, 2002.
Williams, Charles. *The Descent of the Dove: A Short History of the Holy Spirit in the Church*. New York: Meriden, 1956.
———. *The English Poetic Mind*. Oxford: Clarendon, 1932).
———. *The Figure of Beatrice: A Study in Dante*. London: Faber & Faber, 1943. Reprinted, 1953.
———. *He Came Down from Heaven*. 1938. Reprinted, Grand Rapids: Eerdmans, 1984.
———. *The Image of the City and Other Essays*. Selected by Anne Ridler. London: Oxford University Press, 1958.
———, editor. *The Letters of Evelyn Underhill*. London: Longmans, Green, 1943.
———, editor. *The New Book of English Verse*. London: Gollancz, 1935.
———. *Poetry at Present*. Oxford: Clarendon, 1930.
———. *Reason and Beauty in the Poetic Mind*. Oxford: Clarendon, 1933.
———. *Taliessin through Logres, The Region of the Summer Stars, Arthurian Torso*. Grand Rapids: Eerdmans, 1974. Reprinted, 1980.
Williams, Rowan. *Lost Icons: Reflections on Cultural Bereavement*. Edinburgh: T. & T. Clark, 2000.
———. *On Christian Theology*. Challenges in Contemporary Theology. Oxford: Blackwell, 2000.
———. "Trinity and Ontology." In *Christ, Ethics and Tragedy: Essays in Honour of Donald MacKinnon*. Edited by Kenneth Surin. Cambridge: Cambridge University Press, 1989.
Wolterstorff, Nicholas. *Divine Discourse: Philosophical reflections on the claim that God speaks*. Cambridge: Cambridge University Press, 1995.
Wordsworth, William. *The Works of William Wordsworth*. In *The Wordsworth Poetry Library*. Hertfordshire, UK: Wordsworth Editions, 1994.

Recommended Further Reading—By Category

Theology, Hermeneutics, Philosophical, and Theological Aesthetics/Christian Poetics

Augustine, St. *On Christian Doctrine*. Translated by D. W. Robertson Jr. Indianapolis: Bobbs-Merrill, 1958, 1979.
Balthasar, Hans Urs von. *The Glory of the Lord: A Theological Aesthetics*. 7 vols.:
    Volume I: *Seeing the Form*. Translated by Erasmor Leiva-Merikakis. Edited by Joseph Fessio and John Riches. Edinburgh: T. & T. Clark, 1982, 1989.
    Volume III: *Studies in Theological Style: Lay Styles*. Translated by Andrew Louth, et al. Edited by John Riches. Edinburgh: T. & T. Clark, 1986.
Barth, Karl. *Church Dogmatics, Vol. IV: The Doctrine of Reconciliation*, Part 3, First Half and Part 3.2. Translated by G. W. Bromily. Edited by G. W. Bromiley and T. F. Torrance. Edinburgh: T. & T. Clark, 1961/1983, 1962/1992.
———. *God in Action: Theological Addresses*. Translated by E. G. Homrighausen and Karl J. Ernst. New York: Round Table, 1936.

———. *The Preaching of the Gospel*. Translated by B. E. Hooke. Philadelphia: Westminster, 1963.
Begbie, Jeremy, editor. *Beholding the Glory: Incarnation through the Arts*. London: Darton, Longman and Todd, 2000.
Blond, Phillip. "Art and the Power of God." *Christian Issue* 99/3 (1999) 12–13.
Brown, David, and Ann Loades, editors. *Christ the Sacramental Word*. London: SPCK, 1996.
———, and David Fuller, editors. *Signs of Grace: Sacraments in Poetry and Prose*. London: Cassell, 1995.
Compier, Don H. *What Is Rhetorical Theology? Textual Practice and Public Discourse*. Harrisburg, PA: Trinity, 1999.
Dawson, David. *Christian Figural Reading and the Fashioning of Identity*. Berkeley: University of California Press, 2002.
Dupré, Louis. *Symbols of the Sacred*. Grand Rapids: Eerdmans, 2000.
Edwards, Michael. *Towards A Christian Poetics*. Grand Rapids: Eerdmans, 1984.
Farley, Edward. *Deep Symbols: Their Postmodern Effacement and Reclamation*. Valley Forge, PA: Trinity, 1996
Frei, Hans. *The Identity of Jesus Christ: The Hermeneutical Bases of Dogmatic Theology*. Philadelphia: Fortress, 1975.
Jasper, David. *The Study of Literature and Religion: An Introduction*. London: Macmillan, 1989.
Lindbeck, George A. *The Nature of Doctrine: Religion and Theology in a Post-liberal Age*. Philadelphia: Westminster, 1984.
Lynch, William F., S.J. *Christ and Apollo: The Dimensions of the Literary Imagination*. Notre Dame: University of Notre Dame Press, 1975.
Milbank, John. *The Word Made Strange: Theology, Language, Culture*. Oxford: Blackwell, 1997.
Prickett, Stephen. *Words and the Word: Language, Poetics and Biblical Interpretation*. Cambridge: Cambridge University Press, 1986/1989.
Scott, Nathan A., Jr. *Modern Literature and the Religious Frontier*. New York: Harper & Brothers, 1958.
———. *Negative Capability: Studies in the New Literature and the Religious Situation*. New Haven: Yale University Press, 1969.
———, editor. *The New Orpheus: Essays toward a Christian Poetic*. New York: Sheed & Ward, 1964.
———. *The Wild Prayer of Longing: Poetry and the Sacred*. New Haven: Yale University Press, 1971.
Steiner, George. *Real Presences*. Chicago: University of Chicago Press, 1989.
Volf, Miroslav. *The End Of Memory: Remembering Rightly in a Violent World*. Grand Rapids: Eerdmans, 2006.
Ward, Graham. *Barth, Derrida and the Language of Theology*. Cambridge: Cambridge University Press, 1995/1998.
Weidle, Wladimir. *The Dilemma of the Arts*. Translated by Martin Jarrett-Kerr. London: SCM Press, 1948.

Christianity and Contemporary Culture, Modernity Critiques, Christian Witness

Baumer, Franklin L. *Religion and the Rise of Skepticism: A History of Western Man's Doubt and of His Search for a Reasonable Faith during the Last Four Centuries.* New York: Harcourt, Brace and World, 1960.

Berger, Peter, Brigitte Berger, and Hansfried Kellner. *The Homeless Mind.* Middlesex, UK: Pelican, 1977.

Beger, Peter, and Thomas Luckmann. *The Social Construction of Reality: A Treatise in the Sociology of Knowledge.* Middlesex, UK: Penguin University Books reprint, 1972.

———. *The Social Reality of Religion.* Middlesex, UK: Penguin, 1973. Published in the U.S. as *The Sacred Canopy.* New York: Faber & Faber, 1967.

Bloesch, Donald G. *The Christian Witness in a Secular Age: An Evaluation of Nine Contemporary Theologians.* Eugene, OR: Wipf & Stock, 2002.

Chang, Curtis. *Engaging Unbelief: A Captivating Strategy from Augustine and Aquinas.* Downers Grove, IL: InterVarsity, 2000.

Clark, Daniel K. *Dialogical Apologetics: A Person-Centered Approach to Christian Defense.* Grand Rapids: Baker, 1993.

Ebeling, Gerhard. *Theology and Proclamation: Dialogue with Bultmann.* Translated by John Riches. Philadelphia: Fortress, 1966.

Forsyth, P. T. *The Preaching of Jesus and the Gospel of Christ.* Blackwood, South Australia: New Creations, 1987/2000.

Gunton, Colin. *The One, the Three and the Many: God, Creation and the Culture of Modernity.* Cambridge: Cambridge University Press, 1993/2000.

Jasper, David. *Rhetoric, Power and Community: An Exercise in Reserve.* Louisville: Westminster John Knox, 1993.

Milbank, John, *Theology and Social Theory.* Oxford: Blackwell, 1990.

Newbigin, Lesslie. *Foolishness to the Greeks: The Gospel and Western Culture.* London: SPCK, 1986.

———. *The Gospel in a Pluralist Society.* Grand Rapids: Eerdmans, 1989, 1991.

———. *Truth to Tell: The Gospel as Public Truth.* Grand Rapids: Eerdmans, 1991.

Newman, John Henry. *Grammar of Assent.* New York: Image Books, 1955/1958.

Niebuhr, H. Richard. *Christ and Culture.* New York: Harper, 1951.

Postman, Neil. *Amusing Ourselves to Death: Public Discourse in the Age of Show Business.* New York: Viking, 1985.

Pippin, Robert. *Modernism as a Philosophical Problem: On the Dissatisfactions of European High Culture.* 2nd ed. Oxford: Blackwell, 1999.

Rubenstein, Richard L., and John K. Roth. *Approaches to Auschwitz: The Holocaust and Its Legacy.* Rev. ed. Louisville: Westminster John Knox, 2003.

Taylor, Charles. *Multiculturalism and "The Politics of Recognition": An Essay.* Edited by Amy Gutmann. Princeton: Princeton University Press, 1992.

———. *A Secular Age.* Cambridge, MA: Belknap, 2007.

Warner, Martin, editor. *The Bible as Rhetoric: Studies in Biblical Persuasion and Credibility.* London: Routledge, 1990.

Westphal, Merold. *Suspicion and Faith: The Religious Uses of Modern Atheism.* Grand Rapids: Eerdmans, 1993.

Wiesenthal, Simon. *The Sunflower: On the Possibilities and Limits of Forgiveness.* Rev. ed. New York: Schocken, 1997.

Literature and Literary Studies—Criticism

Acheson, James, and Romana Huk editors. *Contemporary British Poetry: Essays in Theory And Criticism.* Albany: SUNY, 1996.

Agenda, Geoffrey Hill Special Issue 17.1 (1979).

Agenda, Geoffrey Hill: Six Essays on Geoffrey Hill's Collected Poems. 23.3–4 (1985/86).

Agenda, Geoffrey Hill Sixtieth Birthday Issue. 30.1–2 (1992).

Annin, David. *Inhabited Voices: Myth and History in the Poetry of Geoffrey Hill, Seamus Heaney and George Mackay Brown.* Somerset, UK: Bran's Head, 1984.

Auden, W. H. *The Dyers Hand and Other Essays.* London: Faber & Faber, 1963.

Bendient, Calvin. "On Geoffrey Hill." *Critical Quarterly* 23.2 (1981).

Bernstein, Charles, editor. *The Politics of Poetic Form: Poetry and Public Policy.* New York: Roof, 1990.

Brown, Merle E. *Double Lyric: Divisiveness and Communal Creativity in Recent English Poetry.* London: Routledge & Kegan Paul, 1980.

Davie, Donald. *Articulate Energy: An Enquiry into the Syntax of English Poetry.* New York: Harcourt, Brace, 1955.

Dodds, David Llewellyn, editor. *Arthurian Poets: Charles Williams.* Suffolk, UK: Boydell, 1991.

Easthope, Anthony. *Poetry as Discourse.* London: Methuen, 1983.

Edwards, Michael. "Quotidian Epic: Geoffrey Hill's *The Triumph of Love*." *The Yale Journal of Criticism* 13.1 (2000) 167–76.

Eliot, T. S. *On Poetry and Poets.* New York: Noonday, 1964.

———. *The Sacred Wood: Essays on Poetry and Criticism.* New York: Methuen, 1928. Reprinted, 1986.

———. *The Use of Poetry and the Use of Criticism: Studies in the Relation of Criticism to Poetry in England.* London: Faber & Faber, 1933.

———. *The Varieties of Metaphysical Poetry.* Edited by Ronald Schuchard. 1993. Reprinted, Orlando, FL: Harcourt, Brace,1996.

Gross, Harvey, editor. *The Structure of Verse: Modern Essays on Prosody.* Rev. ed. New York: Echo, 1979.

Hadfield, A. M. *Charles Williams: An Exploration of His Life and Work.* Oxford: Oxford University Press, 1983.

———. *An Introduction to Charles Williams.* London: Hale, 1959.

Horne, Brian, editor. *Charles Williams: A Celebration.* Herefordshire, UK: Gracewing, Fowler Wright, 1995.

Horner, Avril. "Geoffrey Hill: English Modernist or Postmodern European?" *Working Papers in Literary and Cultural Studies* 7 (January 1994).

Jennings, Elizabeth. *Every Changing Shape: Mystical Experience and the Making of Poems.* Manchester: Carcanet, 1996.

Lewis, C. Day. *The Poetic Image: The Creative Power of the Visual Word.* 1947. Reprinted, Los Angeles: Tarcher, 1984.

Lewis, C. S., editor. *Essays Presented to Charles Williams*. 1947. Reprinted, Grand Rapids: Eerdmans, 1966, 1974.

Lyon, John. "'Pardon?': Our Problem with Difficulty (and Geoffrey Hill)." *Thumbscrew* 13 (Spring 1998).

McLaren, Scott. "A Problem of Morality: Sacramentalism in the Early Novels of Charles Williams." *Renascence: Essays on Values in Literature* 56.2 (2004) 109–27.

McNees, Eleanor J. *Eucharistic Poetry: The Search for Presence in the Writings of John Donne, Gerard Manley Hopkins, Dylan Thomas, and Geoffrey Hill*. Lewisburg: Bucknell University Press, 1992.

Ricks, Christopher. *The Force of Poetry*. Oxford: Clarendon, 1984.

———. *Geoffrey Hill and 'the tongue's atrocities'*. The W. D. Thomas Memorial Lectures, University College of Swansea, Feb. 15th, 1978. Swansea, UK: University College of Swansea pamphlet, 1978.

Sayers, Dorothy L. "Charles Williams: A Poet's Critic." In *The Poetry of Search and the Poetry of Statement and Other Posthumous Essays on Literature, Religion and Language*. London: Gollancz, 1963.

Silkin, Jon. "The Poetry of Geoffrey Hill." In *British Poetry Since 1960: A Critical Survey*, edited by Michael Schmidt and Grevel Lindop, 143–64. Oxford: Carcanet, 1972.

Walker, Peter. "'Accurate Music': Geoffrey Hill's Anatomy of Melancholy." *The Cambridge Review* (May 1997) 34–38.

———. "The Poetry of Geoffrey Hill." *The Cambridge Review* (June 1985) 101–6.

———. "'The Triumph of Love': Geoffrey Hill's Contextures of Grace." *Sewanee Theological Review* 44 (2001) 275–98.

Williams, Miller. *Patterns of Poetry: An Encyclopedia of Forms*. Baton Rouge, LA: Louisiana University Press, 1986.